MASTERPIECES IN THE BROOKLYN MUSEUM

MASTERPIECES IN
The Brooklyn Museum

THE BROOKLYN MUSEUM

in association with

HARRY N. ABRAMS, INC., PUBLISHERS, NEW YORK

FRONTISPIECE:
*Tête de Jeune Homme
(Head of a Boy)*
PABLO PICASSO
(Spanish, 1881–1973)

1923
Grease crayon on pink Michallet laid paper
24 1/2 × 18 5/8 inches (62.1 × 47.4 cm)
Signed lower right, *Picasso*
39.18, Carll H. DeSilver Fund

ON THIS PAGE:
Brooklyn Bridge (Mosaic)
JOHN MARIN
(American, 1870–1953)
1913
Etching and drypoint
11 1/2 × 9 inches (29.2 × 22.9 cm)
50.166.2, Dick S. Ramsay Fund

PROJECT DIRECTOR
Margaret L. Kaplan

EDITOR
Mark D. Greenberg

DESIGNER
Michael Hentges

This publication was organized at
The Brooklyn Museum by Rena
Zurofsky, Vice Director for Marketing; Elaine Koss, Managing Editor;
and John Antonides, Editor.

Library of Congress
Cataloging-in-Publication Data

Masterpieces in the Brooklyn Museum.

 Includes index.
  1. Art—New York (N.Y.) 2. Brooklyn Museum.
I. Brooklyn Museum. II. Harry N. Abrams, Inc.
N620.B6A64 1988 708.147′23 88-6110
ISBN 0–8109–1528–6
ISBN 0–8109–2400–5 (pbk.)

Published in 1988 by Harry N. Abrams, Incorporated, New York
All rights reserved. No part of the contents of this book may
be reproduced without the written permission of the publisher

A Times Mirror Company

Printed and bound in Japan

Contents

Foreword

Robert T. Buck

DIRECTOR
THE BROOKLYN MUSEUM

WHEN IT OPENED IN 1897, The Brooklyn Museum building was the finest achievement of the leading American architects of the late nineteenth century, the New York firm of McKim, Mead & White. It reflected a new era in America in which social responsibility and cultural awareness were intertwined with the inauguration of a large number of civic projects that were seen as uplifting and enriching a devastated and divided society, scathed by the Civil War only a few decades earlier. Indeed, the new museum was to be located just east of Brooklyn's Grand Army Plaza, which surrounds one of the nation's most striking triumphal arches, dedicated to the victory of the Union armies—no coincidence but rather planned in the spirit of the times by urban planners. Simply put, it was to be the largest cultural edifice in the world and the ultimate statement in this country of the civilized achievements of mankind in an institutional setting.

The Brooklyn Museum as we know it today is the product of a steady evolution resulting in a remarkable amassing of over a million works of art housed in seven curatorial departments and displayed in a grand structure of 450,000 square feet. Acknowledged for its major holdings in Egyptian art and American painting of the eighteenth and nineteenth centuries, the Museum is also a storehouse of extraordinary treasures in a large number of other areas, including fine examples of European painting from the fourteenth to the nineteenth century and contemporary painting and sculpture. In the Department of Costumes and Textiles, one of the largest and finest collections of nineteenth-century Russian women's festive wear forms part of a total holding of more than thirty thousand complete outfits from many cultures and periods. In the Department of African, Oceanic, and New World Art is kept one of the nation's outstanding collections of the art of the Southwest American Indians. These objects, many of startling quality, frequently entered the collection as the result of Museum expeditions undertaken by curators whose work in many instances represents the only written record of the trading habits of the peoples involved.

The Museum's Oriental Department has special strengths in the areas of Indian painting and sculpture and Islamic art, with noteworthy Qajar holdings in the latter. On the Museum's fourth floor, twenty-eight superb American period rooms, from the South to New England, unfold to reveal two hundred years of evolution in interior design and treatment and constitute the nucleus of one of America's major collections of decorative arts. Lastly, the Prints and Drawings Department has a long, distinguished record of first-hand involvement with graphic artists, building its collections especially through its National Print Exhibitions, which will soon be joined by a Drawing National.

The Brooklyn Museum Master Plan Model, 1986, designed by Arata Isozaki and James Stewart Polshek. View of south facade from the Brooklyn Botanic Garden.

Midway through the tenth decade of its existence, The Brooklyn Museum anticipates celebrating its one hundredth anniversary as a very changed institution, poised to enter the twenty-first century after an intense period of self-inspection and analysis. In the spring of 1986, the Board of Trustees announced an architectural competition to commission a master plan for the renovation and expansion of the McKim, Mead & White building. The winning team—a joint venture of Arata Isozaki & Associates of Tokyo and James Stewart Polshek and Partners of New York—designed a stunning building that looks as sensitively to the past as it does daringly to the future.

Trusting that brilliant architecture, like all great art, is at moments the bearer of truth and may have therefore an element of inevitability contained within, The Brooklyn Museum community of board members, city officials, volunteers, Museum members, staff, and supporters in general has embarked together with the greater New York cultural community on a future full of opportunity of a unique kind. Paramount in our approach from the start of the institution's master planning has been the consideration of the Museum building as a masterpiece in its own right and therefore an integral part of the Museum's collection. Nowhere else in New York—indeed in the nation—is there an institution of such size and history that still remains unfinished from the previous century. By forging the sensibilities of two centuries into one of the most thoroughly researched museum projects of recent date, we have an opportunity to construct one of the great museum structures of all time. The treasures illustrated in this book are deserving of no less a home.

View of north (front) facade.

History of the Collections

Linda S. Ferber

CHIEF CURATOR

ON INDEPENDENCE DAY 1825, General Lafayette, on a triumphant tour of the United States, boarded one of the Fulton and South Ferry Company's steamboats for the short trip across the East River to the village of Brooklyn. The thriving community—then quite independent from its sister city on Manhattan Island—is depicted in Francis Guy's painting of 1820. Accompanied from the Brooklyn ferry landing by a great throng of "citizens, trade societies and Sunday Schools," the hero of the Revolution presided over the laying of the cornerstone of a large brick building, the Brooklyn Apprentices' Library—the ancestor of The Brooklyn Museum—at the intersection of Cranberry and Henry streets in today's Brooklyn Heights.

FRANCIS GUY (American, 1760–1820)
Winter Scene in Brooklyn, circa 1817–20
Oil on canvas
58³/₄ × 75 inches (149.2 × 190.5 cm)
97.13, Gift of The Brooklyn Institute of
   Arts and Sciences

Only two years earlier, in the summer of 1823, a group of public-spirited citizens had met at William Stephenson's tavern to establish the village's first free circulating library. The idea was William Wood's, a merchant who had already founded libraries in his native Boston and in New York. The proposed audience was a specific one—young working-class men—and the mission was both practical and social: "Extending the benefits of knowledge to that portion of our youth, who are engaged in learning the mechanic arts, and thereby qualifying them for becoming useful and respectable members of society."

In 1824 these citizens incorporated the Brooklyn Apprentices' Library Association not only as a library but as "a repository of books, maps, drawing apparatus, models of machinery, tools, and implements." These somewhat disparate collections grew rapidly in temporary quarters on Fulton Street, and by summer 1825 a building for the Apprentices' Library Association was under construction.

The initial course of lectures was held in the new building early in 1827, and the first painting commissioned in 1831: William Dunlap's *Portrait of Robert Snow*, founding president of the Association. The building functioned as a center for the village, housing the Library as well as a number of civic functions. After a decade of activity public support waned, however, and in 1835 the Library closed and the books were stored. The building was sold to the city in 1836 for public use and demolished in 1857.

Sometime during 1838, the Library Association was revived and classes in mechanical, architectural, landscape, and figure drawing were begun in rooms rented in the Brooklyn Lyceum Building on Washington Street, north of the Heights and "then the center of the wealth and culture of our young city." The Brooklyn Lyceum, organized in 1833, was a local manifestation of the popular national lyceum movement, which, like the Apprentices' Library, promoted intellectual improvement and advanced the cause of public education through classes, lectures, and, at Brooklyn, a natural history collection as well.

The move to the Lyceum's elegant granite Greek revival building, completed in 1836, was to prove significant. In 1842 Augustus Graham, a prosperous manufacturer of white lead, a founder of the Library and by then the President, bought the building for the Association, thus reestablishing a permanent home for the institution that provided adequate space, not only for a library that exceeded 2,500 volumes but for other activities as well. The popular lecture courses were continued, and the first annual exhibition of paintings was held in October. In 1843 the charter was amended and the Library Association was renamed The Brooklyn Institute because the original name conveyed "too limited an impression of . . . usefulness." That same year, Library and Lyceum were consolidated as The Brooklyn Institute. The Institute's natural history department was established then with the acquisition of

The Brooklyn Institute, 1840s–50s
182 and 184 Washington Street near
  Concord Street
Photograph from Wallace Goold Levison,
  "Reminiscences of The Brooklyn Institute
  and some Early Collectors," The Brooklyn
  Museum Archives

HISTORY OF THE COLLECTIONS

the Lyceum's collection: "birds . . . reptiles in jars in alcohol; a few mammals; various fishes beautifully mounted . . . a considerable number of shells . . . and some minerals." The second annual Institute exhibition, held later that year, offered further evidence of the broadening scope of activity, consisting of "models of machinery, curious specimens of nature and art, a fine collection of prints, and flowers . . . pieces of sculpture, with many superior works in painting." These annuals were composed almost entirely of works and objects loaned by the citizens of Brooklyn, suggesting an abundance of local collectors who must have inspired the Institute directors to announce during the fifth annual in 1846 their intention of establishing a permanent art collection.

In 1848 Augustus Graham paid off the mortgage on the Institute building. While Graham was one of a number of library promotors, his traditional recognition as the founder of the Museum is due not only to his dedication to the infant institution during his lifetime, but also to his provision for its future. Graham died late in 1851 and was interred on Vista Hill in Greenwood Cemetery. His confidence in the Institute's future was embodied in a bequest. Along with funds to support the library, lectures on secular and religious subjects, classes in drawing, and the work of the department of natural history, Graham left a sum that marked the formal establishment of a Gallery of Fine Arts. Like a good mission statement, his endowment outlined what would remain the primary intellectual and social commitments of the institution until the mid-1930s, although the Museum's massive collections were not to be formed until the early years of the twentieth century.

The first Graham commission was extended in 1855 to Asher B. Durand, whose *First Harvest in the Wilderness* is a landscape allegory in tribute to the Institute and its benefactor, "that pioneer in the wilderness," as *The Crayon* hailed Graham. However, despite *The Crayon*'s optimism, by 1878, when a group of friends presented Guy's picture to the Institute, momentum had declined and the permanent collection consisted of only fifteen works, all of them American and seven of them portraits of officers. A report on the state of the "nucleus of a Fine Art Gallery" observed that, in the twenty-six years since Graham's bequest, "the value of works of Art have been enhanced greatly, and the value of money reduced." Thus the fund was "inadequate to purchase every year a work of Art worthy of the Institute."

By the mid-1860s, the activities of the Natural History Department were also on the wane, a state that was generally indicative of the depressed condition of the Institute itself. The Washington Street address was no longer fashionable. The center of cultural activity had moved to Montague Street, where buildings for the recently established Academy of Music and Brooklyn Art Association were completed in 1861 and 1872.

In an effort to keep up with the times, the Institute building was completely remodeled in 1867, incurring a debt whose repayment over the next twenty years absorbed nearly all income. As a result, the Institute entered "a long period of suspended activities."

Brooklyn, however, was on the move. The years between 1850 and 1880 had seen the establishment of many rivals for public support and attention: a short-lived Brooklyn Art Union (1851), the Brooklyn Sketch Club (1857), the Graham Art School (1858), the Brooklyn Art Social (1859), the forerunner of the very successful Brooklyn Art Association (1861), the Brooklyn Academy of Design (1866), the Brooklyn Art Club (1878), and the Rembrandt Club (1880). All testified to the lively art and cultural life of what was by then a large and busy city.

Optimism ran high about Brooklyn's future. The consolidation act of 1855 had enlarged the boundaries of the city to include the village and town of Bushwick and Williamsburgh, increasing the population to more than 200,000. Thousands commuted daily by ferry to businesses in New York. A substantial building boom took place from 1860 to 1880. Prospect Park, designed by Frederic Law Olmsted and Calvert Vaux on farmland, stimulated the development of nearby Park Slope, Brooklyn's own Gold Coast. By 1860

Brooklyn was the third largest city in the country. The ultimate harbinger of a glorious destiny for the City of Churches seemed embodied in John A. Roebling's Great East River Bridge, under construction by 1869.

An excerpt from Joshua Van Cott's 1881 address on the dedication of a building for yet another urban amenity, the Long Island Historical Society (now the Brooklyn Historical Society), captures the ambitious and competitive optimism of Brooklyn at the time:

It is obvious to anyone who will think about it that the business of New York must, in a few years, draw out of New York its residences, except those of the plainest and cheapest description. The great warehouses of New York, the great shops and factories will drive the more elegant residences of New York out of the city. . . . The great Merchants of New York with their accumulations will have to cross over the great bridge. . . . Every person who has seen the growth of New York knows that New York is to be abandoned in less than a half century, and the residences of the rich financiers will have to go to New Jersey or to Brooklyn. We are now at the beginning of a great movement of that kind when this City of Brooklyn of ours—no longer to be called the City of Churches but the Home City of America . . . —is to be aggrandized, to be built up in institutions, is to have its university, its great libraries, its great collections of art, is to have everything that adds to the sweetness of life and the moral and intellectual excellence of a great city.

This same spirit also galvanized supporters of the nearly defunct Institute—Van Cott among them—to ambitious and even daring plans once the final payment on the disastrous mortgage was made in 1887. The following year, the proceedings of a Citizens' Committee on Museums of Art and Science were outlined in *The First Year Book of the Brooklyn Institute:* "Boston has the Lowell Institute, a Society of Natural History and an Art Museum; . . . Philadelphia has the Franklin Institute, an Academy of Sciences and a Gallery of Fine Arts, and . . . New York has the Metropolitan Museum and the American Museum [of Natural History]," yet, the writer lamented, "Brooklyn has nothing corresponding to these institutions." Committee members spoke eloquently of "the educating and uplifting influence of true Art" and of the importance of securing "a collection of casts . . . that would not only indicate what was true in Art, but would also teach the history of its development." To the conventional pieties of "educating and refining" the working class, the citizens added the "element of enjoyment": "that people whose day's labor was long and severe, should find in a museum that which would give them rest and pleasure." Members reported on the origins and history of the successful Metropolitan Museum of Art (founded in 1870) and the American Museum of Natural History (founded in 1869).

Early in 1889, George Brown Goode, Assistant Secretary of the Smithsonian Institution, spoke before the Institute and the Citizens' Committee on "The Museum of the Future":

The founding of a public museum in a city like Brooklyn, is a work whose importance can scarcely be overestimated. The founders of institutions of this character do not often realize how much they are doing for the future. Opportunity such as that which is now open to the members of the Brooklyn Institute occur only once in the lifetime of a nation. It is by no means improbable that the persons now in this room have it in their power to decide whether in the future intellectual progress of this nation, Brooklyn is to lead or to follow far in the rear.

Brooklyn, the Committee decided, was to lead with a unique amalgam combining the best elements of The Metropolitan Museum of Art and the American Museum of Natural History, an institution that would, through its collections and programs, explore and present the entire spectrum of natural history and human achievement to the citizens of Brooklyn and "people from the other side of the river and from a distance." The directors therefore "determined to make the property of the Institute the nucleus of a broad and comprehensive institution for the advancement of science and art, . . . laboring not only for the advancement of knowledge, but also for the education of the people through lectures and collections in art and science. It was felt," they concluded, "that Brooklyn should have an Institute of Arts and Sciences worthy of her wealth, her position, her culture and her people."

The old Institute, the germ of this grand scheme, was expanded into sixteen departments (which by 1897 had grown to twenty-five). Some were independent organizations that joined the Institute, like the Art Association and the Academy of Music. The loose combination resembled a large university, "each department forming a society by itself, and yet enjoying all the privileges of the general association." The Brooklyn Academy of Music, Brooklyn Botanic Garden, and Brooklyn Children's Museum were departments of the Institute until the 1970s. Sites for programs were located all over the city of Brooklyn while the existing collections were still mostly housed in the old Institute building on Washington Street.

It was obvious, however, that these existing facilities were inadequate to house this grand design, especially after a fire in 1890 damaged the building and destroyed part of the collection and library. By 1891, under the energetic leadership of President John B. Woodward (1835–1896), the Institute made plans to build a large museum, a complex that would house nearly all departments of the newly incorporated (1890) Brooklyn Institute of Arts and Sciences in a single structure. The City of Brooklyn, authorized by the state legislature to lease to the Institute the site on Prospect Heights just east of Olmsted and Vaux's great park, also appropriated funds for the construction of the building, a responsibility assumed by the City of New York when Brooklyn became a borough in 1898.

The land now occupied by The Brooklyn Museum, the Brooklyn Public Library, and the Brooklyn Botanic Garden was part of a 320-acre tract bisected by Flatbush Avenue that had been set aside earlier in the century as the future site for a public park. In 1866 Frederick Law Olmsted and Calvert Vaux submitted a report to the Brooklyn Park Commission suggesting that the wedge of land east of Flatbush Avenue be reserved for "Museums and other Educational Edifices" and that the area west of Flatbush Avenue continue to be developed as Prospect Park. Olmsted and Vaux conceived of this cultural and recreational complex as an organic unit to be connected to outlying areas of Brooklyn by a system of parkways—a term they coined in 1868—to the south (Ocean Parkway) and to the east (Eastern Parkway). Their grand urban plan was realized and remains intact today.

Prospect Park was opened in 1866 and some twenty-nine years later the Institute's directors and City officials were prepared to implement the rest of Olmsted and Vaux's scheme. On Saturday afternoon, December 14, 1895, Charles A. Schieren, Mayor of Brooklyn and soon to be an Institute Trustee

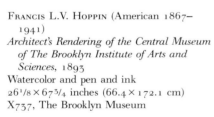

FRANCIS L.V. HOPPIN (American 1867–1941)
Architect's Rendering of the Central Museum of The Brooklyn Institute of Arts and Sciences, 1893
Watercolor and pen and ink
26 1/8 × 67 3/4 inches (66.4 × 172.1 cm)
X737, The Brooklyn Museum

The Hall of Casts, 1898–99
West Wing, third floor

and donor, laid the cornerstone for the West Wing of the Central Museum of The Brooklyn Institute of Arts and Sciences with the aid of William R. Mead of McKim, Mead & White, architects of the building, and P. J. Carlin, contractor for construction. Francis Hoppin's 1893 rendering presents the imposing Beaux-Arts building as originally proposed. Meant to house comprehensive collections of art, natural history, and science, as well as myriad education and research activities, the plan—if completed—would have been the largest museum structure in the world.

With the decision to concentrate most of the departments beneath a single roof and with building plans under way, the loosely amalgamated departments of the Institute required central administration. In 1890 Woodward appointed Franklin W. Hooper (1851–1914) first Director of the reorganized Institute. Hooper, a Harvard-trained scientist who had studied natural history with Louis Agassiz, taught in the 1880s at Brooklyn's Adelphi Academy (now Adelphi University), was active in the scientific endeavors of the old Institute, and had served on the Citizen's Committee. Hooper was very much the driving force in the development of the expanded Institute.

When the West Wing of the Central Museum was opened in 1897 the collections moved from storage to Eastern Parkway to be installed and enlarged as new sections of the building were opened in coming years. The organization and growth of the collections in the new museum building were regulated at the turn of the century by three departments: Fine Arts; Ethnology, newly established in 1903; and Natural History.

The Fine Arts Department came to the new museum building with a collection hardly larger than that recorded in the 1878 inventory of paintings. The "Opening Exhibition" of European and American paintings in June 1897 consisted almost entirely of loans from private collections. William Henry Goodyear (1846–1923) presided as Curator over the department for almost twenty-five years. A graduate of Yale University, Goodyear studied law, history, and art history in Europe before embarking on a career as an archaeologist, architectural historian, and educator. Called "America's first art historian," Goodyear had served from 1882 until 1888 as Curator at The Metropolitan Museum of Art. In 1890 he came to Brooklyn, first as Titular Curator and the architect of successful and long-lived educational programs and then, in 1899, as Curator of Fine Arts. He was Hooper's match in the boundless energy and conviction with which he took up the Institute's cause of public education. Goodyear's range as a scholar was extraordinarily broad. He published widely on art history and vigorously advanced his theory of architectural refinements—intentional departures from geometrical uniformity to enhance optical interest—with extensive travel, articles, lectures, and photographic documentation of monuments from ancient Egypt to the 1900 Paris Exposition. Goodyear's primary focus on European art and architecture did not prevent him from taking a strong interest in American art—an enlightened attitude at the time. He wrote regularly on these and other art topics in early issues of the Museum *Bulletin*.

Major gifts of these early years included the bequest in 1906 of Caroline Polhemus, a collection that included sixty-one nineteenth-century American and European paintings and watercolors. A portion of the estate of her brother, William Herriman, which included eleven works by Elihu Vedder as well as an important work by Jean François Millet, was given in 1921. While Goodyear was Curator of Fine Arts, collector and connoisseur A. Augustus Healy (1850–1921), who succeeded Woodward as President in 1895, masterminded major painting and sculpture acquisitions during these early years. One of the earliest purchases was secured by a campaign Healy led to raise funds for 344 gouaches by James Tissot illustrating *The Life of Christ*. In 1906 Healy and George Hearn purchased Henri Fantin-Latour's important *Portrait of Madame Léon Maître* (1882) for the Museum from the artist's Memorial Exhibition in Paris. Both purchases were probably made with the advice of Healy's friend John Singer Sargent, whose watercolors Healy saw to it were purchased for the Museum in 1909. In 1910 the Cyrus J. Lawrence collection of over one hundred bronzes by French animalier Antoine Louis Barye was purchased at auction.

Collections of European glass, ceramics, ivories, and metalwork were then also held in the Fine Arts Department, while Oriental materials were transferred early on to the Department of Ethnology. Original works were supplemented by nearly one hundred casts of Classical and Renaissance monuments as well as hundreds of Goodyear's photographs and lantern slides of European architecture. Goodyear worked closely with Susan A. Hutchinson, both librarian and curator of prints, from 1899 to 1934, acquiring Homer watercolors, Rembrandt and Whistler etchings, and other treasures, establishing what would become in 1937 an autonomous Department of Prints and Drawings. Goodyear died in 1924, an eminent art and architectural historian who was lauded as "one of the few survivors of a type of American genius which expressed itself in aggressive action with an intense fervor of intellectual conviction." Perhaps his greatest contribution was as a dedicated educator and tireless promoter of Institute programs.

The Institute Department of Ethnology, established in 1903, reflected the intention of planners not only to include traditional European fine arts but also to collect productions of non-Western European cultures, especially those of North and South America. The first curator, Robert Stewart Culin (1858–1929) was, like Hooper and Goodyear, a remarkable figure. A self-trained ethnologist and folklorist, he assumed a museum post at the University of

*Installation of Pomo Indian Collection in
California Hall, 1911
West Wing, third floor*

Pennsylvania, where he established himself during the 1890s as an expert on folk culture and games of the world. After an initial focus on Oriental cultures, Culin turned to the art and artifacts of the North American Indian and in 1900 made the first of many collecting expeditions to the American west, a collecting practice he continued after coming to found the department at The Brooklyn Institute three years later. The energetic Culin immediately began to expand the meager holdings of the old Institute by means of a series of field trips through the Southwest, California, and Northwest Coast regions, acquiring and carefully recording information about thousands of objects.

Although Culin was dedicated to the systematic documentation of North American Indian cultures, his interests were by no means limited to those geographic areas. After 1910 he traveled to the Orient and Central Europe acquiring collections of paintings, sculpture, decorative art, and costume from a wide range of cultures. He was adept not only at collecting but also at display. His exhibits were admired and his clear labels praised. Sensitive to aesthetic issues, he saw objects in terms of their formal qualities and technical finesse as well as in terms of material and use. One of the notable early acquisitions of the department was a large collection of Central African objects Culin purchased in Belgium in 1922—today still the great strength of the Museum's African holdings. The interpretation of these objects as works of art in a landmark exhibition the following year marked the Museum as a pioneer in the reevaluation of such material—previously interpreted as anthropological specimens— as worthy of aesthetic appreciation on a par with European art.

The thousands of specimens Culin acquired on Museum expeditions provided the pool of objects later to be dispersed into four curatorial departments that have since been further developed and refined into collections that are today among the strongest and best documented in the Museum. These include the direct descendant of Ethnology—African, Oceanic, and New World Art—and some of the most important holdings in today's Department of Costumes and Textiles and Decorative Arts. From Culin's travels in the Far and Near East came the objects that formed the core of the Oriental Art Department: Japanese, Ainu, and Korean holdings as well as the first Indian art collections.

A small collection of Oceanic materials had been deposited at the Institute as part of the Natural History Department prior to Culin's arrival. While Culin's Museum field expeditions did not include this area, these holdings have continued to grow over the years and today include a number of important objects.

The Department of Natural History, Institute Director Hooper's own primary interest, was the oldest department, established in 1843, and in 1903 by far the largest collection, with more than 71,000 specimens. Vestiges may occasionally still be found in the corner of a remote storeroom. As construction of the building continued, the galleries in the West Wing would be largely reserved for exhibits of shells, animal habitats, and marine mammals, all of which were among the Museum's most popular displays for decades.

Hall of Invertebrates, 1920s
West Wing, fourth floor

When the Brooklyn Botanic Garden was originally established as a department of the Institute in 1910, the existing botanical collections and library were eventually transferred to the garden site just south of the Museum building. The Garden was intended by McKim, Mead & White's master plan to function not only as the parklike repository of a living collection but also as the setting for a monumental entry and stairway dominating the south facade of their great Beaux-Arts Museum building.

In 1914, when Hooper died, all recognized that an era had come to an end. His title—Director of the Institute—was retired, and three directors were appointed to guide the Museums (Central and Children's), the Botanic Garden, and the Education Division. William Henry Fox (1858–1952), engaged to oversee the Museum—a post he would hold for two and a half decades—paid tribute in his *Memoires* to the dynamic founding director of the Institute, characterizing him as a man of "energy and vision," a "spellbinder" whose "plans had no limits" and whose "ideas were colossal." As a practical administrator, however, Fox also recognized the unrealistic ambitions of the original promotors of The Brooklyn Institute of Arts and Sciences. Hooper was, in Fox's words "afflicted with the impractical." "Sheer size," he continued, seemed to be Hooper's "standard of excellence" with "no sense of economy whatever." Soon after his arrival in 1913, Fox appears to have understood that the projected "biggest museum building in the world," now the ward of New York City with several other major collecting institutions, had little chance of completion. The central portion of the facade had been added in 1905, and in 1907 the East Wing and Grand Staircase were completed. The original building campaign would come to a final halt in 1927, just four years after the Centennial of the Apprentices' Library, with only one-sixth of McKim, Mead & White's original conception realized.

Seeking both to define and to consolidate the collections of what he called this "composite museum," Fox early on entertained the "heretical idea" of placing the natural history collections elsewhere. The Board, then presided over by A. Augustus Healy, had, in fact, requested upon Fox's engagement that he seek, in the President's words, to "restore the balance between the art and science displays which at present is heavily scientific." Fox recalled Healy's words at that initial interview in 1912: "most of us on the Board of Trustees . . . have a greater personal interest in art than in science and we feel that it would be better for . . . Brooklyn if more attention were paid to the development of this branch of the Museum." Franklin Hooper's death soon afterward removed a primary obstacle to such a reordering of Museum priorities.

Fox accepted the challenge. Trained in law, with museum experience as director of the Herron Institute (now the Indianapolis Museum of Art), he had served as fine arts administrator of two international expositions. His vivid recollection of his first visit late in 1912 to what he described as "a massive Romanesque structure on the wide Parkway" is worth quoting at length:

The first few rooms we passed through were heavily scientific. The objects were quite well, if conventionally arranged. But they gave out an air of over-importance and when we carried our inspection further, of overbalance. . . . The Japanese hall through which we passed offered a kind of protest to the overwhelming force of natural science exhibits. This was part of the ethnological collection—and taste had been exercised in its arrangement and we thought the effect excellent. Naturally we were concerned with the section of the art exhibits which Mr. Healy had in mind, so we inquired our way to the gallery of paintings. The scene that assailed our eyes was awful. The walls of a room one hundred and ten feet long by forty wide with smaller galleries adjacent were covered with three rows of paintings, without regard to their relation to each other, a veritable maelstrom of clashing harmonies, color, subject, and school, resting heavily on a wooden cimaise. . . . In a connecting room Tissot's life of Christ was hung on both sides of permanent screens, forming a barrier to anything like revolving exhibits and was partly in the dark. In another gallery stood a lurid full length portrait of the Kaiser . . . which was so conspicuous as to prevent the other canvases from being noticed.

Painting and Sculpture Gallery, before 1904
West Wing, fifth floor

The director-to-be's interests ranged further afield in his conviction that "there was vast room for improvement in the art section" and in his and Mrs. Fox's interest in the decorative arts: "On another floor there was a loan exhibit of lace which Catherine pronounced to be very ordinary," he wrote, "and this, as far as we could then see, was the Brooklyn Museum's only representation of the applied arts." Catherine Fox was to play an important role in the development of these collections. A common passion for lace seems to have been the basis for a friendship with Theodora Wilbour which was to yield great benefits to the Museum. In 1931 Catherine Fox arranged for Mr. and Mrs. Edward S. Harkness to purchase the Shabelsky collection of Russian costumes and textiles for the Museum.

Fox characterized the "veteran" curator Goodyear as "somewhat impractical," but "a fine cabinet scholar," whose passion for research obviously outweighed installation skills. Characteristically, Culin was away on expedition when Fox arrived, but stories of his "eccentricities" abounded. Fox described him as "an odd character" who "preferred to be an independent figure in his special department with a minimum of control." When in residence, he occupied "a little dark den of an office" near the Japanese Hall that was book-lined, with a picturesque mass of objects littering the floor.

Fox's own exhibition philosophy called for "a compact and scientific installation, presenting each class of exhibit as a single unit." Such an arrangement was not only "convenient to the public," he wrote, but "a necessity" in making "the story of art clear and impressive." Fox admired Culin's skills in installation and turned first to those areas most in need of his attention—the "veritable maelstrom" that was the painting and sculpture galleries. Mindful of his mandate to "raise the art of the museum to the same standard set by the scientific section," Fox sought to establish a distinct field of endeavor for the Museum that would not compete with the "excessive old master atmosphere" of the Metropolitan Museum but, rather, guide the Museum's energies toward the exhibition and collection of modern or contemporary art, "as it was then understood," that is, primarily French Impressionist and Post-Impressionist works and American early modern works. Fox even proposed that the two museums "divide the Museum field in Greater New York"—the Metropolitan emphasizing "works of the past" and Brooklyn concentrating on later periods. Although the offer was declined for reasons of "insurmountable difficulties," the plan was pursued at Brooklyn, with the support of Healy, himself most interested in nineteenth-century French painting. In 1920, the President presented the Museum's first work by Monet, *The Doge's Palace*. In the following decade important works by Lautrec, Gauguin, Pissarro, Degas, Sisley, Cezanne, and Morisot entered the collection.

Healy's passing in 1921 and Frank L. Babbott's (1854–1933) assumption of the presidency may have checked the momentum of the modernist trend in Brooklyn. Fox was to lament lack of trustee support in his later quests for the Lillie P. Bliss and Havemeyer collections (now at The Museum of Modern Art and the Metropolitan Museum respectively), and although Katherine S. Dreier's Société Anonyme exhibited at the Museum in 1926, the collection went to Yale. Nevertheless, Babbott's own collecting proclivities were ultimately beneficial to the Museum's limited but choice "old master atmosphere." His fine collection of early Italian panel paintings, purchased between 1911 and 1916, would come to the Museum as gifts from his children over a span of some four decades.

Trustee enthusiasm and connoisseurship had positive results in other collecting areas as well. Fox had declared Museum interest in the "applied arts" early in his tenure, citing with pride the fact that the Museum was "early in the field" in building collections of "rarity and originality." The year after his arrival, in 1914, a Department of Colonial and Early American Furniture was established, predecessor of today's Decorative Arts Department, and most probably the idea of a new Trustee, Luke Vincent Lockwood (1872–1951), a Brooklyn attorney who was a noted authority on and pioneer collector of American furniture and decorative arts.

The Museum's intention was to interpret objects of the American past through the device of period rooms—then a relatively new idea in museum installation and a concept that has largely determined the growth of the Museum's strong collection to the present. Although acquisitions of objects and architectural elements began immediately, final installation of period rooms was not possible until the central portion of the building and the East Wing were completed in 1927. Over the next two years, under Lockwood's direction, twenty-one American period rooms of the seventeenth and eighteenth centuries were built. When they opened in late 1929, they formed the central focus of the collection and remain one of the Museum's most popular exhibitions. Continuing the tradition, the Museum in 1953 became the first art museum in America to install a series of nineteenth-century period rooms. Today the installation includes twenty-eight rooms ranging in date from a 1675 Dutch house from Flatlands, Brooklyn to a 1928 Art Deco library from a Park Avenue apartment. Like other portions of the Museum's collections, these rooms have been reinterpreted and reinstalled a number of times since 1929 in attempts to achieve more accurate approximations of the past. At this time, two other Trustee collector-scholars, John Hill Morgan (1870–1945) and Walter Crittenden (1859–1947), were also in advance of popular antiquarian taste and scholarship. They saw to it that the Museum began to build a fine collection of Colonial American painting in the 1910s and 1920s to parallel Lockwood's American decorative arts. Complementing the period rooms is one of the best American ceramic collections in the country in addition to strong collections of American furniture, glass, silver, pewter, and other metalwares as well as European decorative arts.

Fox retired in 1933 after a long career, during which time the building was completed and the major growth of the collections took place. The 1930s were to prove a decade of reevaluation, a turning point for the Museum and its collections.

Fox's successor, Philip Newell Youtz (1895–1972), trained as an educator and was a practicing architect and a committed modernist. He was to have a profound impact on the Museum during a short but highly active tenure, implementing a radical five-year plan that marked the emergence of the Museum as we know it today.

In 1934 the Board adopted a new collection policy, allowing Youtz to carry out Fox's "heretical design" of distributing the natural history specimens to other New York institutions, bringing to a close the era of the "composite museum" and laying to rest the nineteenth-century encyclopedic ambitions of the founders by finally abandoning science for art. The remaining collections were eventually organized into seven curatorial units, dividing the holdings of the Department of Ethnology between a Department of American Indian Art and Primitive Cultures and a Department of Oriental Art. The history of Western art was organized chronologically in departments of ancient, medieval, renaissance, and contemporary art—later consolidated as the Department of Painting and Sculpture—while print collections remained a division of the Library. The plaster casts, so prized by the Citizen's Committee of 1890, were discarded. Modern museum administrative practices and systematic collection care were introduced with the appointment of a registrar and the establishment of the conservation laboratory.

In his conviction that the "museum of today must meet contemporary needs," Youtz sought to encourage practical use of the collections not only for traditional educational purposes but as a research source for modern industry and manufacturing interests. Such practical application of the collections to the improvement of modern life was not new to the Museum. In fact, the original audience for whose benefit the Apprentices' Library had been founded was one of artisans and workers. While the Institute's constituency broadened rapidly, this initial impulse was not forgotten. As early as 1909, Culin considered the possibility of the Museum's collections being used by artists and designers working with industry. One motive for the acquisition of an African collection was Culin's conviction that this unfamiliar art form, as well as the other "exotic" objects he collected, would provide inspiration for American industrial designers and manufacturers.

Herbert J. Spinden (1879–1967), Culin's successor, was of the same opinion: "It has already been demonstrated that the ethnological collections in our museums contain the best source materials in applied arts. . . . We should make it the slogan of American industry that the finest products of all ages and peoples are welcome ingredients but that all these must be reborn to fit the needs and ideals of our modern civilization." Fox, too, had promoted the growth of Museum collections of decorative arts: "I have always," he wrote, "tried to project this phase of creative effort in design up to the prestige enjoyed by the arts of painting, sculpture and architecture. . . . They are of equal value and the history of their development is just as important."

It would be Youtz, however, who organized these long-term Museum commitments into an institutional plan, proposing in 1935 that an Industrial Center for Greater New York be established at the Museum, to be funded by the Public Works Administration. While the project as Youtz envisioned it was not pursued, the collections of costumes, textiles, and jewelry were largely consolidated at that time into an Industrial Division, which encouraged use and research on these materials by member firms. This service developed in the late 1940s into the Edward C. Blum Design Laboratory, named in honor of the Institute Trustee who served from 1911 to 1946. Housed in the Department of Decorative Arts, the Lab was transformed by 1973 into today's Department of Costumes and Textiles, one of the most important costume collections in the United States.

Under Youtz's leadership, not only were the collections and their uses redefined but the building itself was reconfigured as well. The most radical change was the removal in 1934 of the Grand Staircase on the northern facade. While justly criticized today as an ill-conceived violation of the original design of the building, this controversial "improvement" was intended as a socially responsible gesture, eliminating the grand ceremonial entry, which literally elevated the visitor to the level of the arts, in order to facilitate public access directly from the street.

Youtz wanted to "turn a useless Renaissance palace into a serviceable modern museum." At his insistence a great deal of Beaux-Arts ornament was stripped from the Museum interior to create the "clean, neutral" gallery space deemed most desirable by modernist standards. The collections themselves were then configured into what was termed "chronological" order—a kind of visitor's art history survey through time and space—beginning with the ahistorical placement of American Indian Art and Primitive Cultures on the first floor and rising to a "gallery of living artists" on the sixth—a floor plan that survives nearly intact today.

In 1932 the children of the pioneer American Egyptologist Charles Edwin Wilbour gave a fund in his honor for the endowment of a curatorial department of ancient art. The collection of ancient art, originally begun under Goodyear's supervision, dates its beginnings from acquisitions of Egyptian antiquities in 1902, some obtained from excavations of Sir William Matthew Flinders Petrie, the father of modern field archaeology. In 1908 the Museum acquired more Egyptian antiquities from the famous private collection formed in the 1880s by Armand de Potter. In 1916 the Wilbour family began giving most of his collection and his library to the Museum. Some three decades later, in 1947, The Museum received Wilbour's important collection of papyri and the following year the Wilbour Fund made possible the acquisition of the Egyptian holdings of the New-York Historical Society. This huge collection complemented the core collection already in place—the Predynastic and Archaic antiquities acquired through early excavations, and the Amarna (New Kingdom) objects from Wilbour's holdings, Old and Middle Kingdom objects, including sculpture and reliefs of relatively large scale.

In the early 1950s, the Museum also acquired a number of important reliefs from The Metropolitan Museum of Art including the tomb reliefs of an

Egyptian Antiquities and Goodyear's
Photographs Demonstrating the Theory of
Architectural Refinements, circa 1904
West Wing, third floor

Egyptian vizier named Nespeqashuty. These reliefs were restored and installed in 1986. Acquisitions since the 1940s have consisted primarily of objects of high aesthetic quality, and the installations have been progressively redefined in displays emphasizing art history rather than ancient history, religion, and archaeology. Today, the collection is housed in nine galleries of pre-Pharaonic and Pharaonic Egyptian art with a tenth gallery devoted in part to the art of Roman and Christian Egypt. Those pieces of purely archaeological interest, once almost all on view, are now part of an important study collection.

The Classical and Ancient Near Eastern collections are much smaller in their scope and number of objects than the Egyptian holdings, but they include splendid Aegean, Greek, and Roman works as well as pieces of equally high quality from various parts of the Middle East. In 1955, with the support of the Hagop Kevorkian Foundation, the Museum acquired from the New-York Historical Society collections twelve monumental reliefs from a palace of the Assyrian king Ashurnasirpal II at Nimrud that are the most spectacular of the holdings of Ancient Near Eastern Art.

Culin's early ethnographic collecting trips to India, China, Korea, and Japan from 1909 to 1914 had established the foundation for what became an autonomous Department of Oriental Art by 1937. From the 1950s the holdings of later Near Eastern or Islamic art, today exhibited in the Department of Oriental Art, as well as the Indian and Southeast Asian collections were enriched through the interest of Trustee-collector Ernest Erickson (1893–1983), who acquired important works in this and other non-European cultural areas. Placed on long-term loan as Erickson acquired them, some 474 objects were eventually given to the Museum by the Ernest Erickson Foundation in 1987. They are among the most important gifts of the last decade in magnitude and over-all impact on the quality of the collections.

Erickson's earliest contact at the Museum seems to have been with Herbert Spinden, Culin's successor in 1929 as curator of Ethnology. By 1937 Spinden was curator of the newly organized Department of American Indian Art and Primitive Cultures created out of Stewart Culin's original Department of Ethnology. He continued to strengthen North American holdings by borrowing and eventually acquiring the New-York Historical Society's important Eastern Plains Indian objects collected in the 1830s by Nathan Sturges Jarvis. However, Spinden had committed his major curatorial energies to establishing Pre-Columbian art as a presence at the Museum based upon his passion for the ancient Americas, especially Andean art and textiles.

Spinden was in advance of collecting taste and scholarship in also acquiring post-Conquest Colonial material at a time when there was little North American museum interest in this aspect of the hemisphere's art history. In 1941 he organized an important exhibition of Colonial and folk art of Latin America. During the 1940s and 1950s, he also acquired Spanish Colonial paintings, sculpture, decorative arts, and costumes for several departments forming a collection unique in American museums.

During the same period, Curator of Contemporary Art John I. H. Baur (1909–1987), a pioneer scholar in the field of American art history, was making crucial additions to the collection of eighteenth- and nineteenth-century North American paintings and sculpture. Paralleling the strengths in American paintings and sculpture is a watercolor collection distinguished by comprehensive coverage of the nineteenth century in particular as well as major holdings in the work of Sargent and Winslow Homer. In 1912 the first twelve Homers were purchased from the artist's brother, and with further additions over the years—including four superb works that had belonged to Babbott given in 1978—the Museum has acquired an important collection of Homer's work in the medium.

The William A. Putnam Memorial Print Room was established in 1937 to honor the Trustee and donor of prints. The creation of this study center marked the separation of the Department of Prints and Drawings from the Library collections, where Carl O. Schniewind had succeeded Susan Hutchinson as Curator-Librarian. Una Johnson assumed the curatorship when Schniewind left for the Art Institute of Chicago, continuing the National Print exhibitions, a biennial survey of current work in the medium begun in 1921. Acquisitions from the Nationals have played a major role in establishing the Museum's strength as a survey collection of five decades of contemporary American printmaking.

Photography has also been an important tool in the Museum educational process from the turn of the century, when Goodyear amassed hundreds of images of European monuments that are today of interest as historical documents in the history of the medium. Although curators began to collect photographs as art objects in the 1930s, they did not persist. Fortunately, acquisition has now resumed with emphasis on current work paralleling the Museum's interest in contemporary art in all media with the recent revival of a curatorship of Contemporary Art.

In 1966 the Museum charted a new collecting area and adopted novel methods of display with the opening of the Frieda Schiff Warburg Memorial Sculpture Garden. This outdoor gallery of nineteenth- and twentieth-century architectural ornament has become a favorite visitor retreat.

In his 1889 address to the Citizens' Committee, the Smithsonian Secretary warned the supporters of the Museum project that, if successful, their work would "never be finished."

When a museum building has been provided, and the nucleus of a collection and an administrative staff are at hand, the work of museum-building begins, and this work, it is to be hoped, will not soon reach an end. A finished museum is a dead museum, and a dead museum is a useless museum.

The measure of the founders' and their successors' achievement at "the work of museum-building" is recorded in this volume. Far from being a static treasure house, nothing—including the building itself—is ever "finished" at The Brooklyn Museum. Change has been the constant. Each collection, each department, has its own story, its own cast of characters, a chain of events—internal and external—that have charted or altered its course. Each has contributed to the history of the Museum as a whole while institutional goals have in turn exerted a powerful influence upon the growth of collections. Curatorial departments have come and gone as holdings have been repeatedly divided, redivided, and reorganized in efforts to define collections more accurately. The collections changed in response to new scholarship and changes in mission and curatorial vision, to new audiences and to the donors and patrons who continue to enrich Museum holdings.

The earlier ethnographic orientation of the Museum has left a rich legacy in the form of the non-Western collections as well as the core of the costume and textile holdings. Many of Culin's pieces came from the field with context intact rather than as isolated art objects. Consequently, the comprehensive nature of the collections made it natural for the Museum to play a major role in the reevaluation of non-European cultures as worthy of aesthetic appreciation—a role the Museum continues to play as successive generations discover and rediscover the extraordinary collections housed here. The diverse collections at Brooklyn reflect a history of taste and of ideas about objects and their makers in a way that those in other museums founded solely as museums of art cannot.

What is today The Brooklyn Museum began in 1823 as an idea—"extending the benefits of knowledge"—embodied in a series of collections through 164 years of constant change. The audience changed, Brooklyn changed, the building changed, and the collection changed. The idea, however, has remained constant as the mission that inspired the founding of the Brooklyn Apprentices' Library, The Brooklyn Institute of Arts and Sciences, and The Brooklyn Museum.

I want to thank Joan Darragh and Leland M. Roth for the opportunity to read their excellent essays before publication in *A New Brooklyn Museum: The Master Plan Competition*. Deborah Wythe offered invaluable support with her expert knowledge of Museum archives. I am especially grateful to Deirdre Lawrence for generously allowing me to consult her manuscript on Museum history and her copious research files and for reviewing and commenting so cogently upon my own effort.

The following members of the staff of The Brooklyn Museum have written the entries in this publication: Richard Fazzini, Curator, Robert S. Bianchi, Associate Curator, James F. Romano, Associate Curator, and Donald B. Spanel, Research Associate, Egyptian, Classical, and Ancient Middle Eastern Art; Diane Fane, Curator, Francine Farr, Assistant Curator, and Ira Jacknis, Assistant Curator for Research, African, Oceanic, and New World Art; Robert Moes, Curator, Sheila R. Canby, Associate Curator, and Amy G. Poster, Associate Curator, Oriental Art; Elizabeth Ann Coleman, Curator, Costumes and Textiles; Dianne Pilgrim, Chairman, Kevin Stayton, Curator, and Christopher Wilk, Associate Curator, Decorative Arts; Linda Konheim Kramer, Curator, Barbara Head Millstein, Associate Curator, and Barry Walker, Associate Curator, Prints, Drawings, and Photography; Sarah Faunce, Chairman, Charlotta Kotik, Curator, Barbara D. Gallati, Associate Curator, Barbara Head Millstein, Associate Curator, Ann Dumas, Assistant Curator, and Teresa Carbone, Assistant Curator for Research, Painting and Sculpture; and Deirdre E. Lawrence, Chief Librarian.

Egyptian,
Classical,
and Ancient Middle Eastern Art

1   EARLY FEMALE FIGURE

Egypt, El Ma'mariya
Predynastic Period, Naqada IIa
  (transitional), circa 3500–3400 B.C.
Terracotta, painted
11 1/2 inches (29.3 cm) high
07.447.505, Museum Excavations 1906–7

Since the 1880s archaeologists have unearthed hundreds of pottery figurines of women in Egyptian Predynastic or prehistoric tombs. This striking image and a nearly identical piece from the same tomb are among the few acknowledged masterpieces of the type. It represents a slender female raising her arms above her birdlike head and bending her attenuated fingers downward in a bold, sweeping gesture. The entire figure is covered with a thin red wash. The craftsman who made it applied a layer of black resin to the head representing a wig or hair. The figure's lower body takes the form of a peg; it has been painted white to suggest a skirt.

The meaning of this statuette is unclear. Painted pottery vessels of this period sometimes have representations of females shown on a much larger scale than their masculine companions. These figures have long conical lower bodies and raise their arms in a manner echoing the statuette. Their exaggerated size suggests that they played a supernatural role, perhaps as a goddess or guardian of the deceased. The unusual head, resembling that of a great bird, enhances the feeling of otherworldliness. Since other Predynastic figurines show naturalistically modeled faces, we may presume that the artisan wished to imbue this figure with a nonhuman, perhaps divine, appearance.

The rounded bottom prevented the figure from standing. Only with the end of the Predynastic Period were statues given bases enabling them to stand upright.

2 RELIEF REPRESENTATION OF A STATUE

Egypt, Saqqara, Tomb D43
Old Kingdom, late Dynasty V (2475–
2345 B.C.)
Limestone, 29¼ inches (74.4 cm) wide
37.25E, Charles Edwin Wilbour Fund

Saqqara Tomb D 43 is dated to late Dynasty V on the basis of its inscriptions, and this dating accords well with the tomb's relief style, including its boldness. The physiognomy of the figure in this particular relief is, however, exceptional, being only partially paralleled in a few other works. Indeed, this face differs so much from the many conventionalized faces of its time that in the last century it was identified erroneously as a depiction of a non-Egyptian. Today this relief remains one significant focus of the ongoing debate over the existence and nature of portraiture in ancient Egyptian art, even though it is not a representation of a person.

Egyptian reliefs of people normally show both shoulders frontally. This relief, however, clearly had shoulders in profile, making it a representation of a statue of its owner, labeled with his two names of Smenkhuptah and Itwesh. The statue's unconventional face has led some scholars to interpret the phrase *shesep er ankh* accompanying the names as "statue according to life" or "lifelike image."

However, most scholars now translate those words as "living" or "receiving statue"—a reference to the sculpture's magical functions. In fact, the relief formed part of the largest known Old Kingdom image of a private person's statue, probably in a scene where the sculpture received offerings for its owner's spirit. Some of the peculiarities of the image presumably reflect the type of sculpture shown, one embodying an ideal state of existence in which the image is what one might call prosperously portly. Nevertheless, there is something indeed "lifelike" about this "living" statue.

3 STATUE OF METJETJI

Egypt, probably from Saqqara
Old Kingdom, late Dynasty V to early
  Dynasty VI, circa 2360–2340 B.C.
Wood, stone, metal, gesso, painted
24¹/8 inches (61.5 cm) high
51.1, Charles Edwin Wilbour Fund

Every large-scale Egyptian tomb contained at least one statue of the deceased. Tomb statues served as substitute bodies, sheltering the spirit if the mummy were destroyed. They also received offerings of food, drink, and clothing brought by the tomb owner's respectful descendants.

Since most tomb statues were sealed in chambers, never to be seen by mortal eyes, Egyptian artisans did not feel compelled to reproduce the subject's actual physical appearance. As long as the sculpture bore an inscription with the correct names and titles, the spirit could recognize it and return to it for refuge and nourishment.

Only on the rarest of occasions do we encounter a statue that breaks away from standard idealizing models and tempts us to believe that we are gazing on a likeness of a specific ancient Egyptian. This statue, representing a high official named Metjetji, is such a piece. The lively face is dominated by huge calcite and obsidian eyes. Their downward cast suggests intelligence and contemplativeness, perhaps characteristics of the man himself. The tautness of the flesh and the head's ovoid shape are rarely seen in the Old Kingdom. The sculptor's decision to fashion a statue of Metjetji with these features seems to indicate that they were distinctive of the man himself.

4 PEPY II AND HIS MOTHER

Egypt, possibly from Saqqara
Old Kingdom, Dynasty VI, circa 2220–
2210 B.C.
Calcite, 15⁷⁄₁₆ inches (39.2 cm) high
39.119, Charles Edwin Wilbour Fund

Pepy II ascended to the Egyptian throne as a child, perhaps at the age of six. An Old Kingdom document seems to indicate that he ruled for ninety-six years; some scholars, however, would shorten his reign to sixty-four years.

This statuette shows Pepy II as a child seated on the lap of his mother, Queen Meryre-ankhnes. No doubt the piece was carved in the earliest years of his kingship. Pepy II appears in the traditional costume of an Egyptian king: the *nemes*-head-cloth, with its protective *uraeus*-cobra, and the short goffered kilt called a *shendyt*. The queen's trappings, including her wig and long dress, recall representations of noblewomen of the Sixth Dynasty. The tiny hole in her forehead, however, testifies to her royal status. It once accommodated a queen's symbol, the golden head of a vulture, the earthly manifestation of the Mother Goddess Mut.

Royal stone statues of the late Old Kingdom are extremely rare. All are quite small and show the artistic tendency, first recognizable in mid-Dynasty V, of carving the arms and legs fully in the round rather than connecting them to the rest of the statue by awkward stone "bridges." This figure of Pepy II is unique among Sixth Dynasty sculpture in its use of two primary views. Normally, Egyptian sculpture was meant to be seen only from the front. By placing Pepy II and his mother at right angles, an innovative sculptor has created a work that must be seen from two distinct views.

5 RECUMBENT DOG

Mesopotamia, perhaps from Babylon
Old Babylonian Period, circa 19th
 century B.C.
Aragonite, 8³/4 inches (22.3 cm) long
51.220, Gift of Mr. and Mrs. Alastair B.
 Martin

A strong tradition of animal sculpture existed for millennia in ancient Mesopotamia (modern Iraq). However, few statues of animals have survived from the major historical periods. Those that we do have seem to come from temples and represent animals associated with specific divinities. The dog was sacred to the goddess Gula, the consort of the great Babylonian god Ninurta. Quite probably this image was a votive offering left in the temple by a pious adherent of Gula's cult. It may have once stood in a sanctuary of that goddess, perhaps in one of the temples of Babylon.

This figure reflects the great attention to naturalism that characterizes the finest creations of the Old Babylonian Period. The sculptor paid great attention to the dog's wrinkled muzzle; heavy jowls; thick, muscular neck; and stout torso. So faithful was his representation of these details that we can recognize the dog as an early form of the modern mastiff. The Mesopotamians used the fearless mastiff to protect their flocks against rapacious predators. The thick collar around the animal's neck signifies ownership.

6 ROYAL WOMAN

Originally from Egypt, found near
Rome, perhaps at Hadrian's villa at
Tivoli
Middle Kingdom, mid-Dynasty XII,
circa 1929–1878 B.C.
Chlorite, 15⅜ inches (38.9 cm) high
56.85, Charles Edwin Wilbour Fund

Some of the finest sculptures of ancient Egyptian women were carved
during the Twelfth Dynasty. Their
faces convey a youthful radiance
with wide-open eyes, fleshy cheeks,
and slender lips. This tendency is
most conspicuous on images of royal
women.

This head is recognizable as a
queen or princess by the hairpin in
the form of a *uraeus*-cobra on her
forehead. A heavy striated wig covers
her head; only a tiny portion of her
natural hair is visible just beneath
the *uraeus*. The statue survives in an
imperfect state. The eyes, originally
made of stone and metal, were pried
from their sockets in antiquity. In
addition, the figure's nose, lips, and
chin have all experienced damage.

Since the end of the wig tails off
toward the horizontal, we know this
head originally belonged to a figure

of a recumbent sphinx. Female
sphinxes enjoyed great popularity in
the court of Dynasty XII. One of
these, showing a daughter of
Amenemhat II named Ita, was found
at Qatna in Syria. Its similarity to the
Brooklyn head suggests that they
were contemporaneous.

The head's recent history begins in
1771, when Galvin Hamilton, a
Scottish painter, acquired it in Rome.
Any Egyptian piece of this size and
quality was probably found at
Hadrian's villa at Tivoli, whence the
Romans brought it from Egypt.

7 SESOSTRIS III

Egypt, probably from Hierakonpolis
Middle Kingdom, late Dynasty XII,
circa 1878–1840 B.C.
Black granite, 21 7/16 inches (54.5 cm)
high
52.1, Charles Edwin Wilbour Fund

At the apex of Egyptian society stood the indomitable figure of pharaoh. Religious tradition taught that he was a god incarnate, the earthly manifestation of the Sky God Horus who ruled and protected Egypt. One of the mightiest of these divine pharaohs, Sesostris III, governed with absolute authority at a time when Egypt was the world's paramount power. Evidence suggests that when faced by an increasingly hostile feudal nobility, Sesostris III simply stripped the landed gentry of all its ancient rights and privileges. This action reduced the nobles to the level of nonentities and consolidated all national power in the king's person.

This impressive statue of Sesostris III shows him sporting the traditional regalia of a king: the *nemes*-headcloth with its protective *uraeus*-cobra, the *shendyt*-kilt, and the bull's tail between his legs. Sesostris III's role as protector of Egypt's borders is symbolized by the nine bows beneath his feet, representing Egypt's nine traditional enemies.

Since the king was seen as divine, royal statues normally have idealizing faces, without the blemishes or lines that mar mortal flesh. During Sesostris III's reign, however, royal sculptors abandoned this perfect model. The king's face now features heavily lidded eyes, deep creases running across his cheeks, and a firmly set mouth. Sesostris III's statues come closer to conveying the impression of a real person than any earlier royal images.

8 STATUE OF SQUATTING MAN

Provenance not known
Thirteenth Dynasty (1781–circa 1650 B.C.)
Brown quartzite, 27¹/₂ inches (69.8 cm) high
62.77.1, Charles Edwin Wilbour Fund

This magnificent statue of an unnamed person superbly illustrates the continued influence of late Twelfth Dynasty royal sculpture on works commissioned by private persons in succeeding generations. Every detail of the facial modeling is the legacy of Sesostris III and Amenemhat III, the two most important rulers of the latter part of the Middle Kingdom. The heavy eyelids, slightly downcast eyes, tightly drawn cheeks, pursed mouth, and especially the flaring ears are the distinctive characteristics of late Middle Kingdom royal and private sculpture. In the Thirteenth and Seventeenth Dynasties, however, these details were simplified and mannered. This statue, for example, lacks the folds and muscles in the cheeks that give late Twelfth Dynasty sculpture its force, although the eyes do have an exaggerated brooding look. The hands are rather large and the fingers flat, and each body part is treated as a distinct component, as if to signify that the artist was paying careful attention to his prototypes. As a reinterpretation of earlier work, this piece is thus an invaluable illustration of the ancient Egyptians' outlook on their own art.

Sesostris III was no doubt highly regarded by his successor, Amenemhat III, and by contemporary and later private persons. As a highly effective ruler who perfectly fulfilled his role as pharaoh, Sesostris III embodied a cosmic principle of equilibrium known as *ma'at*. Little wonder, then, that later persons sought to advertise their own virtue by copying the features of such a revered ancestor.

9 Minoan Jug

Originally from Crete
Purchased by Dr. Henry Abbott before
1852 (reportedly from Lower Egypt);
formerly in the New-York Historical
Society Collection
Late Minoan IB Period, circa 1575–
1500 B.C.
Pottery, wheel-made, fired, burnished,
and painted,
8 11/16 inches (22.2 cm) high
37.13E, Charles Edwin Wilbour Fund

Of all the potters of the ancient world, those of Minoan Crete perhaps came the closest to achieving a perfect harmony between painted decoration and vessel shape. The Minoans' most common motifs feature lively maritime scenes. On this vessel, five nautili are framed by various species of marine flora. The animals' hard shells occupy the space just beneath the vessel's widest point, calling attention to the jug's solidity and volume. The long, graceful tentacles of the nautili, however, extend upward toward the neck and spout, adding a sense of lightness to the pot's upper half.

In keeping with preclassical drawing conventions, the painter combined two viewpoints in a single-fig-ure frieze. The nautili appear in pure profile while the water plants are seen from above. Such a merging of views also characterizes Aegean wall painting, including frescoes from the island of Thera.

This jug was found in Egypt, where it was, no doubt, sent as part of the trade that flourished between Crete and the Nile Valley during the sixteenth century B.C. Its transference to Egypt is responsible for the vessel's remarkable state of preservation. Minoan pottery found in the damp Cretan soil frequently shows severe surface deterioration. Burial in the drier soil of Egypt spared this masterpiece of the potter's art from such a fate.

10 HEAD OF A KING

Egypt, exact provenance not known
New Kingdom, Dynasty XVIII, circa
1554–1504 B.C.
Sandstone, painted, 24¼ inches
(61.8 cm) high
37.38E, Charles Edwin Wilbour Fund
(formerly in the Abbott and New-York
Historical Society Collections)

With the expulsion of the Hyksos, Asiatics who ruled Egypt for more than a century, Egyptian sculptors faced the challenge of reviving an art form that had been largely dormant during the long period of foreign occupation. Since very few statues were made in the final decades of Hyksos rule, artisans working for the first kings of Dynasty XVIII, Ahmose (circa 1554–1526 B.C.) and Amunhotep I (circa 1529–1505 B.C.), were not obliged to perpetuate a flourishing style. Instead, they were free to seek inspiration from Egypt's long artistic past.

These artists devised sculptures with details hearkening back to the style of the early Middle Kingdom. No doubt the historically conscious Egyptians wished to draw a parallel between that remote era, which marked the beginning of a glorious age in Egyptian history, and their own fledgling dynasty.

So similar is the art of earliest Dynasty XII and Dynasty XVIII that for many years this uninscribed head was attributed to the Middle Kingdom. We now know it to be an Eighteenth Dynasty piece with a treatment of the eyes, eyebrows, and mouth deliberately recalling early Middle Kingdom royal sculptures. Its open, ingenuous expression and curious half-smile, however, are characteristic of the New Kingdom and seem to invoke the sense of confidence that pervaded Egypt following the reestablishment of native rule. In all probability the head represents Ahmose or his son and successor, Amenhotep I.

11 STATUE OF SENENMUT

Egypt, Armant
New Kingdom, Dynasty XVIII, reign of
  Hatshepsut (1479–1458 B.C.)
Gray granite, 18½ inches (47.2 cm)
  high
67.68, Charles Edwin Wilbour Fund

Senenmut, one of the most powerful officials of the time of the female pharaoh Hatshepsut, had at least twenty-five statues made of himself. These display a variety of innovative types, including that of a private person offering a divine symbol or image.

According to its inscription, this statue depicts Senenmut offering an image of Renenutet, a goddess of the city of Armant, on behalf of the well-being of his sovereign and in the hope of eternal blessings for himself. However, as the cobra resting on a pair of upraised human arms and crowned with cow horns and a solar disk is also a rebus for Maat-ka-Re, the throne name of Hatshepsut, the entire statue, made to stand visible in a temple, can be "read" as a statement that Senenmut offers the name of his sovereign. For the same reason, the statue can be viewed as a declaration of, and an appeal for, loyalty to a controversial female pharaoh, who was likened to a goddess of nourishment in accord with the traditional concept of pharaoh as sustainer of Egypt.

Stylistically the statue's oval face, arched eyebrows, widely opened eyes, narrow and straight mouth, and aquiline nose relate it to several royal sculptures of its era. This explains why scholars still debate the question of whether any of these features reflect Senenmut's actual physiognomy rather than the influence of a royal atelier, whence the statue may have come.

12 THE LADY THEPU

Egypt, Thebes, Tomb 181
New Kingdom, Dynasty XVIII, late
    reign of Amunhotep III–very early
    reign of Amunhotep IV (circa 1360–
    1349 B.C.)
Painting on gesso over mud plaster
14¾ inches (37.6 cm) high
65.197, Charles Edwin Wilbour Fund

Although painting, as distinct from painted relief, was used for Egyptian tomb decoration from very early to very late times, it was seemingly most popular during the New Kingdom in the cemeteries in the cliffs at the southern capital of Thebes. There, where the stone was not always suitable for carving, artists evolved styles of painting that exploited many of the medium's potentials.

One apogee of this painting tradition was reached in the reign of Amunhotep III and survived into the very early part of the reign of Amunhotep IV (Akhenaten), a time that also witnessed the first flowering of the art of the Amarna Period. Amunhotep III ruled over an Egypt made wealthy and cosmopolitan by its military, commercial, and cultural contacts with other lands, a fact that helps account for the sophisticated elegance and opulence evidenced in much of the art of his era, such as this painting of the Lady Thepu, with her elaborate wig and floral headband, lavish jewelry, and fancy, diaphanous garment.

This image comes from a scene in which Thepu accompanied her deceased son, Nebamun, a Chief Sculptor and Administrator of Workshops, in making burnt offerings to the gods as part of an annual religious ritual of great magical benefit to the noble dead. Although Thepu appears to have been depicted as still alive, in keeping with the Egyptian desire to represent the ideal, essential, and eternal essence of a subject, she is shown as young and beautiful despite the fact that she must have been advanced in years.

13 NEFERTITI

Egypt, Karnak (Amun Precinct)
New Kingdom, Dynasty XVIII, circa
1365–1361 B.C.
Sandstone, painted, 16⅝ inches
(42.3 cm) wide
78.39, Gift of Christos G. Bastis

In Year 5 of his reign, Amunhotep IV changed his name to Akhenaten and moved the Egyptian capital from Thebes to El Amarna. By then Amunhotep IV had already drastically altered traditional Egyptian art and religion. Prior to his kingship pharaohs appeared as perfect beings with flawless faces and slender, well-conditioned torsos. Similarly, the major gods of earlier times often assumed some combination of human and animal form.

Amunhotep IV soon abandoned these conventions. In the precinct of the god Amun at Karnak he erected several sanctuaries to the Aton. This mysterious version of the sun god looked like no other Egyptian deity. It appeared in purely iconic form: a sun disk whose projecting rays ended in tiny hands. Images of the king and his consort, Nefertiti, show a similar rejection of classic style. The royal couple appears with elongated eyes set at an unnatural slant, long straight noses, emaciated cheeks, thick lips, lantern jaws with knobby chins, and attenuated necks. Both king and queen invariably show bodies with swollen, almost feminine breasts, a distended abdomen, and spindly arms and legs.

This relief represents Nefertiti presenting offerings to the Aton; the tiny *ankh*-sign before her nose is proffered by one of the Aton's rays. The block probably came from the *Hewt-benben*, the Aton's Karnak sanctuary where Nefertiti served as principal celebrant. The hieroglyphic inscription behind the queen mentions Princess Meryt-Aton; no doubt her figure originally appeared behind her mother.

14 Statue of Sa-Iset

Egypt, Assiut
New Kingdom, Dynasty XIX, reign of
Ramesses II (1279–1212 B.C.)
Wood, 22¹/₂ × 5¹/₂ × 6 inches
(57.0 × 14.0 × 15.5 cm)
47.120.2, Charles Edwin Wilbour Fund

Were this sculpture uninscribed, it
would be attributable to Dynasty
XIX (1291–1185 B.C.) on the basis of
the style of its finely detailed wig, its
elaborately pleated garments, and its
physiognomy, although its face—
once enlivened by inlaid eyes and
eyebrows—deviates to some extent
from more conventional faces of that
era. Happily, the statue's inscriptions
not only place it in the exceptionally
long reign of Ramesses II and associate it with the city of Assiut, they also
identify it as belonging to Sa-Iset,
Royal Scribe and Overseer of the
Granaries of Upper and Lower
Egypt. Although two like-named
and like-titled men—grandfather
and grandson—are known from Dynasty XIX Assiut, it is most probable
that this statue is of the second Sa-
Iset, who held office during the latter
part of Ramesses II's reign and the
very beginning of the reign of Mer-
enptah (1212–1202 B.C.). Much
more problematic are the questions of
whether, as has been argued, the
faces of the Brooklyn Sa-Iset and a
few other statues of, or probably of,
Sa-Iset the Younger deviate sufficiently from artistic conventions of
their time to warrant the label "por-
traitlike" and whether they resemble
each other sufficiently to help attribute them all to the second Sa-
Iset.

Sa-Iset is represented here holding
a divine staff, a pose that in private
statuary was limited to the New
Kingdom and was particularly common in the time of Ramesses II. The
inscriptions indicate that it was a staff
of Wepwawet, chief god of Assiut,
and that one function of the sculpture was to help ensure that Sa-Iset
would enjoy his god's aid in achieving a long lifetime and a blessed existence in the hereafter.

15 CARTONNAGE OF NESPANETJERENPERE

Egypt, Thebes
Third Intermediate Period, probably
 Dynasty XXII (945–718 B.C.)
Cartonnage (linen or papyrus mixed
 with plaster), inlaid with glass and
 lapis lazuli (eyes and eyebrows)
69¾ inches (177.0 cm) long
35.1265, Charles Edwin Wilbour Fund

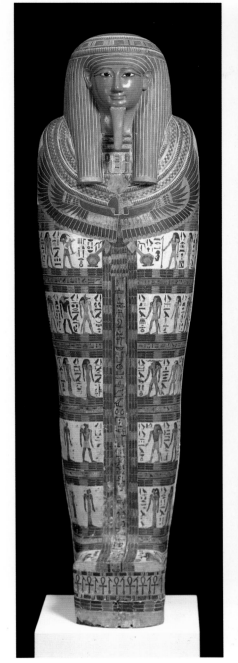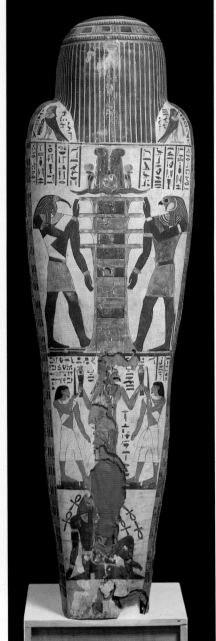

A mummy cartonnage is a container for a body and was normally interred within a coffin or sarcophagus of more durable material. This cartonnage was made for a man named Nespanetjerenpere, whose priestly titles suggest he lived in the southern capital of Thebes. The cartonnage's date is based on its medium, general style (including the almond-shaped eyes and slightly arched eyebrows), and scheme of decoration. Every aspect of its form and decoration had the magical purpose of helping to ensure a happy hereafter for its owner.

A depiction of Nespanetjerenpere wrapped as a mummy, the braided and curled "divine beard" indicates an intention to associate the deceased with the gods. This intention is also evident in the image of the ram-headed solar deity on the chest and the scene of Horus and Thoth erecting the *djed*, symbol of enduringness, and the god Osiris, on the back. More unusual is the decoration of the front panels, which for the most part consists of deities whose accompanying texts identify each of them with a part of Nespanetjerenpere's body. The priest also appears in human guise in these panels and on the back, where he is shown receiving life-giving water twice from a goddess and then kneeling under a flow of life signs.

This massing of divine images, propitious symbols, and magical texts in lively colors on a white ground is characteristic of funerary furnishings of Nespanetjerenpere's era, when, in part as a reaction to widespread tomb robberies, prominent and well-decorated sepulchers were not made.

16   WINGED GENIE

Iraq, Nimrud (Assyria), from Room H
of the Northwest Palace
Reign of Ashur-nasir-pal II, circa 883–
859 B.C.
Alabaster, 91 inches (231.1 cm) high
55.153, Gift of Hagop Kevorkian

Beginning in the reign of Ashur-nasir-pal II, Assyrian kings decorated the lower portion of their palace walls with monumental alabaster reliefs. These reliefs show the king performing the official duties of an Assyrian ruler: fighting, hunting lions, governing, overseeing the crops, and participating in religious rituals. The Brooklyn Museum possesses twelve of the earliest Assyrian palace reliefs; all were removed from Ashur-nasir-pal II's royal residence at Nimrud in 1853 but did not reach Brooklyn until 1955.

This slab depicts a great winged genie who attends the king at a religious ceremony. He holds a single ritual object, a pail, which may have contained liquid used to purify the "Sacred Tree," a major icon of Assyrian religion. The genie's long braided hair and beard are in keeping with the fussiness of Assyrian royal art. He wears a fringed shawl draped over his knee-length, tasseled tunic. The ensemble is enhanced by an elaborate array of jewelry, including a rosette on his forehead, earrings, bracelets, and a beaded necklace. The handles of two daggers project from beneath the genie's shawl.

A long cuneiform text appears across the center of this and other scenes from Ashur-nasir-pal II's palace. This "Standard Inscription" recounts the major events in the illustrious reign of the self-proclaimed "King of the World."

17 AMUN-RE AND MUT

Egypt, Thebes, Karnak
Dynasty XXV, circa 760–656 B.C.
Sandstone, 29 × 31 × 1 3/4 inches
(73.5 × 79.0 × 4.5 cm)
87.184.2, Charles Edwin Wilbour Fund

In the first quarter of the first millennium B.C. a powerful state arose in Kush (modern Sudan), far to the south of Egypt proper. This state was to survive for centuries to come. Far shorter lived was the conquest and control of Egypt by six of its kings, who are counted as Egypt's XXVth Dynasty. While their own civilization rapidly accommodated Egyptian influences, in Egypt these Kushite kings played the role of traditional pharaohs, a fact clearly reflected in the Egyptian art created for them. To be sure, some Egyptian depictions of their Kushite overlords are decidedly un-Egyptian in terms of their physical appearance and royal regalia. Nevertheless, most Egyptian art of Dynasty XXV is characterized by the continuing evolution of native styles that reflect Kushite influence

in some details of costume or—though not always—hints of a Kushite physiognomy in the depiction of heavy noses, prominent cheekbones, and full mouths. Those same features could also be used for representations of other individuals and even the gods. Such is certainly the case with the relief illustrated, especially the figure of the goddess, which is in all respects a splendid example of royal relief at the southern Egyptian capital of Thebes during the second half of Dynasty XXV.

The great god Amun-Re and his consort Mut were worshiped throughout Egypt and Kush, but their traditional and most venerable Egyptian cult places were at Karnak at Thebes, also the location of many of the most important building projects of Dynasty XXV in Egypt.

18 RELIEFS FROM THE TOMB OF THE VIZIER NESPEQASHUTY

Egypt, Thebes, Tomb 312
Late Period, Dynasty XXVI, reign of
Psamtik I (664–610 B.C.):
Limestone, section illustrated:
29¹/₂ inches (75.2 cm) high
52.131.1–.32 and 68.1, Charles Edwin
Wilbour Fund

In the upper register of the section of reliefs illustrated here is part of a depiction of funeral ceremonies for the vizier Nespeqashuty. Though the ancient Egyptians believed death might be followed by life eternal, they were not anxious to leave the existence they knew. Hence the presence here of female mourners who, as in much Egyptian art, convey their messages—aversion to death, the pain and loss of separation, the affluence of a man whose family could afford numerous professional mourners—much more by poses, gestures, and garb than by facial features. Here the women are wearing a mourning garb with a tie at the waist, leaving the breasts bare, but their faces are virtually expressionless. The man with a quiver of arrows at the left was presumably part of a procession of figures bearing to Nespeqashuty's tomb the funerary equipment he might wish or need in the hereafter.

While the existence of related female figures in works made well after Dynasty XVIII (1550–1291 B.C.) suggests that these figures are part of a living artistic tradition, they also clearly owe some debt to works of that much earlier age. This archaizing, a tendency displayed by much art of Nespeqashuty's time, is also apparent in the lower register of female offering-bearers. Derived ultimately from depictions as early in date as Dynasty IV (2600–2475 B.C.) of personifications of estates established by kings to furnish their spirits with offerings of food and drink, Nespeqashuty's figures are related to their New Kingdom descendants, that is, to depictions of offering-bearers of less exalted status.

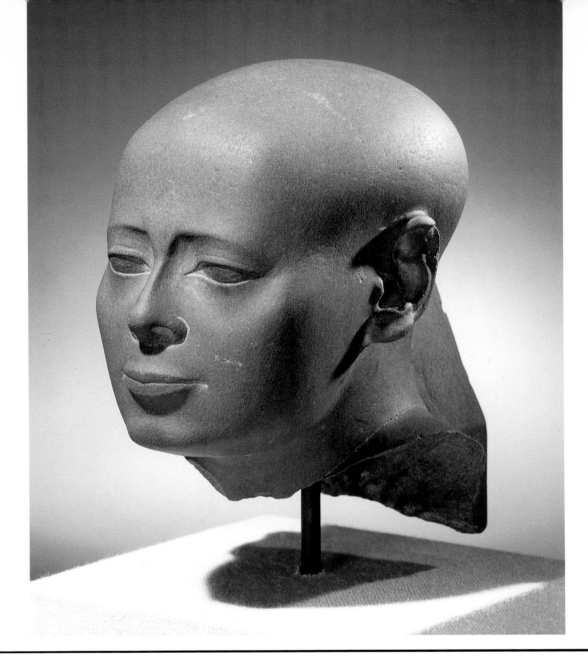

19 PORTRAIT OF WESIRWER

Egypt
Dynasty XXX, 380–342 B.C.
Green schist, 6 1/16 inches (15.4 cm)
 high
55.175, Charles Edwin Wilbour Fund

The identification and dating of this head were the result of a continuing international collaboration aimed at developing a more complete assessment of the true aesthetic achievements of ancient Egypt. In the 1960s a European Egyptologist noticed that the top of the back pillar of the statue is decorated with a figural scene depicting the deity Osiris seated on a throne, the side of which is decorated with a swallow. Upon reflection it was noticed that the god and the bird are, in and of themselves, hiero-glyphs that read "Wesir-wer," or "Osiris is great," and that that phrase is a rebus, or visual pun, for the name of a man who had been identified in the inscriptions on a headless statue in the Cairo Museum. Since the dimensions of the breaks of both head and body are identical, it appeared that the pieces belonged together—a hypothesis confirmed when casts of the originals were joined break to break.

The history of the statue could now be determined. It had been erected originally in the Temple of Amun at Karnak during Dynasty XXX. At a somewhat later time, however, the priests of the temple reverently bur-ied it along with hundreds of others during a routine weeding out of the dedicatory statues then cluttering the site. Subsequently the head seems to have been broken off and separated from its body—that is, until the 1960s, when for a short time, head and body were reunited at The Brooklyn Museum.

The modeling of the portrait is both abstracted and mannered, executed with subtly merging planes. Earlier academic formulas have been adapted and modified in a schematic way so as to produce a masklike image that, although divorced from reality, still engages the spectator's interest.

20 STATUETTE OF ALEXANDER THE GREAT

Egypt
Probably 1st century B.C.
Alabaster, 4¹/₈ inches (10.5 cm) high
54.162, Charles Edwin Wilbour Fund
Right: actual size

In 332 B.C. Alexander the Great entered Egypt without a struggle. The native Egyptians heartily welcomed him as the liberator who would free them from the oppressive yoke of the Persians then ruling the country. He was subsequently crowned as pharaoh at Memphis, the religious capital of the land, traveled to the remote Oasis at Siwa in the Western Desert, and laid out with his own hands the foundations for Alexandria, a city destined to become the undisputed cultural center of the classical world. For the next nine years he set about completing his conquest of the known world. When he died in Babylon in 323 B.C., he had changed the course of history and had brought the culture of Greece to the nations of the East. His body was ceremoniously laid to rest in his beloved Alexandria in a sumptuous tomb, which has yet to be discovered.

Alexander the Great not only changed the course of history but also affected the subsequent development of Western art history. He was the first Greek ever to commission his portrait during his lifetime. Fair of complexion, exceedingly handsome, and boyish in appearance with a full head of hair that his contemporaries likened to a lion's mane, Alexander had features that clearly distinguished him from all other men. Of his contemporary portraits, none was more famous than that created by the court sculptor Lysippos. The Roman biographer Plutarch, writing in Greek in the second century A.D., described that image in his *Life of Alexander* as one depicting Alexander with a melting gaze in his eyes and his head inclined to one side over his left shoulder.

This remarkably well-preserved statuette is based on that famous work. Because of its small size, it was probably the focal point of a private shrine erected in honor of Alexander by a wealthy Egyptian. Conforming to the luxurious tastes of the times, the white alabaster bust was initially set into a draped body sculpted from a different-colored stone. That sense of color was enhanced by the addition of a diadem representing the rays of the sun, each metal spike of which was affixed to the head by means of tiny drill holes that are still visible. The sculptor was an accomplished master and has crafted the piece with jewel-like precision, as is evident from the rendering of the irises and pupils of the eyes. The sketchy, almost impressionistic rendering of the hair is but one indication that this statuette could have been sculptured in late Hellenistic times when the memory of Alexander was linked to Egypt's renewed imperial aspirations.

21 THE BROOKLYN BLACK HEAD

Egypt
47–44 B.C.
Diorite, 16¼ inches (41.3 cm) high
58.30, Charles Edwin Wilbour Fund

This head, named for the hard, black diorite from which it is sculpted, is a quintessentially Egyptian work that owes nothing to Graeco-Roman artistic traditions. In keeping with pharaonic sculptural principles of the Late Period, the artists have consciously endeavored to juxtapose the smoothly polished surfaces of the face with the rough surfaces of the hair, only the first three rows of which have the individual strands articulated. The remaining curls are only roughly blocked out. The hair does not grow organically from the scalp, as in classical works, but rather rests on the head like a cap. From such observations, it is evident that this classical coiffure, with its crab-claw configuration of locks lapping the forehead, is rendered by purely pharaonic stylistic means. The same conclusion applies to the sculpting of the features of the face, which are modeled as a series of subtly merging planes enhanced by linear adjuncts. So, for example, the subtle undulations of the forehead and cheeks are punctuated with faintly incised lines that effectively paint a picture of a mature man. That maturity is emphasized by the gaunt, sunken cheeks, by the naso-labial furrows emanating from the wings of the nose to the corners of the mouth, by the thin, pencil-lined horizontal lips, and by the heavy, upper lids of the typically rendered Egyptian wide-open eyes.

All these physiognomic features are evident only in the frontal view and are not developed in the profile views. This absence of an integration of the front and side views of a face, wholly lacking in developed Hellenistic and Roman portraits, is a hallmark of Egyptian art in all periods. All the features of the head, when taken singly, can be paralleled on other Egyptian portraits of the Late Period.

Probably from Tuna el-Gebel (Greek
Hermopolis, modern Ashmunein)
Ptolemaic Period (305–30 B.C.)
Gilded wood, rock crystal, gold, and
silver
23¹/₂ × 15 inches (58.7 × 38.2 cm)
49.48, Charles Edwin Wilbour Fund

Most likely from the vast animal
cemetery of Tuna el-Gebel in Middle Egypt, this beautifully fashioned
coffin once held the mummified remains of ancient Egypt's most sacred
bird. The ibis was the more common
manifestation of the god Thoth, who
is sometimes also depicted as a ba-
boon. Indeed, Tuna el-Gebel has
yielded the mummies of thousands of
ibises and baboons.

Thoth was the god of scribes and
was equated by the Greeks with
Hermes. Perhaps because writing
was considered an activity reserved
for the elite, he was also associated
with wisdom in general. In fact, in
some New Kingdom texts, Thoth is
the creator of all languages, not just
Egyptian. As a scribe, he is often
shown in vignettes of illustrated funerary papyri, such as the *Book of the
Dead*, at the judgment of the deceased, tallying the results on his
notepad as the dead person's heart is
weighed against the feather of truth.

This coffin is fashioned from silver
and wood overlaid with gold leaf.

The eyes are rock crystal set in gold
bands, and the head, legs, and tail
are made from pure silver. Dating to
the Ptolemaic Period, the coffin is not
unique but is nonetheless an especially fine, large, and well-preserved example of its type. The artist
has adroitly captured the sinuous
curve of the beak and neck, and the
highly detailed legs are evidence of
the ancient Egyptian craftsman's careful observation of anatomy.

Even today, an occasional ibis can
be seen in rural Egypt, strolling
freely through the fields and irriga-
tion canals of the Nile Valley. Now, as
then, the ibis is a treasured bird.

23 FUNERARY CARTONNAGE OF A LADY OF MEANS

Egypt
Roman Imperial Period, 1st century A.D.
Linen, painted and gilded gesso, with
  various inlays
22³/₄ inches (57.8 cm) high
69.35, Charles Edwin Wilbour Fund

Despite their conquest of Egypt in 30 B.C., the Romans were initially unable to alter the cultural fabric of the country. Wealthy Egyptians continued to practice their millennia-old religious beliefs, and the pious habitually interred their deceased with all the traditional funerary paraphernalia. Nevertheless, the use of gold and wood for anthropoid, or human-shaped, sarcophagi gradually gave way to cartonnage, a combination of layers of papyrus and/or linen coated with gesso, or plaster, which resembles modern papier-mâché. The cartonnage was modeled by hand to depict the features of the deceased and while still wet could be inlaid with various materials, as seen, for example, in the eyes and eyebrows, which are made of glass and faience, a typically Egyptian glazed material. The finished object could then be both painted and gilded.

The deceased here is depicted as a wealthy and fashionable Roman matron. Her coiffure is elaborately arranged as a series of three rows of tightly twisted spiral locks that frame her forehead and are set off by a series of corkscrew locks at either side of her face. Her accessories, most of which are known from actual examples in gold, reveal just how accurate the artist was in his depiction of jewelry. These include a pair of stunning U-shaped earrings and two necklaces. The first is a string of green beads and the second a lavish, bejeweled creation, most of the inlays of which are, unfortunately, no longer extant. In addition, the figure wears two finger rings, two bracelets, and an armlet, all of which are serpent-form. Her right palm presses a hand garland of rose-colored petals against her chest while her left hand clasps a cluster of ears of wheat. Her costume consists of an opulent Egyptian three-piece ensemble, the fringed shawl of which is knotted to her wraparound skirt at her breast.

To the ancients, the serpent, who annually shed its skin, and wheat, which would sprout again from seed stored during the winter season, were symbols of rebirth in the hereafter. These attributes, like the entire cartonnage itself, were gilded in an attempt to imitate gold, a material itself imbued with the symbolic values of incorruptibility and permanence. Thus, this anonymous Roman matron is ostentatiously dressed with the means to ensure her resurrection.

24 HEAD OF THE
OMPHALOS APOLLO

Greece, Athens
Roman copy after an original of 460–450 B.C.
Marble, 12¾ inches (32.4 cm) high
18.166, The Woodward Fund and a gift
from A. Augustus Healy

One of the cultural characteristics of the Roman Imperial Period was the propensity to collect copies of famous Greek works of art, some of which were made over five centuries earlier. The originals have, for the most part, disappeared with the passage of time, but a knowledge of and an appreciation for those works is provided by the Roman replicas, which often survive in numbers. Such is the case for the so-called *Omphalos Apollo*, replicas of which have been identified in The Brooklyn Museum, London's British Museum, Paris's Louvre, and Athens's National Museum. The statue is named after an altar, in the shape of a stylized everted navel, or *omphalos*, with which it was found in 1862 in the Theater of Dionysos beneath the South Slope of the Acropolis in Athens. This *omphalos*-shaped altar was a conscious allusion to Delphi, the most famous oracular center associated with Apollo. That site was anciently considered to be in the center of the known world in the same way that the navel was regarded as the center of the body, midway between the crown of the head and soles of the feet.

Apollo, the Greek god of music, archery, prophecy, medicine, and to a lesser degree the care of flocks and herds, was also associated with the loftier, ethical aspects of civilization.

He was invoked whenever law codes were ratified and was habitually offered as an example of both the highest moral principles and uncompromising religious tenets. This unsullied, upright god was represented in art as the ideal of youthful, but postpubescent, male beauty, an image consummately captured in this head of the *Omphalos Apollo*. The god is depicted with his head turned slightly to one side, and with his long locks, characteristically parted in the middle of his brow, tied up in a series of braids visible at the back. The eyes and mouth, with its parted lips, are no longer arranged on strictly horizontal planes, a feature that departs from earlier traditions and anticipates that found later in the sculpture of the high classical period. The subtle modeling of the facial lineaments has been somewhat obscured by a disquieting coating of the surface in the nineteenth century with a resolutely unremovable material that attempted to mask the infelicitous restoration of a nose that has since been removed. The treatment of the hair, especially the drill holes in the ends of the locks on the forehead, indicates that this head is a copy of the second century A.D. of a bronze original attributed to the Attic sculptor Calamis.

25 BEASTS OF PREY AND THEIR QUARRIES

Egypt
Roman Imperial Period, circa A.D. 300
Painted limestone
14 × 51 inches (35.6 × 129.5 cm)
41.1266, Charles Edwin Wilbour Fund

This frieze, or band of sculptural decoration, is so well preserved and unweathered that it must have once adorned an interior wall of a building. The sculptors have used several different types of drill bits and chisels to sculpture the stone in order to achieve the desired effect of light and shadow across the surface of the composition. Notice how the contours of each of the five beasts stand out vividly from the scarcely visible dark background. That effect would have been originally heightened by the application of paint, faint traces of which are still visible here and there if one looks carefully. The skins of the beasts have been embellished with a variety of lines or dots that would have been filled with black pigment in order to depict each beast as distinctively as possible.

The five animals are, from left to right, a wild boar chasing a hart, a hyena stalking a canine, and a spotted beast. A floral motif, perhaps to be identified as laurel, surrounds each animal and contributes to the feeling that the chase is taking place in a dense forest. Moreover, the attitudes of the weaker animals with their heads turned back are echoed by the S-curve of the tendrils, which likewise turn back toward the spectator's left. Such a compositional device is artfully employed to suggest the ultimate outcome in which the boar and hyena will fell their prey.

In the past, such relief representations have been considered examples of Coptic art, that is, creations of the early Christians in Egypt. Such a designation is inappropriate because much of what has been labeled Coptic art has great affinities in both style and theme with the artistic production of the Roman Empire as a whole. The close parallels between this relief and that commissioned by the Roman Emperor Diocletian for his palace in Split, Yugoslavia, show that this wonderfully playful piece is better regarded as a product of the late Roman Empire.

African,
Oceanic,
and New World Art

26 GONG

Nigeria; Benin people
16th century
Ivory
$14^{1}/_{8} \times 3^{3}/_{4} \times 2^{1}/_{4}$ inches
   ($35.8 \times 9.5 \times 5.4$ cm)
58.160, A. Augustus Healy and Frank
   L. Babbott Funds

One of only five in existence, this intricately carved ivory gong is an exquisite record of the great political and artistic florescence of the Benin Kingdom in the sixteenth century. Because ivory was also carved for visiting Portuguese, it is important to bear in mind that it was in the mid-fifteenth century, before the arrival of Europeans, that a particular king (*oba*) encouraged ivory carving and consolidated the visual vocabulary of Benin divine kingship that lasted for five hundred years.

The medium, function, and iconography of this rare gong unequivocally connote royal power, wealth, and purity. The front of the gong depicts the *oba* supported by two retainers. Except for the large bead necklace worn by the *oba* and the snakes that issue from his waist, the figures are identical. The bead necklace may be a reference to the conflict between the sixteenth-century *oba* Esigie and his brother Aruaran, who fought for ownership of a special coral bead granting the power to make proclamations. The color and economic value of the ivory in addition to the representation of crocodiles, snakes, and mudfish are symbols of Olokun, the sea god, who is the *oba*'s equal in the spirit world. The function of this gong was presumably similar, if not identical, to that of the undecorated gong used in the present-day *Emobo* ceremony in which the *oba* annually purifies and strengthens the Benin nation by dancing and striking the gong to eradicate malevolent spirits.

27 HORNBLOWER

Nigeria; Benin people
17th century
Leaded brass, 23 1/2 × 7 1/2 inches
(59.5 × 19.0 cm)
55.87, Gift of Mr. and Mrs. Alastair B.
Martin

This freestanding representation of a courtier playing a side-blown horn is an outstanding example of the famous bronzes of the Benin Kingdom of southern Nigeria. The casting of bronze and brass objects was very much a royal prerogative, for only the king (*oba*) could commission objects from the casters, who were organized into guilds. The *oba* would have kept this beautifully cast and engraved hornblower on the altar of one of his forefathers.

According to Benin oral tradition, brass casting was introduced by the neighboring Kingdom of Ife around the end of the fourteenth century. Recent scholarship suggests, however, that brass casting had an earlier and more dispersed origin in Nigeria.

The circle with four projecting leaves decorating the hornblower's costume refers to the river leaves of Olokun, the Benin god of the waters, and is also associated with the four cardinal directions. This quatrefoil design may have been adapted from European or Islamic design for use in Benin symbolism. Other symbols include human and animal heads and the moon. The leopard's head motif on the skirt front alludes to the association of the *oba* with the powerful leopard—each a king in its respective domain.

28 BOM BOSH

Zaire; Kuba people
Mid-18th century
Wood (*Crossopterix febrifuga*)
19¹/₂ inches (49.4 cm) high
61.33, Gift of Mr. and Mrs. Robert E.
  Blum, Mr. and Mrs. Alastair B.
  Martin, Mr. and Mrs. Donald M.
  Oenslager, and the Mrs. Florence E.
  Blum Fund

This commemorative portrait of King Bom Bosh is the oldest of eleven such figures known in the world. One hundred years after his reign, Bom Bosh became the first Kuba king to be memorialized in this form. The tradition of these effigies, called *ndop*, was instituted by King Bope Pelenge between 1760 and 1780 as a means of materially expressing an increased authority of Kuba divine kingship. More specifically, Bope Pelenge abolished the national cult of nature spirits, of which the king was viewed as a mere priest, in favor of a cult of the king as paramount nature spirit. Thus, where previously there had been no ancestor cult among the Kuba, the equivalent of one was introduced with Bom Bosh as its first locus.

Bom Bosh is not a portrait per se but rather a conventionalized effigy with distinguishing attributes. All *ndop* in fact share the same basic features as *Bom Bosh:* a visorlike coiffure, a hand-held state knife, a cowrie-shell belt, a lumbar-pad, a paunch, bracelets, and a decorated platform. Likewise characteristic of the type are the smooth polished patina and the *tukula* powder-filled crevices that indicate its traditional method of preservation. Finally, this historic *ndop* is unmistakably distinguished by the drum emblazoned with a severed hand, the symbol of Bom Bosh's fame as a great military leader who expanded the boundaries of the Kuba kingdom.

29 GRAVEMARKER

Zaire or Angola; Kongo people, Ba
 Boma subgroup
Late 19th century
Steatite, pigment, 22 1/2 × 5 7/8 inches
(57.2 × 15 cm) high
22.1205, Museum Expedition

Stone is used relatively infrequently as a medium for sculpture in sub-Saharan Africa. Only in the case of the *nomoli* and *pomtan* figures of Sierra Leone and Guinea is it carved with as much stylistic variety and dynamism as the gravemarkers of the Bakongo ba Boma people who live on both banks of the lower Zaire River. The funerary monuments these Kongo people carve are called *bitumba*, a derivation of the old Portuguese word for tomb. They originated in the second half of the nineteenth century as a product of the wealth and power accumulated by longstanding trade with Europeans and were probably inspired by the narrative tombs of Europeans in Kongo cemeteries. The common departure from frontality, as in this superb example, can also be attributed to European influence.

The high price of commissioning a *tumba* from one of the many workshops in the area meant that a person had to be quite affluent to have one placed on his grave. The detached but dignified chief represented here is distinguished by his cross-legged position and looped fiber cap as well as by his necklace and bracelets. The posture is a variant of the "thinker" theme. In Kongo body language, the chief is distancing himself from the noise of the mundane world in order to concentrate on important matters. Insofar as royal objects are believed to record their owner's thoughts, this chief may be communicating with his predecessor by smoking his pipe.

30 MOTHER-AND-CHILD FIGURINE

Zaire, Middle Kasai region; Luluwa
 people
19th or 20th century
Wood, metal, 14 × 3⁵/₈ inches
 (35.6 × 8.5 cm)
50.124, Frank S. Benson Fund

The ethereal delicacy and grace of
this mother-and-child figurine sets it
apart from all others conceived by
the Luluwa of south-central Zaire.
The sensitive carving of the head
and neck of the mother is especially
remarkable for the slight forward tilt
of the perfectly shaped face, the
gently attenuated neck, the con-
fidently and idiosyncratically modeled nose and mouth, the oversized,
half-cast eyes, and the characteristically sinuous scarification patterns.
Noticeably exaggerated are the mother's hands and navel and the position
of the child's legs, respectively con-
noting protection, fertility, and flex-
ibility. The luminous black surface
of the figurine is created by native
application of palm oil.

A Luluwa figurine like this one,
whose lower portion is pointed and
nonfigurated, is called *buanga bua
tshibole* and is used in the territories
of Demba, Kazumba, Luebo, and
Dibaya. It is carried in the belts or
loincloths of pregnant or lactating
women for protection.

31 CEREMONIAL SHIELD

Solomon Islands, Santa Isabel
Circa 1852
Basketry, nautilus shell inlay on resin
  base
32⅝ × 9¼ inches (83.0 × 23.5 cm)
59.63, Frank L. Babbott and Carll H.
  DeSilver Funds

The unparalleled virtuosity of the Solomon Islanders in the art of shell inlay is clearly demonstrated by this rare and richly embellished war shield collected before 1852 by Surgeon Captain James Booth of the British Royal Navy. There are only about twenty of these shields extant today.

Shell-inlaid shields were based on the more common elliptical wicker shield wielded by the peoples of Guadalcanal, Florida, Santa Isabel, and New Georgia islands. Guadalcanal islanders, the sole producers of these wicker shields, sold them to others, including the Santa Isabel islanders, who decorated the shields with highly abstract linear designs created with small notched pieces of nautilus shell. This shield, bearing the characteristic design format dominated by an anthropomorphic figure with upraised arms, is distinguished by two detached heads and a face and a set of four double arrowlike points.

Excessive warfare in this region, particularly headhunting, dictated the shield's imagery and its use in the acquisition and display of male prestige. Beautiful and fragile, this shield was probably never used in battle but served instead as the ceremonial insignia of a chief.

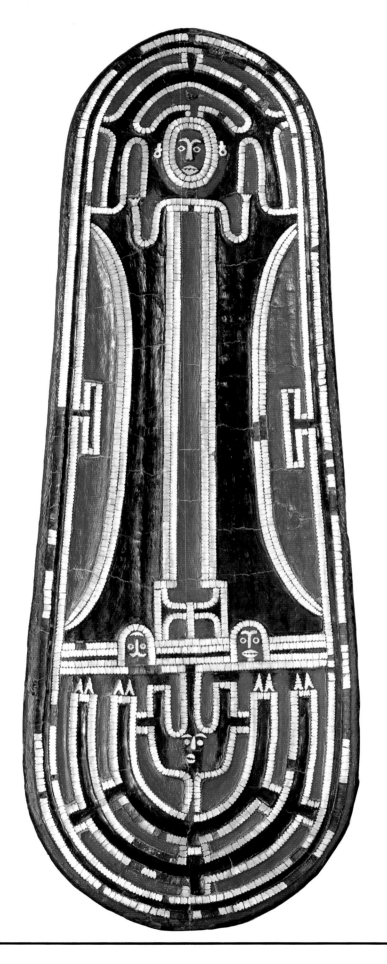

32 SUSPENSION HOOK

Papua New Guinea, Middle Sepik;
  Sawos people
Wood, pigment
61 × 16 × 5 inches
  (155.0 × 40.6 × 12.7 cm)
Formerly in the Bremen Museum
  Collection
86.229.13, Gift of Mrs. Evelyn A. J.
  Hall and Mr. John A. Friede

Although suspension hooks are ubiquitous in the area of the middle Sepik River and its southern tributaries, few are as elegant and well aged as the one here. The degree of refinement of this hook may be explained in part by the fact that it is made by the Sawos people, who appear to use hooks more frequently than other groups in the area. The dominant human figure of the hook represents a male ancestor spirit (*wagen*). The pig's head in high relief on the hook proper refers to the Sawos's regard for domesticated pigs as their own children. Judging from its size and artistic elaboration, this hook was hung in the men's cult house, where it would have served both ceremonial and utilitarian purposes such as storing net bags of sago flatbread and activating spirits responsible for the welfare of the village. In the latter case, an attendant eats the chicken and betel nut hung for him on the hook, enters into a trance, and then speaks on behalf of the hook's apotropaic spirit.

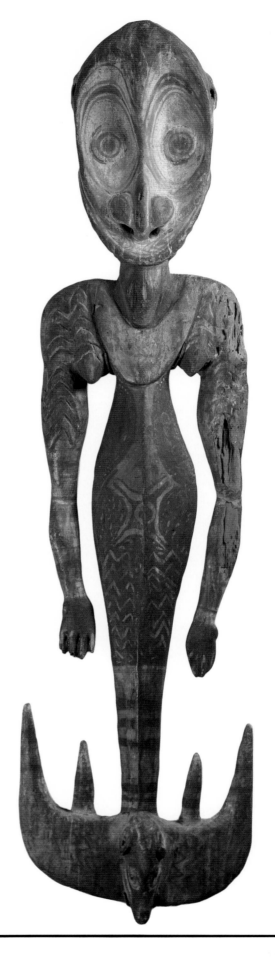

33 MALE FIGURE

Papua New Guinea, Gulf Province, Era River, Koiravi Village
Wood, pigment, 26¹/₂×9 inches (67.4×23.0 cm)
Collected by John W. Vandercook, 1929
51.118.9, Gift of John W. Vandercook

The highly animated figure reproduced here is the work of an exceptionally gifted artist from the Wapo/Era area of the Gulf province of Papua New Guinea. Small silhouette figures of this type, called *bioma*, are usually placed near the floor within the partitioned men's ceremonial house in proximity to trophy skulls of pigs and crocodiles. Characteristically, *bioma* figures from this area are flat with two sets of limbs, one upraised, one lowered, and ridged edges along the outer sides. The extraordinary vitality of this figure is a result of its having been cut from a curved slab of wood that was probably part of an old canoe.

This figure is one of fifty-eight objects, most from the Pacific Islands, donated to the Museum in 1951 by John Womack Vandercook. Vandercook traveled extensively in the Pacific Islands, collected works of art, and wrote books and articles on his travels. Although this figure is not mentioned specifically in his illustrated book *Dark Islands* (1937), Vandercook vividly describes direct encounters with the art and people of the Papuan Gulf.

34 CANOE BREAKWATER

Papua New Guinea, Massim region,
  Trobriand Islands
Wood, pigment, 52⅜ × 32⅝ inches
  (133.0 × 83.0 cm)
80.2, Gift of Mr. and Mrs. Milton F.
  Rosenthal

In the Massim region of southeastern New Guinea the seagoing outrigger canoe is vital to the interisland network of ceremonial gift exchange called *Kula*. As such, the canoe is the object of elaborate ritual and ornamentation. The canoe breakwater (*rajim*) is set transversely across the prow, closing the ends of the well of the vessel. It is considered a medium for supernatural powers activated by magical spells cast when it is set in place and thereafter by other spells for specific occasions. In this way the canoe breakwater is assigned the dual purpose of protection of its owners and aggression toward their *Kula* trade partners.

The finely crafted canoe breakwater here marvelously exemplifies the most diagnostic of Massim stylistic traits. The clean contour is filled with complex curvilinear patterns in very low relief on a flat pigmented surface. That most famous of Massim motifs, the scroll, here curls upward, forming two equal-sized lobes that ripple outward as continuous bands and depict the opposing frigate birds supporting the upper section. These zoomorphic and geometric elements, and possibly the overall shape of the breakwater, symbolize flight and its attendant success to the Trobriand Islanders.

35 FIGURINE

Mexico, Campeche; Maya, Jaina style
600–900
Ceramic, paint, 8¹/₄ × 1¹¹/₁₆ inches
  (21.0 × 4.8 cm)
70.31, Dick S. Ramsay Fund

This extraordinary combination of man and flower has been modeled with such sensitivity and grace that the form appears to be entirely natural. Hundreds of figurines in this style, mold-made as well as hand-modeled, have been found on the island of Jaina, just off the Campeche coast of Mexico, a place that is presumed to have functioned as a necropolis for the Maya of the Late Classic Period (600–900). At this burial ground one or two figurines were placed in the arms of the dead along with other offerings including seashells, musical instruments, and ornaments. The subject matter of the figurines is varied, but the majority represent elaborately dressed humans. They have been interpreted as portraits of the Maya elite or protagonists in an elaborate Underworld mythology that is also recorded on painted ceramic vases.

Human figures emerging from flowers constitute a special class of Jaina figurines. There are variations in the type of flower depicted and in the gender and age of the individual within the bloom. In this example a slender youthful male rises in an attitude of calm authority from a water-lily pod. Because the water lily is associated with the Underworld in Maya art, this figurine may symbolize the renewal of life after death. As such it would have been an especially appropriate burial offering.

36 JAGUAR

Mexico; Aztec
1440–1521
Stone, 4¹⁵/₁₆ × 5¹¹/₁₆ × 11 inches
  (12.5 × 14.5 × 28.0 cm)
38.45, Carll H. DeSilver Fund

Some of the finest Aztec carvings are naturalistic representations of plants and animals including squash, cacti, snakes, grasshoppers, and jaguars. Often small in scale, these compact sculptures tend to be made from a hard, dense stone and are frequently polished. This jaguar is an excellent example of the type. Every part of the animal is carefully carved, including the underside where the paw pads are represented in low relief. The alert position of the head and the emphasis on the oversized claws aptly express the jaguar's latent energy and destructive power.

The jaguar had both political and cosmological associations for the Aztecs. As the most feared and powerful predator in Mexico, it was closely identified with the ruler; it also symbolized the earth and the realm of darkness. Aztec kings sat on thrones draped with jaguar skins and commanded armies of "jaguar" warriors, representing the terrestrial aspects of the world, as well as "eagle" warriors, associated with the celestial sphere.

Unfortunately no jaguar sculptures have been found in situ. It is likely, however, that they served as palace or temple furnishings. Although the provenance of this jaguar is unknown, it is in the metropolitan style and must have been carved in one of the major cities in the basin of Mexico in the fifty years preceding the Spanish Conquest.

37 LIFE-DEATH FIGURE

Mexico, Veracruz; Huastec
900–1250
Stone, 62¼ × 26⅜ inches
(158.0 × 67.0 cm)
37.2897, Henry L. Batterman and
Frank S. Benson Funds

The dualism that permeates Mexican art is perfectly exemplified by this great Huastec statue from northern Veracruz. The life-size figure represents a youthful male wearing a conical hat, large ear ornaments, a pendant, and a cloth knotted around his waist. Parts of his chest and arms and his lower legs are covered with a dense pattern resembling the designs painted on Huastec pottery. Compressed within the youth's broad back is a skeletal figure with the same conical hat and clawed hands and feet. The significance of this remarkable juxtaposition of life and death is not known. It has been variously interpreted as a cult statue of the god Quetzalcoatl, who was closely associated with the Huastec region, or as a representation of the apotheosis of a Huastec ruler. Although other Huastec life-death figures exist, this is undoubtedly the most complete and the finest depiction of the theme.

Linguistically related to the Maya, the Huastec created their distinctive style of stone carving with an emphasis on freestanding figures and

dual imagery between the tenth and fourteenth centuries. Huastec sculptures may well have inspired the Aztec, whose imperial art style developed after they had conquered the Huastec region in the mid-fifteenth century.

The collection history of this sculpture is unusually complete. In 1844 B. M. Norman, an American traveler to Veracruz, contracted malaria and was nursed back to health by Ann Chase, the wife of the American Consul at Tampico. On his recovery, Mrs. Chase presented him with three "interesting relics" that a previous American traveler had brought to Tampico from the vicinity of San Vincente Tancuayalab. The life-death image was included in the group. Norman brought the large sculptures back to New York and donated them to the New-York Historical Society. In 1937 The Brooklyn Museum exhibited these pieces for the first time and, in 1950, was able to purchase them. This figure has been the focal point of the Mesoamerican installation at the Museum ever since.

38 STELA

Costa Rica, Central Highlands–Atlantic
 Watershed, Mercedes
1200–1500
Stone, 22 1/16 × 16 inches
(56.0 × 40.5 cm)
34.5094, Alfred W. Jenkins Fund

Although Costa Rica's stone carvings are not as well known as its gold pendants (the abundance of which gave the country its name, "rich coast"), they are artistically and technically just as interesting. In the Central Highlands–Atlantic Watershed region, stone sculptural forms include elaborately decorated metates, pedestal tables, bowls, and freestanding figures. A rare type found in this region is an upright slab carved with figures on the top, presumed to have been used as a grave marker. A combination of low- and high-relief carving, these grave markers show that the pre-Columbian artists in this area had mastered a wide range of stone-carving techniques.

This example from the site of Las Mercedes was collected in Costa Rica by Minor C. Keith, the founder of the United Fruit Company, in the early part of this century. It is unusual in the simplicity of the slab and lively posture of the figures—qualities that make it especially appealing to modern taste. The twin figures, precariously balanced on a raised band, appear to be about to climb over the upper edge of the slab. They have infantile bodies with the vertebral column delineated as a graceful curve, enhancing the sense of movement. Each figure wears round ear ornaments and has a circular pattern carved on the crown of the head representing a hairdo or headdress.

39 PLAQUE

Panama, Coclé Province, Sitio Conte
700–1100
Gold, 9 × 8¹/₂ inches (22.9 × 21.6 cm)
33.448.12, Peabody Museum Expedition
  to Coclé Province, Panama

In 1931 The Brooklyn Museum sponsored archaeological excavations conducted by Harvard University at the site of Sitio Conte on the banks of the Rio Grande in Panama. As a result, the Museum has an exceptionally well-documented collection of Panamanian goldwork and ceramics. This plaque of hammered gold came from one of the largest and most lavishly furnished graves at Sitio Conte. Nested with another nearly identical plaque, it had been placed near the head of the body of what must have been an important local chief.

In contrast to cast objects, which were made with a mixture of gold and copper, sheet-metal objects were fabricated of almost pure gold. The goldsmith hammered the metal to a thin sheet and then, working over a resilient surface such as leather or sand, embossed the designs on it.

The frontal saurian-human figure on this plaque appears on painted pottery and cast goldwork as well as on plaques of various shapes.

Salient features of this composite creature are the serrated crests that emerge from his head, the big staring eyes, the prominent teeth, and the clawed hands and feet. The creature is usually flanked by reptilian profile heads attached to a belt or streamers emanating from the figure itself. Bristling with spiky appendages, the image confronts the viewer in an attitude of aggression and defense. In the literature this figure is often referred to as a "crocodile god," but recently scholars have interpreted it as a mythical warrior or culture hero.

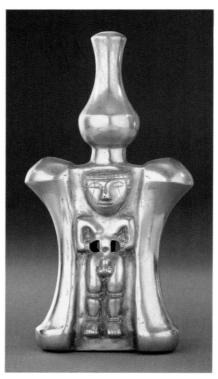

40 LIME CONTAINER

Colombia, Middle Cauca Valley;
Quimbaya
500–1000
Tumbaga (gold-copper alloy),
8 × 4¹/8 inches (20.3 × 10.5 cm)
35.507, Alfred W. Jenkins Fund

Cast by the lost-wax technique, this lime container has a male figure on one side and a female figure on the other. Both figures are nude except for ornamental bands around their heads, wrists, knees, and ankles. The hands, which were cast separately and attached through the holes at the wrist, are now missing. Male and female have the same broad face and serene expression. This idealized human countenance is found on Quimbaya pottery as well as on gold flasks and pendants.

In the Quimbaya region of southwestern Colombia there was considerable experimentation in metallurgy, perhaps because gold was less abundant here than on the Pacific slopes. Lost-wax casting reached its zenith in this area with the production of these elegant vessels with figurative imagery. A separate core was required to cast hollow forms; on this piece there are four plugged core support holes, two on the bottom and two on the top of the lateral flanges.

Lime containers were used in coca-chewing rituals. A spatula or pin would have been required to reach the lime through the bottle's narrow neck. The lime would then be mixed with a quid of coca leaves and chewed. Some gold containers have been found with the powdered lime still inside.

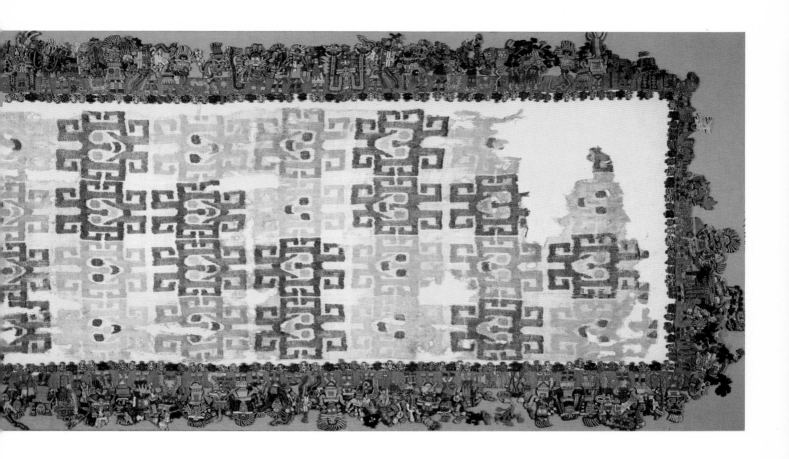

41 MANTLE

Peru, Paracas Peninsula
Circa 100 B.C.
Wool, cotton
58³/₄ × 24¹/₂ inches (149.2 × 62.2 cm)
38.121, J. T. Underwood Memorial
 Fund

The most famous piece in the Museum's Peruvian collection is undoubtedly this small rectangular mantle known as *The Paracas Textile*. Discovered in 1910 at the site of Cabeza Larga on the Paracas Peninsula on the south coast of Peru, it is said to have been the piece that inspired Julio Tello, the great Peruvian archaeologist, to begin scientific excavations on the Peninsula in 1925. There Tello found the necropolis site, a complex of subterranean rooms containing over four hundred mummy bundles composed of layer upon layer of spectacular embroidered cloths as well as gold and feather ornaments.

The best evidence we have of the beliefs and practices of the people who buried their honored dead on the Paracas Peninsula between 500 B.C. and A.D. 100 comes from the designs embroidered on the textiles. The border of this mantle, consisting of more than ninety individual figures created by needle-knitting, is uniquely varied and detailed. Included are elaborately dressed humans, gesturing animals, fantastic figures, and vegetation in various stages of growth. The human figures, all male, are portrayed wearing the type of costumes and ornaments that have been found archaeologically on the Paracas Peninsula. We can assume, therefore, that these figures represent ritual leaders in Paracas society, dressed for a major ceremony. With its emphasis on activity and the descriptive clarity of the individual figures, the border vividly illustrates the way in which the Paracas people envisioned the relationship between man, nature, and the supernatural.

42 HAT

Peru; Huari
500–1000
Cloth, reeds, feathers
6¹¹/₁₆ inches (17 cm) high
41.228, A. Augustus Healy Fund

Feathers were highly prized by the ancient Andean peoples and were used to create a great variety of costume elements including shirts, mantles, and hats. Sometimes the natural shape of the feathers was incorporated into the design, but in other instances the feathers were used solely for color and texture. On this hat they have been attached and cut to create a design of exceptional brilliance and beauty.

Square hats are characteristic of the Huari culture, but they are usu-

ally made of wool. The designs on this rare featherwork version are similar to those found on both the wool hats and fine Huari tapestry shirts. Profile feline heads alternate with a pattern of squares and triangles on all four sides of the hat. In keeping with the geometricization of natural forms in Huari art, the felines' heads and snouts have been squared off. A different four-part stepped design appears on the top of the hat.

43 TUNIC

Peru; Huari
Circa 600
Wool, tapestry weave: warp 19, weft 100
  per cm
38 × 28 3/8 inches (96.5 × 72.0 cm)
86.224.109, Gift of the Ernest Erickson
  Foundation

Huari tapestry tunics are technically and artistically among the finest textiles produced by ancient Andean weavers. More than prestige garments, they are complex statements of political affiliations and religious beliefs.

Although the center of production of these extraordinary tapestries seems to have been at or near the site of Huari in the South-Central Highlands of Peru, the imagery woven into the shirts is similar to that on the monumental stone sculpture of Tiahuanaco in Bolivia, a great religious and commercial center during the Middle Horizon Period (500–1000). On the stone doorway known as the "Gateway of the Sun" at Tiahuanaco, the main deity is represented flanked by rows of profile attendants running with staffs in their hands. Variations of these attendant figures appear in brilliant color on Huari tunics, arranged in precise vertical bands.

Six bands of eight figures each decorate the main body of this shirt. Like the Sun Gate attendants, the figures carry staffs and are in active postures. Although all the figures are the same, their direction alternates and they are patterned by four different color combinations. These variations make the overall design seem rich and complex.

This shirt is unusual, but not unique, in having sleeves and a fringe at the bottom. It is also exceptional in the fineness of the weave. With a thread count of 100 wefts per centimeter, the designs are so tightly woven that they appear to have been painted.

44 MIRROR HANDLE

Peru, North Coast; Chimu
Circa 1200
Wood, gold, turquoise, traces of paint
11⁵/₈ × 5⁹/₁₆ inches (29.5 × 14.2 cm)
86.224.4, Gift of the Ernest Erickson
 Foundation

Although the Chimu culture is best known for its textiles and metalwork, wood was also an important expressive medium for the people who dominated the North Coast of Peru during the Late Intermediate Period (1000–1400). Chimu wood carvings range from roughly carved statues to elegantly finished artifacts like this mirror handle, which portrays a well-dressed individual holding a trophy head in each hand. The elaborate headdress, serpent-headed collar, and sleeved tunic clearly identify the individual as a member of the ruling class. They also testify to a relatively realistic carving style: costume elements similar to the ones depicted have been found in Chimu burials. The trophy heads and the distinctive facial markings may indicate a special prowess in battle.

The carving has been enriched with inlays of highly prized materials: tiny turquoise beads on the handle, collar, and headdress, and gold painted over with red in the eyes of the central figure and his victims. A shallow concavity in the back of the carving probably once held a mirror made of pyrite. Unfortunately, practically nothing is known of the function of mirrors in ancient Andean civilization. Judging by the elaborateness of this handle, however, and considering the subject depicted on it, it seems likely that it was part of a ruler's regalia.

45 Water Jar

North America, New Mexico, Zuni
1800–50
Ceramic, slip
12⁷/₁₆ × 13³/₁₆ inches (31.5 × 33.5 cm)
03.132, Museum Expedition, 1903

Pottery making's long history in the American Southwest is characterized by remarkable continuity in materials and techniques and creative experimentation with forms and designs. A special vessel type that can be traced back to the early nineteenth century, for instance, is the large globular jar for carrying and storing water. Each village developed its own repertory of designs and shapes for water vessels; many of these regional preferences are still apparent in the work of Pueblo artists today.

Because systematic collecting of Pueblo pottery only began in 1879, few vessels from the early part of the century have survived. This fine jar is a rare example of the early nineteenth-century Zuni style. Distinct features are the high, flat shoulder

and the ridge at the bottom, which isolate the mid-body of the vessel as a field for painted designs. Here the artist has created a striking pattern of architectural forms that alternately enclose and support a stylized butterfly. The fine-line hatching within the dark borders of the stepped design has its roots in the prehistoric pottery painting tradition and is also found on the more spherical water jars that the Zuni began to make after 1850.

R. Stewart Culin, the Museum's first curator of ethnology, purchased this jar in Zuni in 1903 from the missionary Andrew Vanderwagen. It may have been still in use in 1898 when Vanderwagen first settled in Zuni. Certainly the rich patina and the wear on the rim suggest decades of handling.

46 SHIRT

North America, Plains; Blackfeet
Early 19th century
Hide, porcupine quills, glass beads, hair,
 pigment
44 × 69 1/4 inches (111.8 × 175.9 cm)
50.67.5a, Frank S. Benson and Henry
 L. Batterman Funds

In the early nineteenth century, when this shirt was made, only chiefs and leading warriors of the Plains Indians wore such garments, but as the century progressed they were adopted more generally. This shirt, acquired by The Brooklyn Museum in 1950, was presented to the New-York Historical Society in 1873. Matched with a pair of leggings, it reportedly belonged to a chief of the Piegan band of the Blackfeet.

The binary shirt is a classic type of Plains men's clothing. The body is constructed of the halves of two animal (usually deer) skins, cut just behind the forelegs, which form the front and back. The top (front leg) portions of each skin were cut in half again and sewn to the body as sleeves.

The complex decoration of this shirt is partly attributable to a collaboration of male and female artists.

A woman made the garment and was responsible for the geometric decoration—painted green and brown dots, beading, porcupine quill embroidery, strands of dyed hair, and cut fringes. The male wearer of the shirt painted the representational designs, depicting his war exploits. Although only the owner knew the precise identification of the motifs, their general meaning is clear. On the front is a row of painted human figures, probably signifying enemies killed in battle, while the back contains a tomahawk, a pipe, two rifles, two quivers, three bows, and an arrow—personal possessions taken on the battlefield. Both sides include a pair of holes with red paint streaming down, perhaps representing a war wound, and rows of marks resembling bird tracks, the significance of which is unknown.

47 Girl's Puberty Basket

MRS. SAM HUGHES
North America, California; Northern
Pomo

Late 19th–early 20th century
Sedge, dyed bulrush, willow, black quail
 topknots and red woodpecker crest
 feathers, clamshell beads
11 × 10⁵/8 inches (28.0 × 27.0 cm)
07.256, Museum Expedition, 1907

The Pomo are widely regarded as the finest makers of basketry in native California. Combining utility and beauty, baskets permeated Pomo life, from fishing and acorn processing to birth, marriage, and death rites. All women wove their own baskets, though some weavers were acclaimed for their skill and expertise. This coiled basket is clearly the work of a master: the sewing is tight and precise, the form regular and elegant, and the design laid out on the surface with imagination and balance. The use of feathers and shell beads signifies that this was a specially made ceremonial basket.

This basket was part of a set of four used by a girl at her puberty ceremony: a basket like this to hold water, a second for bathing, a third as a drinking cup, and a fourth for food. The girl was secluded in a reed hut for eight days, during which time she was not permitted to comb her hair or feed herself. Women continued to use these baskets during their periods of menstruation, often handing them down to their daughters.

This basket traveled a circuitous route on its way to the Museum. Its maker, Mrs. Sam Hughes of Potter Valley, California, sold it to a local druggist who in turn sold it to the proprietor of a hotel in Ukiah, California. In July 1907 Brooklyn curator Stewart Culin purchased it out of the hotel showcase, writing at the time that it was "the finest obtainable specimen of its kind."

North America, California; Maidu
Circa 1855
Native hemp and commercial cotton
cordage, mallard duck and acorn
woodpecker scalp feathers, white glass
beads
74 1/16 × 4 3/4 inches (188.0 × 12.0 cm)
08.491.8925, Museum Expedition, 1908

The Indians of central California were renowned for their ceremonial featherwork, used on headdresses, headbands, cloaks, baskets, and belts. In the mid-nineteenth century all important and wealthy Maidu possessed belts like this one. Women were given belts by their grooms at marriage, though men wore them as well. Used principally during the cycle of world-renewal dances in the winter months, feather belts were wrapped twice around the waist of the dancer.

Belt making was such a laborious and time-consuming craft that it was practiced by only a few men. In feather belts all the feathers were individually inserted into interlaced weaving strands, completely covering the surface of the fiber structure. For the red sections of this belt the scalps of about 125 woodpeckers were needed. Trade materials included here are the commercial cotton string weft and white glass beads, which replaced the native hemp and shell beads of earlier times.

Although the belt's design was associated with distinct motifs, these were regarded more as design names than as representations. According to native experts, the triangular red elements stood for wild grape leaves, the two narrow green bands for the tongs used to remove hot stones from the cooking fire, and the green rectangle for a large grasshopper.

Such elaborate belts were rarely seen by or sold to whites, and when Stewart Culin, Brooklyn's first curator of ethnology, purchased this belt in 1908, he was told that the last maker had died some years before. Highly valued by the Maidu, only a handful of such belts still exist, and of these, Brooklyn's example is without doubt the finest.

49 CHEST

North America, British Columbia; Haida
19th century
Cedar wood, pigment
20 × 22 1/4 × 35 3/4 inches
 (50.8 × 56.5 × 90.8 cm)
08.491.8903, Museum Expedition, 1908

The Indians of the Northwest Coast are renowned for their woodworking. Perhaps their most distinctive form was the kerfed, or bent-corner, box, whose sides were constructed of a single plank of wood, notched, steamed, and bent to shape, sewn or pegged on the fourth edge, and fitted with a top and bottom. Like California baskets, Northwest Coast boxes were used both domestically—for food storage—and ritually—to hold masks and dance paraphernalia.

The decoration on this chest follows the classic "formline" style of the northern coast. The primary structure of the design is painted in a swelling, bold, black line, while the secondary design elements are painted red and lightly carved out. Though each side is bilaterally symmetrical, the front and back are different. The central element of the design is a large head, below which is its body, with appendages to the sides. Visual punning is a common trait of Northwest Coast art. Here many of the "eye" motifs serve as body joints, while the eyes of the major frontal face are themselves constructed of small faces. Similar patterns fill the two sides.

Generally the motifs of Northwest Coast art represent creatures from ancestral myths, but box and chest designs were often ambiguous. Even at the turn of the century native testimony as to the meaning of these designs was inconsistent. Some scholars have suggested that the designs on the front of a chest represent the front parts of a creature, while the back side represents the behind.

This chest was collected by Charles F. Newcombe in Masset, Queen Charlotte Islands, British Columbia, probably in 1906, and purchased for the Museum in 1908. Its back has a section cut out and loosely replaced, which Newcombe explained was due to the chest's use in a performance "in which a child had been put in the box and knives thrust through, like the well known Hindu basket trick."

50 HOUSE POST

North America, British Columbia; Bella
  Bella
19th century
Cedar wood, 111 1/2 × 38 5/16 inches
  (283.0 × 97.0 cm)
11.696.1, Museum Expedition, 1911

The totem pole is synonymous with the art of the Northwest Coast natives. In a society based on the accumulation of wealth and the demonstration of ancestral privilege, such crests or family emblems played a central role. Of the several varieties of totem pole, the house post was probably the earliest form. Four carved posts supported the framework of the great plank community houses occupied by extended families.

The house owner inherited the right to carve on his posts a set of figures featured in the founding myth of his family. This story would be recited to guests at great feasts. Without knowing the specific story, we can only speculate as to the identity of the creatures on this post, but the principal figure is certainly a supernatural bird, perhaps a thunderbird, and it clasps a small human before a shield on its chest. These ceremonial shields, called "coppers," were symbols of wealth. This set of motifs was common to the Kwakiutl, of whom the Bella Bella are a northern group.

The competition to collect totem poles was fierce at the turn of the century, but objects from the Bella Bella are relatively rare in museum collections. Brooklyn's set of four posts was collected in 1911 by the Victoria physician-turned-collector Charles F. Newcombe.

Oriental Art

51 RITUAL VESSEL, TYPE KUANG

China
Shang Dynasty, 12th century B.C.
Bronze
6¹/₂ × 8¹/₂ inches (16.5 × 21.6 cm)
72.163, Gift of the Guennol Collection

Kuang is the ancient Chinese name for this form of vessel, a ewer with a lid having an animal head on the front. *Kuang* were used for serving and making offerings of rice wine. Like virtually all extant examples of ancient Chinese bronzes, this *kuang* has been recovered from a tomb. The bright silvery yellow surface of the metal has acquired a handsome blue-green patina from burial.

This *kuang* is typical of Shang ritual vessels: its surface is covered with zoomorphic designs. The designs suggest spirit animals rather than animals of the real world. They probably represent powerful spirits meant to be propitiated by the rituals in which these vessels were used, for example, spirits who were crucial to early agriculture, such as the dragons who controlled rain. A dragon appears on either side of the spout on this *kuang*. As usual, the spirit animals are surrounded by a squared-spiral pattern derived from ancient pictograms for thunder and suggesting the storm clouds in which rain dragons dwell.

The face on the front of the lid suggests a mythical tiger with flask-shaped horns. A somewhat more realistic ox head with curling horns may be seen on top of the handle. On either side of the main body of the vessel is a *t'ao-t'ieh* (literally "glutton") motif, the masklike face of a fierce guardian monster whose exact meaning is no longer known.

52 HORSE

China
T'ang Dynasty, 7th–8th century
Glazed earthenware
17³/₄ × 18¹/₂ inches (45.1 × 47 cm)
37.128, Exchange

The tombs of Shang Dynasty kings (1523–1028 B.C.) have yielded the skeletons of chariot horses who were killed and buried near their ruler in order to continue serving him in the spirit world. Numerous human skeletons nearby indicate that many of the king's retainers were also dispatched to the spirit world with him. Confucius (551–479 B.C.) is said to have taught that this practice was unworthy of virtuous rulers and to have recommended the burial of inanimate figures as substitutes for live retainers, explaining that they would serve the same purpose in the spirit world.

The earliest examples of Chinese tomb figures (Warring States Period, 480–221 B.C.) were made of painted wood. By the Han Dynasty (206 B.C.–A.D. 221) it was usual to make them from clay. Han and Six Dynasties Period examples (221–581) are usually made of gray earthenware polychromed after firing. During the T'ang Dynasty (618–907), when tomb figures became exceedingly popular, important tombs were furnished with dozens, and even the tombs of lesser personages often contained a few. Some T'ang examples are unglazed, and some have a cream-colored glaze, but the most spectacular ones are adorned with colored glazes: amber, green, blue, cream, and brown in various combinations.

War horses like the one depicted here were the pride of T'ang noblemen and military officers. The best came from Bactria, a kingdom at the western end of the silk trade routes through Central Asia.

53 A Bodhisattva

China
Chin Dynasty, 12th–13th century
Wood
56 1/2 × 17 3/8 inches (143.5 × 44.1 cm)
37.223, Gift of Frank L. Babbott

Bodhisattvas are Buddhist saviors, deities who have postponed their own salvation (Buddhahood) until all sentient beings in the universe have been saved. They work constantly and diligently to bring that about. In contrast to a Buddha, who wears the simple robe of a Buddhist monk, bodhisattvas wear the elaborate drapery, flowing scarves, and sumptuous jewelry of an Indian prince.

The Bodhisattva depicted here might be Avalokitesvara (Chinese: Kuan-yin), the most compassionate, and therefore the most popular, bodhisattva. However, the diminutive figure of Amitabha Buddha that is usually present in the diadem worn by Avalokitesvara is not seen here, and because the forearms are missing the deity cannot be identified by the attributes he may have held.

This image was produced under the aegis of the Jurched Tatars, fierce Central Asian nomads who conquered North China in 1126, forcing the Sung emperor to flee south. The Jurched established their own dynasty, the Chin, which lasted until the Mongols conquered North China in 1234.

Buddhism had first gained a foothold in China under the sponsorship of another nomad group, the T'o-pa Tatars, who adopted it as their state religion. The T'o-pa conquered northwestern China in the late fourth century. Buddhism spread from there to other parts of China, then on to Korea and Japan.

54   Blue-and-White Jar with a Design of Fishes and Water Plants

China
Yuan Dynasty, 14th century
Porcelain
11 3/4 × 13 3/4 inches (29.8 × 34.9 cm)
52.87.1, Gift of the Executors of the
Estate of Augustus A. Hutchins

Blue-and-white ware, that is, ceramic ware decorated with cobalt-oxide painted designs covered with a clear glaze, seems to have been invented in Iraq during the ninth century. The technique was imitated in Iran at the time, but on a limited scale, since Iranian cobalt seems to have been controlled by the regime in Iraq. Although for some reason the technique died out, it was revived in the eleventh-twelfth century and spread throughout the Islamic world, where it has been widely used ever since.

The technique came to China from Iran in the thirteenth century as a result of the Mongol conquests of Iraq and Iran in 1219–20 and China in 1279. These conquests put the Mongols in control of an area extending from Eastern Europe through Central Asia to China and Korea. Goods and ideas flowed across this vast expanse more readily than ever before.

At first the cobalt oxide used in China was imported from Iran and referred to by the Chinese as "Mohammedan blue." But soon cobalt was being mined in China to meet the demand. This jar has the intense, almost purple, color of the imported cobalt. The painted design fits and enhances the powerful, swelling form of the jar to perfection. Blue-and-white porcelain subsequently became a standard Chinese ceramic ware of the Ming Dynasty (1368–1644) and has been produced in large quantities ever since.

55 LANDSCAPE

LAN YING
(Chinese, 1585–1664 or later)

China
Ch'ing Dynasty, dated in accordance
  with 1653
Ink and color on silk
66 × 26½ inches (167.6 × 67.3 cm)
84.72, Purchased with funds from
  Stanley Herzman and the General
  Acquisitions Fund

The Chinese have always loved jade, bronzes, and porcelain, but only painting and calligraphy are classified as art. In Chinese painting, landscape has been the primary subject since at least the tenth century—not landscape as a graphic equivalent of actual scenery, but landscape as created in the artist's mind, often based on his study of earlier masters, but interpreted in a personal way, as an expression of his own poetic sensibility. A Chinese landscape painting is usually an idealized view of hills, lakes, trees, rocks, and an isolated cottage, the sort of place to which a scholar-artist might hope to retire one day.

Lan Ying was a major landscape painter of the late Ming Dynasty (1368–1644) and early Ch'ing. He was a professional artist, as opposed to the supposedly amateur scholar-artists whose paintings and writings were so fashionable at the time. Lan was born and raised in Hang-chou, the former capital of the Southern Sung Dynasty (1127–1279). Although his teacher is unknown, Lan Ying was trained in the landscape tradition of the Southern Sung Imperial Painting Academy and its Ming Dynasty successor, the Che School. In his early twenties he began to study the paintings of old masters associated with the literati (scholar-artist) tradition as well. His mature work combines the best of both traditions.

56 Yaksa (Bhaisajyaguru)

Korea
United Silla Period, 8th century
Bronze
7¹/₈ × 2 inches (18.1 × 5.1 cm)
74.165, Frank L. Babbott Fund

The identity of the specific Buddha represented by this image is indicated by the attribute *(laksana)* held in his left hand. It is a bowl *(pātra)*, not the alms bowl held by certain Buddhist deities, but a medicine bowl, or medicine jar, that holds ointment to cure all the ills of mankind; sometimes shown with its cover on, it is here represented with the lid removed.

The full, if not to say plump, face of this image is a stylistic element derived from Chinese Buddhist sculpture of the T'ang Dynasty (618–907). The style of the image as a whole is based on that of the early T'ang Period, for the body has not yet developed the ponderous massiveness characteristic of late T'ang Buddhist sculpture. The *Yaksa* could pass for a late seventh-century Korean sculpture but for the fact that the hollow figure was cast with two large, oval openings on the back of the body and another on the back of the head. This is typical of eighth-century Korean images but not of seventh-century ones.

The alert and compassionate facial expression of the *Yaksa* conveys a feeling of profound spirituality, as well as the caring, healing capacities of the Buddha of Medicine.

57 CELADON EWER

Korea
Koryo Dynasty, first half of the 12th
  century
Porcelain
9⁷/₈ × 9¹/₂ inches (25.1 × 24.1 cm)
56.138.1, Gift of Mrs. Darwin R. James III

Celadon is a high-fired, porcelaneous ware having a gray clay body covered with a translucent gray-green feldspathic glaze. The green color of the glaze results from the presence of iron oxide in a reduction kiln (one in which only a limited amount of oxygen is available during firing). Celadon was developed in China at the beginning of the Sung Dynasty (960–1279) and introduced to Korea by Chinese potters in the tenth-eleventh century.

The rich, lustrous glaze on this ewer is the "kingfisher blue" color found on only the best twelfth-century Korean celadons. The body of the ewer is carved with a design of overlapping lotus petals framing leaf sprays. The handle is in the form of a lotus stalk bound at the top with reeds, the lid in the shape of an upside-down lotus blossom, and the lid knob in the form of a lotus bud just beginning to unfurl. A tiny butterfly is modeled in relief on the back of the lid. Dots of white slip (liquid clay) accent the ornamental motifs.

This kind of restrained use of painted white slip under the glaze to heighten incised decoration seems to have been an important step in the development of slip-inlay techniques by Korean potters during the first half of the twelfth century. Slip-inlay became the characteristic Korean ceramic decorating technique of the twelfth to sixteenth centuries.

58 SCHOLAR CONTEMPLATING A CASCADE

ATTRIBUTED TO YI CHONG
(Korean, 1578–1607)

Yi Dynasty, 16th century
Album-leaf painting mounted as a
 hanging scroll, ink on silk
11 1/4 × 10 7/8 inches (28.6 × 27.6 cm)
75.130, Museum Purchase

Sixteenth-century Korean ink-wash paintings are extremely rare outside major museums in Korea. Only a handful have reached the West, usually by way of Japanese collections. Most of these have been misidentified as Chinese, since they follow Chinese models quite closely. Recently the Japanese scholar Shimada Shujirō has been active in reattributing many of them to Korea.

The supposed artist of this painting, Yi Chong, was the grandson of Yi Sang-jwa, a slave in the household of a scholar-official who developed such phenomenal artistic skill that the king appointed him to the Bureau of Painting. Yi Chong was trained from early childhood in the use of the brush. By the age of ten he had become a competent landscape painter and was also skilled at figure subjects. Although he decided to become a Buddhist monk at eleven and

joined a monastery in the Diamond Mountains, an area famous for its spectacular granite pinnacles, he continued to paint throughout his short life. He was noted for his independent ways and difficult personality, painting only when and what he wanted to and turning down commissions from powerful persons if they did not suit him.

This painting follows the style of the Imperial Painting Academy of Southern Sung Dynasty China (1127–1279) as interpreted by artists of the Che School during the Ming Dynasty (1368–1644).

59 IRON-PAINTED DRAGON JAR

Korea
Yi Dynasty, 17th century
Porcelain
12 3/8 × 14 5/8 inches (31.4 × 37.1 cm)
86.139, Gift of the Oriental Art Council

The dragon on this jar seems naive, eccentric, and amusing, yet powerful and mysterious. His function was to protect food inside the jar from evil spirits as well as to attract good fortune for the jar's owner. The dragon was painted on the surface of the jar with iron-oxide brown-black pigment prior to the application of the clear glaze. The jar's dynamic shape enhances the visual impact of the dragon. The diamond-shaped profile results from forming the top and bottom halves separately on the potter's wheel and then joining them rim-to-rim.

The potters who made these utilitarian storage jars were members of one of the lowest classes in society during the Yi Dynasty (1392–1910). They had to work quickly and produce serviceable pots in large quantities just to eke out a meager living. The pots they made are natural, direct, and spontaneous, free from pretense or self-consciousness. The few iron-painted dragon jars that have survived are among the most aesthetically satisfying pots ever made.

The dragons on Korean blue-and-white porcelain jars made for use in the royal palace and in Confucian temples were more fully realized paintings based on Chinese models of the Ming Dynasty (1368–1644). While awesome and majestic, these "official" dragons are not nearly as lively, mysterious, and spiritlike as the "folk" dragons on iron-painted dragon jars.

60 DŌTAKU

Japan
Yayoi Period, 2nd–3rd century
Bronze
34¹/₂ × 11¹/₂ inches (87.6 × 29.2 cm)
67.198, Gift of Mr. and Mrs. Milton
  Lowenthal

The Yayoi Period (circa 300 B.C.–
circa A.D. 300) was Japan's Bronze-
Iron Age. It is clear from skeletal
evidence that the Yayoi people were of
Mongoloid racial stock, unlike their
Jōmon predecessors, who were Cau-
casoid. The Jōmon people had
crossed to the northern islands of
Japan from the coast of Siberia by
dugout canoe beginning around
10,000 B.C. and gradually spread
southward throughout the archi-
pelago. Their culture was proto-
Neolithic: they made pottery and polished stone tools but had no agriculture. The Yayoi people migrated to
Japan from the mainland by way of
the Korean peninsula, which forms a
land bridge to within 128 miles of
Kyūshū. They grew rice and made
both bronze and iron tools and
weapons. Thus they easily displaced
and dominated their Jōmon predecessors.

Dōtaku are bell-shaped bronze
ritual objects. Their shapes suggest
the bronze bells of late Chou Dynasty
China (480–221 B.C.), but the walls
of *dōtaku* are too thin to resonate.
Groups of *dōtaku*, lying on their
sides, were buried on hills overlooking rice paddies as offerings intended to propitiate the nature spirits
whose goodwill was essential to Yayoi farmers, hunters, and fishermen.

61 HANIWA FIGURE OF A SHAMANESS

Japan
Tomb Period, 5th–6th century
Earthenware
18 × 8³/₄ inches (45.7 × 22.2 cm)
79.278.1, Gift of Mr. and Mrs. Stanley
  Marcus

By the beginning of the fourth century, a new group calling themselves the Yamato people were migrating into Japan from Korea. They had one tremendous advantage over the Yayoi people and the remnants of the Jōmon people they encountered in Japan: war horses. After taking control of Kyūshū, the Yamato clans moved northeastward through the Inland Sea to the Nara-Kyoto-Osaka area, where they set up one of their chieftains as the first emperor of Japan.

The Yamato people built mound tombs for their important dead, the largest tombs being for emperors. The tomb chambers were filled with luxury goods meant to serve the deceased warriors in the spirit world. These artifacts are nearly identical to those from Kaya and Silla kingdom tombs in southern Korea.

Haniwa, however, are unique to Japan. They are large, hollow earthenware cylinders, either plain or shaped like weapons, buildings, animals, or human figures. They were placed in a circle around the shoulder of the tomb mound, or else on top of it. In Korea figures of tomb guardians were made of granite.

This *haniwa* represents the Shintō priestess who presided over the funeral ceremony, which went on for several days, with eating, drinking, and entertainment. The feast was meant to continue indefinitely in the spirit world, with the clay priestess presiding.

Japan
Kamakura Period, early 13th century
Japanese cypress with traces of
 polychrome
21 × 11¼ inches (53.3 × 28.6 cm) each
85.171.1 and 85.171.2, A. Augustus
 Healy Fund, Frank L. Babbott Fund,
 Dr. and Mrs. Robert Feinberg, Mr. and
 Mrs. Alastair B. Martin, and Mr. and
 Mrs. Milton F. Rosenthal

These energetic guardian lion-dogs originally stood on the veranda of a Shintō shrine. They are called *koma-inu* after *Koma*, an alternative Japanese name for the Koryo Dynasty of Korea (918–1392), and *inu*, the usual Japanese word for "dog." The more familiar *kara-shishi* (mythical lions) of Japan usually appear in a secular context, while *koma-inu* have a hieratic guardian function.

Lions are not native to Japan. Depictions of them were brought to Japan with Buddhism, which was introduced from Korea in 552 by way of China and India, and *shishi*, the Japanese word for lion, is derived from the Sanskrit word *simha*. In India, where it is indigenous, the lion often served as a symbol of the Bud-dha, whose throne was called the Lion Throne, and in China early Buddhist sculpture often showed a pair of mythical lions guarding the Buddha's throne. In spite of the widespread popularity of Buddhism in Japan from the mid-sixth century onward, the oldest known Japanese depictions of lions date from no earlier than the Fujiwara Period (897–1185). The theme did not become popular until the Kamakura Period (1185–1334), when *samurai* (the hereditary military class) took over the government. This pair of lion-dogs is from the very beginning of the tradition and displays remarkable realism, strength, vigor, and grace. Later examples have curled manes instead of straight.

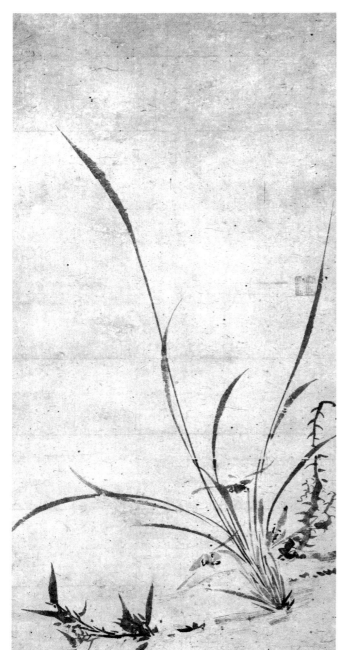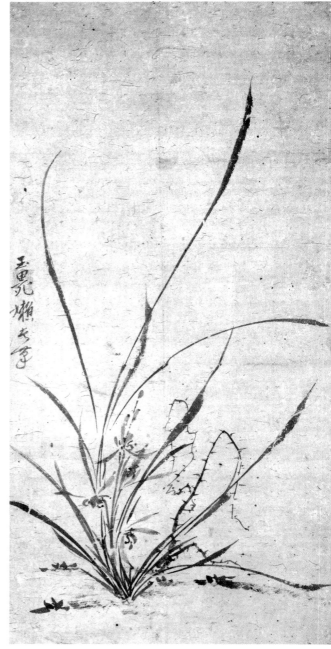

63 ORCHIDS, BAMBOO, AND THORNS

GYOKUEN BOMPŌ
(Japanese, 1348–after 1420)

Muromachi Period, early 15th century
Ink on Korean paper
25 × 12¼ inches (63.5 × 31.1 cm) each
73.123.1, Gift of The Roebling Society
73.123.2, Purchase, Oriental Art
  Acquisitions Fund

Ink-wash paintings of orchids have been fashionable in China since at least the thirteenth century. Scholar-artists trained in the Confucian clas-sics associated the flower with Con-fucian ideals of refinement and vir-tue, while Ch'an (Japanese: Zen) priests, for whom orchids carried no symbolism, also liked to paint them.

During the first half of the four-teenth century, large numbers of Japanese Zen student monks went to China, where many of them mas-tered Chinese literature and cal-ligraphy as well as Zen philosophy. Gyokuen Bompō came from the next generation, fewer monks of which studied in China, and so he never made the trip. Nevertheless he be-came quite famous in Japan for his skill in Chinese poetry, Chinese cal-ligraphy, and ink paintings of or-chids. His orchid paintings followed the style of the Chinese master Hsueh-ch'uang and the Japanese Tesshū Tokusai.

Gyokuen Bompō was one of the great *bunjin-sō* (literati monks) of the early fifteenth century. After ser-ving the priest Shunoku Myōha first at the Tōshōji monastery in Ka-makura and then at Nanzenji in Kyoto, he became the abbot of Ken-ninji and later of Nanzenji. The Shōgun Ashikaga Yoshimochi was his patron.

64 The Actor Segawa Kikunojo III in the Role of Oshizu

TŌSHŪSAI SHARAKU
(active 1794–95)

Japan
Edo Period, Kansei 6 (1794), 5th month
Woodblock print
14⅞ × 9¼ inches (37.8 × 23.5 cm)
42.83, Gift of Mr. and Mrs. Frederic B.
  Pratt

Much has been written about the artist Sharaku, yet after decades of research and speculation little is known about his career. A Noh actor in the service of the lord of Awa, now Osaka, he is credited with producing more than 150 print designs of *kabuki* actors for one publisher within a nine-month period from May 1794 to February 1795. All his actor prints fall within two distinct groups: facial portraits and portraits of actors in full view on stage. The respect with which he treats the face of each actor was never attempted by the other artists of Edo. However similar in format to other prints of his day, his works are completely different in conception and quality.

This print of the actor Segawa Kikunojo III is one of Sharaku's most celebrated portraits of an *onnagata* (male actor in a female role). Dated to May 1794, it portrays the sardonic expression of a character in the Genroku play *Hanaayame Bunroku Soga*, a drama that tells the true story of the vengeance of ten brothers twenty-eight years after their father's assassination in 1701.

65   A Cherry Blossom Viewing Picnic

Japan
Edo Period, Kan'ei era (1624–44)
Ink, color, and gold leaf on paper
39 3/8 × 105 7/8 inches (100 × 266.7 cm)
39.87, Gift of Frederic B. Pratt

In the late sixteenth, early seventeenth century, the merchant class rose to prominence in Japan, although it continued to be held in contempt by the ruling military aristocracy. A new subculture of courtesan districts, bath houses, and *kabuki* theaters sprang up to service the merchants and their employees in the large cities—Edo (modern Tok-

yo), Kyoto, and Osaka. This subculture came to be called *Ukiyo*, the Floating World, parodying an old Buddhist term describing the misery and brevity of life in the real world. By the late seventeenth century, novels and woodblock prints began taking the Floating World as their theme. *Ukiyo-e* prints developed from a late sixteenth-century genre painting tradition depicting the pleasures of ordinary people.

A Cherry Blossom Viewing Picnic is the right screen of a pair; the left screen is in the Yawata Yōtarō collection, Tokyo. The young woman in the red *kimono* (third from the left in the right screen) is probably the daughter of a *samurai*. She is surrounded by six female attendants and followed by a young *samurai*, apparently her lover, who is accompanied by seven male retainers. The eighteen women in the left screen are low-ranking courtesans, many of whom acted in women's *kabuki* before it was banned by the government. The central courtesan is dressed in fashionable male attire and is the object of a lascivious glance by the girl in the red *kimono*.

66 SEATED BUDDHA TORSO

India, Andhra Pradesh, probably
  Nagarjunakonda
Ikshvakhu Period, late 3rd century
Pale green limestone
16³/₄ × 15 inches (42.5 × 38.1 cm)
86.227.24, Gift of the Ernest Erickson
  Foundation

Representations of the historical Buddha, Sakyamuni, first occurred in the iconographic scheme of Buddhist monuments in India in the first century. The events of Sakyamuni's life were signified by the position, hand gestures, and attributes of the Buddha figures. Here for instance, the two deer in the center of the throne indicate that the scene depicted is the Buddha's first sermon in the deer park at Sarnath.

This Buddha is probably from Nagarjunakonda, one of the Buddhist centers of southern India that flourished in the Guntur district and adjacent areas of the eastern Deccan (modern-day Andhra Pradesh) from as early as the second century B.C. until the fourth century A.D. These centers were important not only for their role in disseminating Buddhism to southern and southeastern Asia but also for their extensive participation in sea trade that originated from as far west as Rome and for the complexes of monuments—primarily religious—erected by their rulers. They are considered among the greatest art centers of ancient India.

Nagarjunakonda, the "hill of Nagarjuna"—named after a great second-century Buddhist philosopher who was responsible for much of the renovation of nearby Amaravati—was discovered in 1926. Although its excavated stupas, monasteries, and chapels are now inaccessible as the result of the recent construction of the Nagarjunasagar dam, most of the remains of its antiquities have been moved to the Archaeological Museum of Nagarjunakonda.

The main artistic activity at Nagarjunakonda grew through the patronage of the Ikshvakhu rulers, who succeeded the Satavahanas at the end of the second century and ruled until early in the fourth century. Hindu and Buddhist monuments coexisted at the site. While the kings of the dynasty were worshipers of the Brahmanical gods and performers of Vedic ritual, the Buddhist monasteries there were largely the interest of the Ikshvakhu queens and princesses whose pious gifts are recorded in the extant donors' inscriptions.

The stone sculptures of Nagarjunakonda, like those of the rest of the surrounding Amaravati region, are of a greenish limestone soft enough to have allowed for subtle carving and precise modeling. Most were reliefs designed to adhere to the brickwork of the monasteries. Free-standing sculpture, however, is also known, including several exquisite late third-century standing Buddhas.

This Buddha, head missing, is seated in the *satamaparyanka asana* position (one foot placed on the other with the sole of the right foot visible), a slightly unusual position that originated at Amaravati. His garment, which covers the left shoulder only, falls in deeply modeled folds. The left hand forms the *dhyana mudra* (gesture of contemplation), while the right arm, now missing, was held away from the body, probably in the *abhaya mudra* (gesture of protection). The wheel on the sole of the Buddha's foot is one of the thirty-two major and eighty minor *laksana*, or signs, of the Buddha and refers to the wheel of law, which he set in motion. The two seated lions with their heads turned back that flank the deer on the front of the throne are associated with royal and heroic virtues.

67 Buddha Meditating under the Bodhi Tree

India, Tamil Nadu, Nagapattinam
Circa 9th century
Granite
69 1/2 × 31 1/2 × 18 1/2 inches
  (176.5 × 80 × 47 cm)
84.132, Gift of Alice Boney

Nagapattinam was once an important town in South India and the first Indian port touched by ships from Malaya and Java. Its history dates from the first century B.C., when it was noted for the region's earliest Buddhist shrines. During the reign of the Pallava and Chola dynasties, religious tolerance and artistic production both flourished there.

Nagapattinam Buddhist images are recognized by certain characteristics, namely the flame-shaped finial above the *ushnisha* (cranial protuberance) on the Buddha's head, the decorated border of his monk's costume, the marks on the palms of his hands, and the shape of his *urna* (forehead mark). All these characteristics are evident in this powerful depiction of the Buddha Sakyamuni attaining Enlightenment underneath the Bodhi Tree, one of the largest and most impressive Nagapattinam Buddhas known.

Sakyamuni is represented in a cross-legged meditative pose on a rectangular throne decorated at the base with a row of lions. Both hands rest in his lap in the *dhyana mudra* (gesture of contemplation). Flanking him are two diminutive attendants, each holding a fly whisk as a symbol of respect. Behind them the Bodhi Tree is represented as a pipal tree with its branches arranged in stylized rows. A parasol emerges in front of the tree.

68 Seated Bodhisattva Lokesvara

India, Bihar, Kurkihar
Pala Period, 10th century
Bronze
5¹/₂×4¹/₈ inches (14×10.5 cm)
72.55, Gift of Mr. and Mrs. Richard Shields

This bronze belongs to a hoard of more than two hundred images and ritual objects discovered buried together at Kurkihar, the site of an ancient Buddhist monastery in the state of Bihar in eastern India. The images range in height from a few inches to several feet and date from the eighth to the twelfth centuries. While the earliest Kurkihar images suggest a close stylistic tie to bronzes from Nalanda, Kurkihar bronzes from the ninth century on exhibit an individual style. The predominant figures are Buddhas with tall peaked crowns and flamed aureoles, often with details indicated by silver or copper inlay.

This figure, however, represents a Bodhisattva (Buddhist savior) seated in princely repose on an elaborate lotus throne supported by two lions. The back of the throne is elaborately carved with a long cushion and is flanked by two rampant lions standing on elephants in turn supported by lotuses. It is inscribed with a donor's name in a circular cartouche, a common Kurkihar device. Behind the Bodhisattva's head is a round halo pointed at the top and surrounded by flames.

Considering its scale, this piece represents a splendid artistic achievement. It is recognized as one of The Brooklyn Museum's most important examples of India's metalcasting tradition.

69   Offering the Weapon Chest to Amir Hamza

Illustration from the *Hamza-nama*
India, Mughal
Akbar Period, 1567–82
Opaque watercolor and gold on cotton
36⅞ × 29⅝ inches (93.7 × 75.2 cm)
24.47, Museum Purchase

Unquestionably the finest Mughal paintings in the collection of The Brooklyn Museum are four pages from the tales of Amir Hamza, the *Hamza-nama*. These paintings, originally intended for a multivolume manuscript with 1,400 illustrations, vividly epitomize early Mughal painting under the patronage of the emperor Akbar (reigned 1556–1605).

The extraordinary pictorial vitality, unusually large scale, and early date of the *Hamza-nama* have sparked much scholarly discussion in this century. In addition to several smaller manuscripts of the same period, circa 1567–82, the *Hamza-nama* has been considered a crucible for the various native Indian and imported Persian styles from which the Mughal synthesis developed. While the heads of the royal atelier in which the *Hamza-nama* was produced, Mir Sayyid 'Ali and 'Abd al-Samad, were Persians, the fifty or more artists who worked for them were apparently predominantly Indian.

What is remarkable about the *Hamza-nama* is that the artists conformed to neither a Persian nor an Indian idiom. Rather, under the intense scrutiny and purported guidance of their patron Akbar, they forged a new style. Not surprisingly, this style reflects the vigor and aggressiveness of Akbar, who was busy conquering India in the period in which the *Hamza-nama* was copied and illustrated.

In the page illustrated here, Amir Hamza is enthroned outdoors under a canopy receiving a weapon chest carried above the raging waters in the foreground on the shoulders of a spotted *div* (demon). The intense colors, lively gestures, detailed patterns of costumes and objects, and dramatic setting of the painting are typical of the most exciting pages of the *Hamza-nama*. The Amir is depicted in a pose and setting associated with Safavid painting of the 1540s, while the *div* derives from the beloved monsters of Persian painting. Even the gesture of the figure at the lower right with forefinger raised to mouth is a stock Persian sign of astonishment. Yet in spite of these Persian elements the painterly treatment of the tree, hills, and swirling water and the wild gesticulation of the bearded figure in the foreground find no counterpart in sixteenth-century Persian painting. Rather, these traits characterize early Akbari painting and perhaps are a result of early European influence.

Another unusual trademark of the manuscript is the variation in scale between different figures. Here the figures on the left of the page are noticeably larger than those on the right, even though the text does not call for such a differentiation. The number 40 in the lower margin and 41 on the verso are page numbers. The text on page 41 would have referred to the illustration facing it, not the one here.

70 HEAD OF SHIVA

Cambodia
First quarter of the 10th century
Tan sandstone
7½ × 3¾ inches (19.0 × 8.9 cm)
83.182.5, Anonymous gift

This handsome head of a male is identified as the Hindu divinity Shiva by his usual attributes: a moon crescent in his headdress and a vertical third eye incised on his forehead. The head, carved in the round, portrays the broad face with stippled beard and upturned mustache typical of figures of the pre-Angkor Period (circa 850–1000). A multitiered tiara is tied at the back of the head, which is marked by a high columnar chignon surmounted by a lotus shape.

The Cambodian attribution is less difficult to ascertain than the exact provenance of this piece, for the sculptural remains at Cambodian sites such as Koh Ker and Bantay Srei are often stylistically similar for this period. There are many inscriptions dedicated to the worship of Shiva at these sites, which would indicate that there was a thriving Shaivite cult in Cambodia at this time.

71 Seated Maitreya

Tibet
12th–13th century
Gilt copper
9 1/2 × 7 1/2 inches (24.1 × 19.1 cm)
67.80, Charles Stewart Smith Fund

This wonderfully preserved image of a Buddha is shown in the gesture of setting in motion the Wheel of the Doctrine. The Buddha is identified as a Maitreya (Buddha of the Future) by the *stupa* (ritual object) in his headdress and by the flanking lotus. The artist has emphasized the hieratic pose of the figure and the stereotyped gesture of the hands while at the same time conveying the Maitreya's authority and withdrawal into meditation.

Although the spiked snail curls of this figure are seen in some Buddha images from western Tibet, the abstract patterning of the folds of the monastic garment are more typical of the Newari workmanship of Nepal. Such differences make attribution and dating of the piece difficult, but it is known that Newari craftsmen were often employed in Tibet to produce bronze statuary.

72 MANDALA OF VAJRASATTVA

Tibet
14th century
Opaque watercolor on cotton
15 1/2 × 15 1/2 inches (39.4 × 39.4 cm)
81.10, E. C. Woodward and various
funds

This *mandala*, or diagram, represents the cosmic universe of Vajrasattva, one of the five manifestations of the Buddha in Esoteric Buddhism. Seated in yogic posture at the center, he is portrayed in his customary color, white, and wearing a red patterned dhoti. He is elaborately ornamented with jewelry and a crown and holds his usual attributes, a double *vajra* (thunderbolt) and a bell.

Surrounding Vajrasattva are the Guardians of the Four Cardinal Directions, each seated in a quadrant facing the Buddha. Clockwise from the top they are Virupaksha, King of the Nagas and Guardian of the West (his color is red, and he holds a serpent); Vaisravana, God of Wealth and Guardian of the North (he is seated on a lion and holds a banner and a mongoose); Dhritarasatra, King of the Gandharvas and Guardian of the East; and Virudhaka, King of the Demons and Guardian of the South (he is blue and holds a sword).

A diminutive female is represented on each side of the outer border. She represents one of the forms of Prajnaparamita, the essence of transcendental wisdom. Vases of immortality are depicted in the four corners, and elaborate lotus scrolls complete the spandrels.

This *mandala* is an outstanding example of Tibetan Buddhist ritual art. Actually a temple banner, or *tankha*, it exemplifies the early Tibetan painting tradition with its pure luminous color, expressive line, and symmetrical composition.

73 SEATED BUDDHA

Thailand
Sukhothai Period, 14th century
Bronze
42¹/₄ × 31¹/₂ inches (107.3 × 80 cm)
82.228, Gift of William Randolph Reiss

The Sukhothai Period (1250–1378) was a great golden age of Thai sculpture. Dvaravati sculpture (6th–10th century) had closely followed Indian models of the Gupta Period (320–500), while Lopburi sculpture (11th–13th century) was based quite closely on Khmer models of the Angkor Period (877–1201). In the Sukhothai Period, however, a truly national Thai style emerged. As we see here, it is a style that somehow managed to combine seemingly incompatible qualities such as compassion and haughtiness, spirituality and sensuousness, delicacy and strength, languid grace and dynamic energy.

This Buddha is seated in the lotus position with his hands in the *bhumisparsa mudra:* the right hand pendant in front of the right knee, palm inward, with the fingers extended downward toward the ground. This ritual gesture refers to the time when the Buddha proved his perfect knowledge. The demon king and his armies attacked the Buddha, but he pointed to the ground and the gods of the earth rose up to destroy the demons.

The hemispherical bump (*ushnisha*) on top of the Buddha's head contains his boundless knowledge (*bodhi*). The flame arising from it represents his fiery energy (*tejas*). His extended earlobes refer to the fact that Prince Siddhartha, the Buddha Sakyamuni before his enlightenment, wore the heavy earrings of an Indian prince.

74 A BLUE IRIS

Signed: Ya Sahib-al-Zaman (O Lord of
the Age) (active second half of the 17th
century), one of the accepted
signatures of Muhammad Zaman
Iran, Isfahan
Dated 1663–64
Opaque watercolor and ink on paper
sheet: 13 1/8 × 8 3/8 inches (33.3 × 21.3
cm); image: 7 1/2 × 4 3/8 inches
(19.1 × 11.1 cm)
86.23, Hagop Kevorkian Fund and
Middle East Special Fund

This exquisite painting is by the seventeenth-century Iranian artist Muhammad Zaman. Signed "Ya Sahib-al-Zaman," or "O Lord of the Age," a pun on the artist's name, and dated A.H. 1074 (1663–64), it is the earliest dated work by the artist in an American collection, his only known depiction of a single flower, and the only work by him in The Brooklyn Museum collection.

Muhammad Zaman, who is known for his Europeanizing style, may well have been inspired by a Dutch or Flemish botanical print. Such prints were increasingly brought to Iran during the seventeenth century by European travelers and merchants. Intended for inclusion in an album, *A Blue Iris* might have been placed opposite a European print of the same subject. Apparently Muhammad Zaman's painting inspired a whole school of flower painting in eighteenth- and nineteenth-century Iran, for several eighteenth-century flower paintings bear false attributions to him. Moreover, almost no painting or drawing of flowers dated before 1663 depicts the subject without a bird or butterfly hovering nearby. Muhammad Zaman's work must have been one of the very first Iranian paintings to make the break from the natural setting.

Works by Muhammad Zaman are somewhat rare and often manuscript illustrations rather than single-page compositions. Departing from the seventeenth-century Iranian norm, he painted several scenes from the New Testament. These paintings and a seventeenth-century Italian chronicler's reference to a converted Iranian traveler of the same name led art historians for most of this century to conclude that Muhammad Zaman was in fact a Christian who worked outside Iran in the 1660s. However, in recent years scholars have reexamined this story and have found that no mention was made of the traveler Muhammad Zaman being an artist. Thus, the decidedly European and, to some eyes, Indian influence on Muhammad Zaman's work must have come from imported works of art rather than from Muhammad Zaman's own perambulations.

A Blue Iris comes to us with an impeccable provenance. Formerly in the collection of the bibliophile Hans P. Kraus, it was first published in 1972. It was subsequently sold to Prince Shahram of the former Iranian royal family and then to the contemporary British painter Howard Hodgkin.

75   NISHAPUR BOWL

Northeastern Iran or Transoxiana
9th–10th century
Ceramic, transparent colorless glaze,
 black slip, white engobe, buff
 earthenware body
4 9/16 × 14 inches (11.5 × 35.5 cm)
86.227.19, Gift of the Ernest Erickson
 Foundation

The type of pottery represented here was produced in the northeastern provinces of Iran, Khurasan, and Transoxiana during the ninth and tenth centuries. By 875 the Samanid family had established an autonomous dynasty in Transoxiana with its capital at Bukhara. In return for defeating the Safarrid dynasty in Khurasan, the Abbasid caliph granted the Samanids the governship of that province in 900. Thus, by the tenth century the Samanids controlled a vast and important area of the Eastern Islamic world, including the major cities of Merv, Samarkand (Afrasiyab), Bukhara, Balkh, and Nishapur. Although wares excavated at Nishapur and Samarkand are the best known from this region today, presumably each of the major Samanid cities had kilns of its own where ceramics similar to the bowl shown here were produced.

This piece is demonstrative of the epigraphic, "black-on-white" type of Samanid ceramics. The clarity of the design is achieved by the use of a white slip covering the pink or buff earthenware body, on which decoration was painted in metallic pigments mixed with slip. By adding slip to the pigments, potters could keep them from running. Designs in dark brown or black are often in slight relief and embellished with incising. Customarily, a clear lead glaze covers the decorated surface.

According to Charles K. Wilkinson's classification, "black-on-white wares" constituted one of the most numerous groups of ceramics excavated at Nishapur. These wares are among the most beautiful of all Islamic ceramics. In general, they consist of three types—those decorated with Arabic writing or pseudo-writing, those with nonepigraphic ornament, and those with a combination of epigraphic and other decoration. As discussed by Lisa Volov (Golombek), the inscriptions on Samanid epigraphic pottery invariably appear in Arabic kufic script and most often express pithy sentiments, such as the inscription here: "Peace is that which is silent and only his speech will reveal the [?] of the man with faults."

Costumes and Textiles

76 ORPHREY BAND

English
Third quarter of the 14th century
Linen embroidered with silk and
 metallic thread
25 × 6.9 inches (62.5 × 17.5 cm)
49.216, Gift of Mr. and Mrs. Alastair B.
 Martin

During the Middle Ages one of the favorite subjects for artists in all media was the earthly genealogy of Jesus, known as the Tree of Jesse after the father of King David (Matthew I). Four figures from this family tree are depicted on this fourteenth-century embroidered fragment. Identified by the scrolls they hold, which are inscribed in Gothic characters, they are Ozias, Azor, Achaz, and Sadoch.

This fragment is part of an orphrey, a decorative band made to ornament a vestment or other textile intended for ecclesiastical use. Two companion pieces are in the Guennol Collection and the Cleveland Museum of Art. All are worked in some of the finest and most distinctive needlework ever executed, a type known as *opus Anglicanium*, which at the time of its creation was exported all over Europe. Such embroidery is characterized by silk split stitch and couched metal thread on two layers of linen. The natural dye silk thread is an untwisted floss, and the metallic thread is silver-gilt foil wrapped around a silk thread core.

The figural composition here can easily be related to late medieval manuscript miniatures in which the subject is enframed by foliate forms. Here a grapevine serves both as an ovoid frame for the various subjects and as the uniting branch of a genealogical tree.

77 WALL HANGING

Norwegian, Gudbrandsdalen or Valdres
 region
Mid-late 17th century
Wool and linen, slit tapestry weave
47¹/₂ × 67 inches (120.7 × 170.2 cm)
25.588, Gift of Frank L. Babbott

For many centuries a traditional subject of rural Norwegian pictorial wall hangings was the Parable of the Ten Virgins (Matthew 25:1–13). Over the years there was little change in the format and depiction of the parable, with, as here, two horizontal rows of people.

The biblical story relates how the women set out to meet a bridegroom (the Lord), here portrayed in the lower left corner. Five wise women took lamps with extra oil, while five foolish ones took only their lamps. The unprepared ran out of oil and did not have enough light to see the Lord. These virgins are shown weeping in an archway on the bottom row. On the upper row the five wisely prepared virgins, torches upraised and ablaze, greet the Lord.

The wool yarns of this hanging are hand spun and dyed, and the weaving is probably the work of a professional. The geometric floral or snowflake designs that abound in Norwegian woven textiles here form a full top and bottom frame and partial side panels. The piece most probably was hung in a church.

78   CRAVAT END

Flemish
Circa 1725
Linen thread, bobbin lace
13⅜ × 13 inches (34.0 × 35.0 cm)
31.778, Ella C. Woodward Fund

Historically, lace-enhanced articles of attire have not been restricted to items associated with the feminine wardrobe. During the seventeenth and eighteenth centuries lace-trimmed personal garments—those worn closest to the skin—were a mark of gentility for both sexes.

For a man, lace might trim his shirt or neck treatment. When cravats and falling bands replaced wide-spreading collars in the early years of the eighteenth century, the ends of both were frequently embellished with fine needle- or bobbin-made lace. The depth and complexity of the lace pattern were indications of both the wearer's status and contemporary fashion.

This cravat end is one of a pair worked in mirror image. Hunting scenes like the one it displays were common subjects for lace but were not generally utilized on objects of attire. When the cravat was worn, the central mounted hunter, who is in pursuit of the deer or hare along the lower right edge, would be lost in pendant folds. The mounted hunter is diagonally framed by a fanciful Eastern bird vendor at the upper right and a spear- and shield-carrying hunter at the lower left. Above and below him are a bird and a dog respectively. In the upper left corner is a feline.

This kind of lace is identified as *Point d'Angleterre à reseau*, a Brussels-type bobbin lace. It was executed on a specially formed circular pillow into which pins were stuck in the outline of the pattern. In a variety of open-ended weaving up to thirty bobbins wrapped with linen thread

were then thrown within the pin configuration. The solid subject motifs—in this instance the human, animal, and bird figures—would be made first and then joined and grounded by a net or mesh. Not all the motifs were necessarily made by a single individual, for several lace makers could be employed in turning out spot motifs. To give additional texture the main figures were outlined with a raised cordonnet.

Like many of the finest lace pieces in American museum collections, this piece and its mate, which is now in the Cooper-Hewitt Museum, passed through the hands of the dealer-collector-lace maker Marion Powys. Because lace patterns are usually repetitive, it was once the established procedure among collectors to separate pieces with identical motifs. Scissors executed many amputations.

79 FAN

European
Circa 1730
Watercolor on paper, carved and colored
  ivory
12¼ inches (31.1 cm) long
49.22.66, Gift of Mr. George Arents in
  memory of Annie Walter Arents

Folding fans were a popular and so-cially useful accessory in the eigh-teenth century. As the century pro-gressed, they increased in number while the figural representations that often adorned them diminished in scale.

In the musical gathering depicted on this fan, the fan leaf painter has balanced two female vocal accompa-nists with two male instrumentalists whose caps indicate the informality of the occasion. In the central com-position another woman, dressed in the pseudo-mythological fashion that was a favored artistic conceit of the period, plays a clavier while one of the men plays a flute.

Supporting the leaf, which is dec-orated on the other side with an un-remarkable pastoral scene, are intricately carved ivory guards and sticks. At the shoulder line of the sticks four mirror-image shepherd couples are framed by gilded car-touches outlined in red foil. These alternate with two painted scenes of temples and flowers.

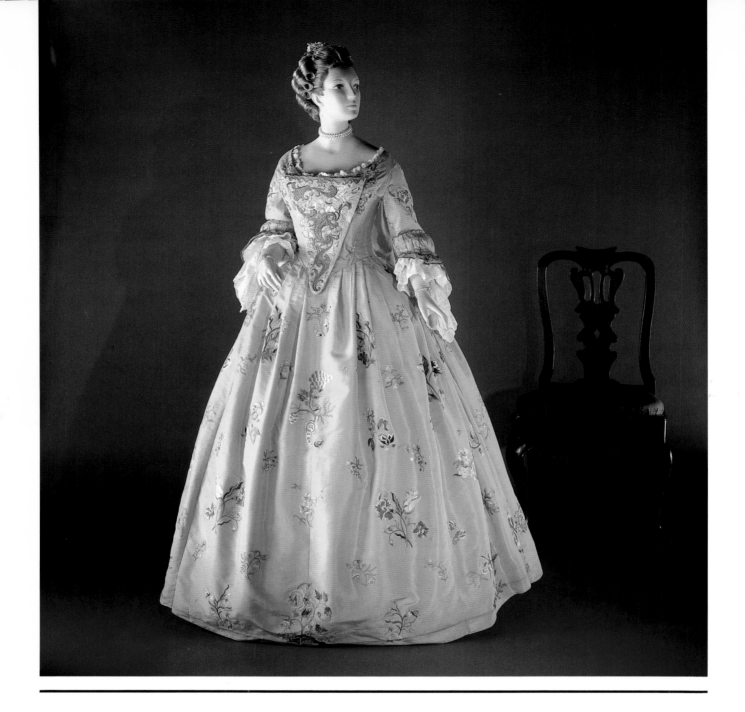

80 CLOSED BRIDAL ROBE

Norwegian
Circa 1760
Embroidered and appliquéd silk
30.955, Ella C. Woodward Fund

Chinese gold, as found in this bridal robe, was a favorite and fashionable textile color in both Western Europe and North America in the mid-eighteenth century. The pattern, instead of being woven, is applied in a typically Scandinavian manner with unpatterned or self-colored patterned silk fabrics in deep rose, emerald green, bright gold, and deep blue. Extant examples of embroidered and appliquéd garments such as this tend to be decorative exterior petticoats, aprons, and baby's layettes that in many instances have been fabricated from earlier garments, probably the mother's own bridal gown. The material was initially embroidered in the rapport manner— the design was worked to the shape of the garment. In this instance the floral sprays increase in scale from shoulder to hem and are symmetrically balanced. Satin stitch worked with a silk twist is used throughout, even securing the appliquéd scraps of silk that form the larger areas of the major floral sprays.

When this dress was acquired for the Museum by its then-Director, Dr. William H. Fox, and his wife on a 1930 buying and vacation expedition to Scandinavia, it was much altered, being in the form of an open robe with petticoat. Careful structural examination revealed up to four major alterations during the life of the garment but fortunately not the one that befell the majority of such wedding wear: it was not cut up for an infant's layette.

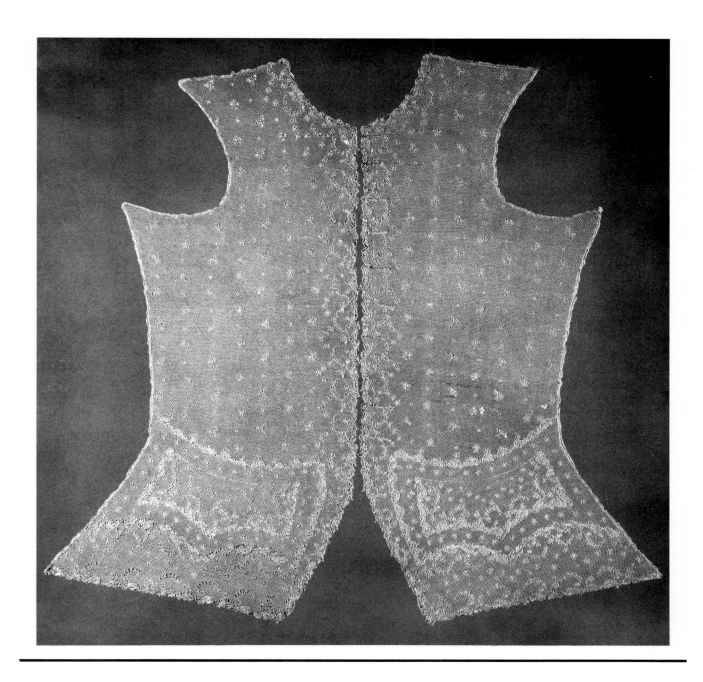

81 Waistcoat Foreparts

French
Circa 1760
Linen thread needle lace
29¹/₈ × 14⁵/₈ inches (74 × 37 cm)
15.86, Gift of Robert B. Woodward

Throughout the eighteenth century the most decorative element of a man's attire was his waistcoat. Although body coats were outlined along the front closure with tightly spaced buttons and buttonholes, they actually only closed with three or four functioning units on the upper chest. Moreover, the torso and skirt of the coat curved away toward the back, leaving the middle section of the body in need of covering. Thus the opportunity for decorative waistcoats.

While many waistcoat foreparts were cut from patterned fabrics, many of the most elaborate were edged with metallic lace, finely quilted, delicately embroidered, woven *en disposition*, or in rare instances made of lace. The expanse and highly visible nature of such pieces would have made them both costly and desirable for a gentleman or courtier who wished to take a basic yet fashionable shape, and make a memorable statement.

This pair of foreparts is constructed in a needle-lace technique known as *Argentan* and, as is characteristic of needle-laces, is built up in a series of buttonhole stitches. Because these fronts were probably applied to a colorful, supportive, functional under waistcoat, neither the buttonholes nor the pocket flaps are operational.

American, Connecticut River Valley
1790
Wool embroidery on wool
86 × 89 inches (218.4 × 226.0 cm)
49.189, Museum Purchase

In an attempt to mitigate the cold of New England winters, late-eighteenth-century residents devised a bed covering that was both decorative and practical. Known as bed ruggs, these wool coverlets usually had enlarged floral motifs. This example, however, along with one in the Henry Francis Dupont Winterthur Museum, has an inner scallop panel and an outer border that resembles waves.

The warmth of these ruggs derived from their structure, here a twill weave wool ground of blanket weight patterned with a greenish-blue and ecru plaid which has been embroidered with a looped, closely spaced running stitch of crewel wool. The yarns of this rugg are hand spun and dyed in three shades of blue with a white highlight thread. The surface has been left uncut; about equal numbers were clipped, and some pieces even display both techniques.

Since the rugg is initialed R.G.E. and dated 1790, it is presumed to have been part of a bridal trousseau and to have been made by and for G.E., whose husband was R. Because of the treasured nature of these bed coverings, they were passed from generation to generation in an informal manner rather than by will.

83 BED VALANCE

Russian, Vologda region
Circa 1800
Embroidered linen mesh
29 × 78¾ inches (79.0 × 195.5 cm)
31.345, Gift of Mrs. Edward S.
 Harkness in memory of her mother,
Elizabeth Greenman Stillman

In the eighteenth and nineteenth centuries Russian females of all classes produced numerous textile objects, many of which were intended to enhance the bed, especially on days when it might be viewed by guests. A valance like this would be attached to the top sheet and hung along the side of the bed in a traditional manner.

The bulbous domes of the buildings depicted here give this piece a distinctive Russian character. The *Peaceable Kingdom* aspect of the composition is standard: domesticated animals mingle with wild. Since many domestic linens have been associated with bridal trousseaus, it is not unreasonable to assume that the central couple is symbolic of the felicitous state all newlyweds anticipate.

While many Russian bed valances are all white or off-white, some are highlighted with color. Many are made up of bobbin lace sections, and a few, like this one, have bobbin lace lower borders.

84 WOMAN'S FESTIVE OUTFIT

Russian, Vladimir region
Early 19th century
Various materials
31.449–453, Gift of Mrs. Edward S.
  Harkness in memory of her mother,
  Elizabeth Greenman Stillman

In 1930 an exiled Russian count traveled around the eastern United States exhibiting a collection of old Russian costumes and textiles and selling to museums as much of the collection as he could interest them in. Thus The Brooklyn Museum, the Museum of Fine Arts, Boston, and the Cleveland Museum of Art came to share parts of an important collection of Russian textile arts that had been assembled in the 1880s and 1890s by a Russian noblewoman named Natalie de Shabelsky. Selections from this collection were considered of such importance during Mme de Shabelsky's lifetime that they were routinely included in World's Fairs—at Chicago in 1893, Brussels in 1894, and Paris in 1900. They also decorated the St. Petersburg Palace of the Grand Duke Nicholas in 1890–91 and were featured as part of the coronation festivities when Nicholas was crowned Czar in 1896.

This outfit from the Shabelsky collection is the festive attire of a Russian peasant woman—a monied peasant, not one who tilled the soil. Such attire is characterized by an exotically shaped headdress (*kokoshnik*), a shirt (*rubakha*), and a long, loose-fitting tunic (*sarafan*). Additional garments might include an apron (*perednik*), a short-sleeved jacket (*dushegreya*), or a short, sleeveless jacket (*epanechka*). At the time this outfit was made the Russian silk industry was advanced enough to produce European-influenced textiles. The Russian addiction to glitter is satisfied with freshwater pearls, paste, and semiprecious stones, and an abundance of metallic embroidery and lace.

85　TEXTILE PANEL

Spanish or Portuguese
Early 19th century
Cut and uncut pile silk satin
21¾ × 39 inches (55.5 × 99.0 cm)
79.238, Gift of Michael Abraham

With its fringed overlay at the lower end, this fabric is identifiable as garment material rather than furnishing fabric. During the second and third decades of the nineteenth century, women's dresses of fashion had a small sprigging on the skirt with a hemline border.

As with many textile items produced on the Iberian peninsula, the fabric displays a certain heavy-handedness. The centered vermicelli garland is rigid and linear, not gracefully swagged, and there is an awkwardness to the landscape, which seems to depict a formal Portuguese garden with a tile-lined, man-made stream. An element of residual chinoiserie influence can be found in the delineation of the water and the columns and rooflines.

The two dueling figures outfitted in eighteenth-century attire seem a little unlikely for representation on cloth that was probably made up into a lady's formal evening dress. Still, with its cut and uncut piles against a shimmering silk satin ground, this material must have created an eye-catching impression as it moved through candlelight.

86 Man's Banyan and Matching Waistcoat

American
Circa 1820
Silk brocade
22.244, Gift of Mr. and Mrs. W.
Sterling Peters

Today with the relative cheapness of clothing and textiles it is sometimes difficult to comprehend the value such goods had in the lives of our ancestors. Many textile items were refashioned, first as fashionable articles, then in pieces of descending scale and importance, before ending up in children's clothes or piecework quilts.

This man's banyan, or dressing gown, for instance, with its shawl collar, slightly full sleeve caps, and ankle-length flared skirt, is stylish for about 1820, but the stylized silk floral brocade of which it is made was probably woven in Lyon, France, about fifty years before.

Although with careful sleuthing it is sometimes possible to determine the previous shapes a textile was made up in, in this case the answer has remained elusive. The matching silk waistcoat reminds us that although the banyan was for informal wear a gentleman could wear it not only at home but also at his place of business.

87　Woman's Dress

French
Circa 1820
Cotton with needle lace and embroidery
26.311a-b, Purchase A. Augustus Healy
Fund

In 1820 the prominent English ladies' journal *La Belle Assemblée* carried a fashion engraving of a "Parisian Summer Promenade Dress" of fine white cambric muslin trimmed with muslin rosettes and openwork embroidery. The dress depicted closely resembles this garment in the Museum's collection, even down to the long sleeves, since the Museum's dress originally came with detachable sleeves so that it might serve for both late day and evening wear.

While the bodice and sleeve construction and decorative treatments are nearly identical, variations are to be noted in the hemline bands. The watercolored engraving shows seven alternating rows of puffed rosettes and a flounced scalloped hemline; the garment has only three rows of fine inset cotton mull petaled rosettes. These are horizontally separated by undulating bands of cotton satin stitched foliate forms entwining snowflakelike needle-lace insertions.

In cut the dress is typical of its period: square neck, medium-high bodice, two sleeve lengths, tubular skirt with a slight flare at the hem and all the fullness gathered to the back. The skill of the needlework techniques and the up-to-the-minute fashion quality of the dress both point to discerning ownership.

88 QUILT

American, attributed to Elizabeth
 Weltch
Circa 1825
Appliquéd cottons
110½ × 109 inches (280.7 × 276.8 cm)
78.36, Gift of The Roebling Society

One of the most remarkable patchwork quilts in The Brooklyn Museum collection is this "liberty quilt" attributed to Elizabeth Weltch of Warren County, Virginia (now part of West Virginia). While unique in neither design nor execution, this quilt makes vivid statements about both. It shows an American eagle sporting a shield and clutching two floral sprays and three arrows. Although this republican motif was probably adapted from the Presidential or Great Seal, in this instance the eagle is surrounded by only eight stars rather than thirteen and holds in its beak a branch rather than a banner. With such a prominent political statement it is possible that the quilt was made in celebration of fifty years of American independence in 1826.

Except for the sawtooth piecework border, the quilt is executed primarily in the appliqué technique. The quilting itself is a simple crosshatch or diamond design. Of special note are the leaves of the flowering corner garlands, which are worked in a complicated reverse appliqué technique in which the white ground fabric is cut away and colored pattern pieces stitched in from the back. These patterned cotton materials are a mixture of yard goods suitable for either garment or household items. Some, as in the sunflower border, even retain their original glaze.

89 SHAWL

French, possibly designed by Anthony
  Berrus or Amédée Courder
Circa 1855
Wool wrapped silk
158 × 64¼ inches (395 × 161 cm)
85.142, Gift of The Roebling Society

When the punch-card system of the
Jacquard loom was perfected in the
early nineteenth century, one of the
primary jobs to which it was applied
was the weaving of "paisley" or
"cashmere" shawls, some of which
were made especially for exhibition.
Such exhibition shawls frequently
had little to do with common examples, which carried the "cone" or
"buta" motif; rather they depicted
naturalistic botanical subjects or exotic motifs populated with animal
and human forms.

The composition and complexity
of this shawl point to its having been
conceived as an exhibition piece,
possibly—as the harlequin banded
border would indicate—for the 1855
Universal Exhibition in Paris. In
weaving this chinoiserie fantasy, a
three-by-one twill, approximately
sixty wefts per centimeter was used.
The Jacquard loom would have been
fitted with about 200,000 punch
cards to direct the weave of the pattern, which is unique over two-
thirds of the shawl. The central subject is a lake over which hangs varieties of exotic vegetation; it is populated by a diverse collection of
equally fanciful beasts, fishes, and
birds, some of which are drawn from
Chinese mythology. Miniature people can be observed plucking fruit
from trees, enjoying tea, hunting, or
going about other daily activities. At
either end of the shawl is a splendidly
outfitted pleasure barge. All these
motifs are set among intermingling
architectural elements of both Chinese and Persian influence.

90 WOMAN'S OPERA CAPE

French, designed by the House of Worth
1890
Silk lampas, velvet, and lace
31.22.19, Gift of the Princess Viggo

In the 1930s the American-born Princess Viggo of Denmark distributed to New York City museums garments from the wardrobes of her late aunts Sarah and Eleanor Hewitt. The Hewitt sisters had been instrumental in developing the design collection at Cooper Union, one aspect of which is today a remarkable selection of textiles. From an early age, as affluent, sophisticated Americans, they had been dressed in Paris by the dean of French fashion, Charles Frederick Worth (1825–1895).

Unequaled textiles were as characteristic of Worth designs as historical reinterpretations, and the parrot tulip lampas used in this cape made for one of the Hewitt sisters is perhaps one of the most remarkable textiles ever used by the House of Worth. Woven in 1889 by A. Gourd & Cie of Lyon, the fabric was distributed in Paris by Maison Morel, Poeckes, & Baumlin. Entitled *Tulipes Hollandaise*, it was included in the section of Lyonnaise textiles at the Universal Exposition of 1889,

garnering a Grand Prix for Maison Gourd. With its thirty-one-inch spread between tulip sprays, it displays among other things Worth's skill at employing fabrics that because of the scale of their motifs might otherwise be considered suitable only as furnishing fabric.

Worth was known to prefer American clients not only because of their seemingly inexhaustible resources but also because "he found that more frequently than in the women of any other nation the Americans had slimness without leanness, leanness, sometimes called scrawniness, that he abhorred." Although, like many of Worth's clients, the Hewitt sisters were physically well endowed, this cape, which sweeps from a squared, slightly raised shoulder line, would elegantly conceal any enlarged figure. A standing neckpiece frilled with black lace softens the break between flesh and fabric. The lining is a dusty rose silk velvet that harmonizes well with the vibrant reds of the baroque tulips.

91 BALL GOWN AND COURT TRAIN

French
1896
Embroidered silk, satin, lace, silk velvet,
and artificial flowers
70.53.5, Anonymous gift

One of the treasured experiences of any late nineteenth-, early twentieth-century American lady was presentation at a European court. Thus Mrs. Washington A. Roebling, the woman who oversaw the completion of the Brooklyn Bridge after the incapacitation of her husband, the bridge's chief engineer, was especially honored in 1896 when she was presented not only to Queen Victoria but also to the Empress of Russia.

On both occasions, Mrs. Roebling wore this garment attributed to the House of Worth. While meeting court etiquette requirements, the ensemble is in memorable colors—bright gold and orchid. The orchid theme is carried through to the selection of the floral trim—cloth orchids outlining the train and dropping from the shoulder. The gilt metallic thread embroidery on the bodice stomacher and the sham underskirt panel are no more than late nineteenth-century adaptations of mid-eighteenth-century styles, as is the styling of the garment itself.

Mrs. Roebling later also chose this ensemble for a formal, full-length portrait by Emile Carolus-Duran and an impressive studio photograph. Such documentation of how a garment looked at its moment of highest fashion is rare.

92 MAN'S COURT PRESENTATION ENSEMBLE

English
1907
Silk velvet, satin, and beaver; cut steel,
and various other materials
50.72.35, Gift of Marion Litchfield

This court presentation ensemble belonged to Edward Hubert Litchfield, son of the head of a prominent Brooklyn family who built, as their home, an Italianate villa that still stands in Prospect Park. Litchfield spent much of his life in London and, like his father, was presented at the Court of St. James. Following the rigid requirements established in *Dress Worn at His Majesty's Court*, he was to appear, if he had no special uniform, attired in black silk velvet tailcoat and breeches, white satin or black velvet waistcoat, black silk hose, and patent leather shoes. His hat, to be carried, was to be a black beaver or silk cocked hat with a steel loop on a black silk cockade. He was also to wear a sword with a steel hilt, a black scabbard, and steel mountings, which was to be held by a black silk web waistband worn under the waistcoat with a black velvet frog for the sword. A white bow necktie and white gloves were the last prescribed articles; nothing was mentioned about the shirt, and buttons were to be of cut steel. Litchfield was outfitted according to regulations, and this suit has both the black and white waistcoats. His hat is silk beaver.

93 ROBE SABA EVENING GOWN

French, designed by Paul Poiret
(1879–1944)
1921
Beaded and appliquéd red silk velvet
Label: Paul Poiret/ à Paris
73.127, Augustus Graham School of
 Design Fund

Splashes of intense color and lean, linear silhouettes are two features that the French designer Paul Poiret is credited with introducing into early twentieth-century fashion. While his days of greatest creative brilliance predate World War I, sparks flash from some of his postwar garments as well. In this *Robe Saba* of 1921, for instance, he used modified kimono sleeves, a medieval girdle and squared train, and two-dimensional decoration—a black silk velvet and gold lamé appliqué and red-and-gold streamered glass bead fringe—to fashion a stylish gown that expresses his passion for theater.

The basic simplicity of the dress is more than offset by the uncontrollable strands of shimmering beads. Like Poiret's finest prewar garments, the gown cries out to be seen in motion. The designer was so satisfied with it that he created an almost identical garment, a *Robe Sabbat*, on which the fleur-de-lis are replaced by a more diminutive beaded waist and hemline decoration.

94 WOMAN'S TABARD

American, designed by Raymond
  Duncan (1874–1966)
Circa 1920
Block-printed and hand-painted cotton
  and wool crepe, 45¹/₄ × 26³/₄ inches
  (115 × 68 cm)
X912, Museum Collection

Although much less well known than
his flamboyant sister Isadora, Raymond Duncan was an artist in his
own right. An accomplished designer and decorator, he had for
many years a Parisian atelier that
specialized in fabrics and embroid-
eries. The garments he produced,
such as this unstructured tabard, reflected a fascination with the civilization of classical Greece. Printed
and brush painted with natural dyes,
the tabard has border and shoulder
bands of a female figure plucking
tree fruit while the remaining rows
are of blocked trees. Duncan is believed to have been assisted by his
brother Augustin in the production of
some of his textiles.

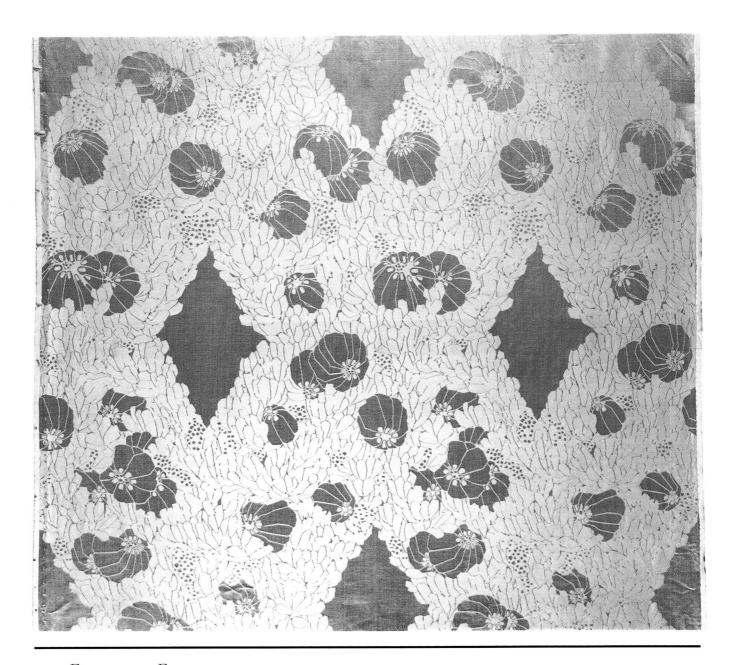

95 Furnishing Fabric

French, designed by Émile-Jacques
  Ruhlmann (1879–1933)
Circa 1923–24
Silk damask, 45.2 inches
  (114.8 cm) wide; pattern repeat 45.5
  inches (115.6 cm)
71.150.13, Museum purchase with
  funds given by Joseph F. McCrindle,
  Mrs. Richard Palmer, Charles C.
  Paterson, Raymond Worgelt, and others

In the spring of 1923 a Lyonnaise industrialist named Weitz hired the Ruhlmann firm of 27 rue de Lisbonne, Paris, to decorate his home. The owner of the firm, Émile-Jacques Ruhlmann, was then fast approaching his zenith as an exponent of Art Deco design, a point he was to achieve at the 1925 Exposition des Arts Décoratifs et Industriels Modernes. His interior design for Weitz called for the intermingling of two of his best-known motifs—a vase of fruits and overall arrangements of stylized roses. These motifs were incorporated into most of the furnishings, including this red and gray silk damask fabric used for both upholstery and wall covering.

When the Museum acquired the salon from the Weitz house in 1972, the fabric was found to have been removed from the walls and stored in the attic during the German occupation of World War II, a move that probably saved it from destruction not only at the time but also during the succeeding years when Art Deco fell out of favor. The silk was probably woven locally, by another Ruhlmann client, Ducharne, as Lyon has traditionally been the silk-weaving center of France. At the time Ruhlmann decorated the house the fabric could be had from his establishment in Paris for 150 francs a meter.

96 Evening Dress

French
Circa 1934
Printed silk crepe
63.121.13, Gift of Mrs. V. D. Crisp

Through the doors of the store Henri Bendel on New York's West Fifty-seventh Street have passed some of the most fashionable women in America. Bendel made his name as, at one time, the largest American buyer of French model gowns. Among the designers whose creations he imported were Callot, Lanvin, Chanel, Mainbocher, and Schiaparelli, whose name has been associated with this garment.

Bendel's imports about 1934 may have included this evening dress of bias-cut oyster silk crepe with a deep hemline panel printed in an abstract feather motif in shaded grays. The feathers are elongated as the panel trails to the back. Within the center back of the train are a pair of eyelets that permit it to be hooked at the waistline. Thus secured, the train forms a cascade of ruffles down the back of the dress and gives it an even hemline. The sash and the deep V-back neckline extending to the waist were fashionable in 1934. The popularity of gowns with trains extended over much of the decade.

97 Evening Dress

French, designed by Madeleine Vionnet
(1876–1975)
1938–39
Appliquéd silk net
69.33.10, Gift of Mrs. Edward G.
Sparrow

The designer of this dress, Madeleine Marie Valentine Vionnet, is one of the premier forces of twentieth-century fashion, her particular contribution being the perfection of bias-cut garments during the 1930s. Born in rural France, Vionnet rapidly worked her way through dressmaking establishments in Paris and London before opening her own Parisian couture house in 1912 on the rue de Rivoli. Having barely begun, she then closed her doors at the outset of World War I in 1914, only to reopen with her former staff in 1918 at 50 Avenue Montaigne. It was at this address, until her retirement in 1940, that she draped her most memorable garments.

Although Vionnet's teachers and mentors included some of the most respected names of the time—Kate Reilly, the Callot sisters, and Jacques Doucet—they could not compete with her assured inventiveness. Utilizing a lay figure, she fashioned fluid garments that moved much more easily with the body because of the elasticity provided by the bias, or diagonal, cut of the fabric. Her interest in the activities of the modern woman included the adaptation of styles for sportswear into formal attire, here seen in this evening dress's halter neck. Much less typical of her style is the dress's billowing, panniered skirt with glued-on appliqué of grape clusters, a reflection of the fashion influence of the 1939 film *Gone With the Wind*. Together the halter bodice and caged pannier skirt support represent a rare melding of nineteenth- and twentieth-century design.

98 NECKLET

French, designed by Elsa Schiaparelli
 (1890–1973)
Autumn 1938
Plastic and metal
8¹/₄ × 7¹/₂ inches (21.0 × 19.1 cm)
55.26.247, Gift of Paul and Arturo
 Peralta-Ramos

One of the most stylish American women of her day was the Standard Oil heiress Millicent Huttleston Rogers. Like a chameleon, she altered her appearance to fit her environment, wearing Tyrolian attire in the Austrian Alps, Southwest American Indian garb in New Mex-

ico, Provençal dress on the Riviera, and witty and sophisticated apparel in the great cultural centers of the world. She was dressed by some of the twentieth century's most creative designers: Charles James, Valentina, Elsa Schiaparelli, and, for her antebellum Southern belle persona, Mainbocher.

The Museum holds many items from Rogers's wardrobe, including this rather astonishing neckpiece on which nineteen embossed and polychromed insects chase one another. Because the insects are applied to

clear plastic, from a distance they seem to wander at will over flesh. Along with a similarly decorated jacket of an afternoon suit now owned by the Museum, the piece was part of Schiaparelli's 1938 autumn-winter collection entitled *Painne,* or Pagan. That collection, which was based on the theme of a primordial forest, reflected Schiaparelli's interaction with the day's leading Surrealists, Jean Cocteau and Salvador Dali. Although in theory drawn from nature, in application it was unbelievable.

99 ABSTRACT OR FOUR-LEAF CLOVER BALL GOWN AND PETAL STOLE

American, designed by Charles James
  (1906–1978)
1953 and 1956
Silk satin, velvet, and faille
53.169.1, Gift of Mrs. Cornelius
  Vanderbilt Whitney
64.254, Gift of Mrs. William Randolph
  Hearst, Jr.

For the Eisenhower Inaugural Ball of 1953, Austine Hearst, the wife of William Randolph Hearst, Jr., commissioned the Anglo-American fashion designer Charles James to create something for her to wear. Although the resulting garment was not, in typical Jamesian manner, completed in time for the function, it has since become one of the icons of mid-century couture and by James's own evaluation, his pinnacle in dressmaking.

Reworking a lobed hemline design of the 1930s and melding it with a quatrafoil millinery model of 1948, James fabricated a gown of four layers—an inner taffeta slip, a structured under petticoat, a matching petticoat flare, and an overdress. The garment expresses James's fascination with geometry and mathematics: while the four lobes are not of equal dimension, they readily fit within a circle. His eye for line and texture is demonstrated by the application of the costliest silks: white duchess satin, black velours de Lyon, and ivory faille.

Here James is a sculptor who happens to have selected fabric as his medium. The garment is constructed from thirty pattern pieces, twenty-eight of which are cut in duplicate, the remaining two singly. Once he had perfected the form he went on to create other similarly shaped garments, some of which were copies, others adaptations. The stole, with its petal outline, is of black silk velvet and white satin. It was adapted from the hipline yoke of a ball gown James created in 1949.

Decorative Arts

100 NORTH ROOM, THE JAN MARTENSE SCHENCK HOUSE

Flatlands (Brooklyn), New York
Circa 1675
18½ × 21½ feet (5.64×6.58 meters)
50.192, Gift of The Atlantic Gulf and
 Pacific Company

When Jan Martense Schenck built his house on Mill Island in the town of Flatlands (now a part of Brooklyn) around 1675, New York had only recently passed from Dutch rule to the English. Schenck himself was Dutch-born, and the two-room house he built is in the Dutch vernacular tradition of the seventeenth century.

Shown here is the north room, which served as a parlor, dining area, and sleeping room. The fireplace is of the Dutch type, with a projecting mantelpiece and no jambs, or sides. The triangular knee braces of the exposed post-and-beam construction are also a Dutch feature, as are the built-in bed boxes against the wall opposite the fireplace. The room is installed as it might have looked after a remodeling of about 1730, and the windows

are typical of this later date. Because the house was greatly altered over the years, some of the details—such as the fireplace and the bed boxes—are reconstructions based on evidence found in this and other early New York houses.

Since Schenck owned a mill that stood near his house and was a relatively affluent citizen, the room is furnished to reflect a comfortable standard of living. The table is covered with a "Turkey carpet" in turn covered by a linen cloth for protection, and the chairs surrounding the table are upholstered in "Turkey work" in imitation of the carpet. The room also includes a number of pieces of ceramics, both Oriental and Dutch Delft, which were made in imitation of Oriental wares.

101 Hall, The Cupola House

Edenton, North Carolina
Circa 1725, woodwork 1756–58
19¹/₂ × 15¹/₂ feet (5.95 × 4.73 meters)
18.170, The Woodward Memorial
Funds

The largest and most impressive eighteenth-century house to survive in Edenton, North Carolina, is the Cupola House. It is believed to have been built around 1725 by Richard Sanderson, a New England sea captain. Its original ground floor—hall, parlor, chamber, pantry, and stair passage—is installed in the Museum. The lavish interior woodwork and the exterior cupola are believed to date to 1756–58, when Francis Corbin bought and remodeled the house.

The fully paneled hall is the most elaborate room in the house. A "hall" is a medieval term used to describe an all-purpose room that was used for dining, but not exclusively so. In America, a room specifically for dining did not occur for the most part until around 1790. The room is installed as if Corbin were about to entertain. The scheme for the over-mantel seems to be from a pattern shown in William Salmon's *Palladio Londonensis* (London, 1748), which was also the inspiration for the fireplace in the Museum's *Russell House Parlor* (see no. 102).

The room conveys the desire of early colonists to display newly found wealth and shows how household goods were imported from both Europe and the other colonies as well.

The richness of colonial life is seen in the use of strong colors for the walls—Prussian blue and red-orange—the wide variety of English ceramics and glass, the Chinese export porcelain, the English silver, and the American Queen Anne and Chippendale furniture. Venetian blinds hang in the windows. They were available in America from the 1760s and were usually painted. On the floor is a painted canvas floorcloth. Although such floorcloths were first produced in England, by the second quarter of the eighteenth century most American cities had at least one maker of painted carpets. Furthermore, upholsterers, paper-hangers, sign painters, and house painters all advertised floorcloths in newspapers. They were the eighteenth century's version of linoleum—durable and appropriate for areas of heavy use. Painted on canvas and then varnished, floorcloths were either a single color or made to imitate marble.

102 PARLOR, THE RUSSELL HOUSE

Providence, Rhode Island
Circa 1772
14 × 14 feet (4.25 × 4.25 meters)
20.956, Purchased with funds given by
the Rembrandt Club

Around 1772 Joseph and William Russell built a fashionable three-story brick house in Providence, Rhode Island. The woodwork from the northeast parlor of this house is the most sophisticated and finely crafted of the Museum's series of eighteenth-century period rooms. As in the *Cupola House Hall* (no. 101), the inspiration for the classical over-mantel seems to have come from William Salmon's *Palladio Londonensis*, published in London in 1748. These English pattern books were a frequently consulted source for architectural details.

In the eighteenth century, rooms were used for a variety of purposes. The Russells, successful merchants and importers, could have entertained, dined, or done business in this elegant, classical space. The room is shown as if not in use, which means that the furniture is lined up against the walls. Until the beginning of the nineteenth century, furniture moved both within one room and throughout the house depending on the need. In the case of the Museum's installation of this room, it was decided to leave the mantel wall empty, except for the Chinese export vase, so the visitor could enjoy and appreciate the beauty of the architecture. Many eighteenth-century English paintings attest to the practice of placing large Oriental porcelain pots in unused fireplaces, particularly during the summer. The sophistication of the woodwork and the occupation of the Russell brothers makes this stylish decoration appropriate. The beautifully executed and carefully ordered woodwork provides a glimpse of the taste of the most affluent colonists on the eve of the Revolution.

103 PARLOR, THE NICHOLAS SCHENCK HOUSE

Canarsie (Brooklyn), New York
Circa 1771, remodeled early 19th
 century
15 1/2 × 17 feet (4.75 × 5.20 meters)
29.1283, Gift of the New York City
 Parks Department

When Nicholas Schenck built his house in Canarsie (a part of the town of Flatlands in what is now Brooklyn) around 1771, much had changed in the area since his Dutch-born grandfather Jan Martense Schenck built a house nearby (see no. 100) nearly a century earlier. By the time Nicholas Schenck, Jr. remodeled the house in Canarsie in the early nineteenth century, the old Dutch families of New York had been Americanized and only traces of Dutch culture remained. Installed at The Brooklyn Museum as it might have looked in the 1820s after fifty years of occupancy by the Schenck family, the parlor of the Nicholas Schenck house reflects this process of change and assimilation.

Although the paneling of the wall surrounding the fireplace dates from the house's construction, the fireplace itself has been closed up and replaced as a source of heat by a more modern and more efficient cast-iron stove. Other new kinds of goods were also available to the middle-class consumer at this period, owing in part to the advances of the Industrial Revolution. The transfer-printed ceramics on the tea table, for instance, were made in the Staffordshire region of England specifically to be imported and sold inexpensively in America. Additional features of the decoration of the room, based on evidence found in period prints, paintings, and watercolors of related interiors, include the use of a French wallpaper of small floral pattern and a vividly striped floor covering called a Venetian carpet. The furniture is a mixture of old and new, ranging from the eighteenth-century tripod tea table to a sofa in the late Federal or Empire style, which was the height of fashion in the 1820s.

Taken as a whole, the Nicholas Schenck parlor represents the way in which the house of a middle-class family might have evolved over decades of continuous use. Together with the Jan Martense Schenck House, it also shows the changes that occurred in Dutch–American culture in New York.

104 PARLOR, THE ABRAHAM HARRISON HOUSE

Irvington, New Jersey
Circa 1818
19½ × 23¾ feet (5.97 × 7.24 meters)
24.422, Museum Purchase

Together with an adjoining dining room from the same house, this parlor from the Abraham Harrison House in Irvington, New Jersey, represents the high-style neoclassical taste popular in America in the early part of the nineteenth century. Sophisticated and restrained, both rooms make use of a limited vocabulary of neoclassical details to accen-

tuate serene and well-proportioned architectural spaces.

The Harrison rooms also serve as a perfect setting for the Museum's collection of New York furniture from the first quarter of the nineteenth century. The spare, elegant chairs flanking the center table in the parlor are attributed to Duncan Phyfe and represent the early phase of his neoclassical style, around 1807, while the window benches, which were made by Phyfe for the Donaldson family around 1823, exhibit the more robust style of his later work.

Certain details of the installation, including woodwork color, carpet,

and window treatments, are based on both technological examination (such as paint analysis) and period documents such as estate inventories, manufacturers' archives, and period publications that provided guidelines for cabinetmakers and upholsterers. For example, we learn from an inventory of Harrison's estate taken after his death that one of the most expensive items in his house was a carpet. The reproduction carpet used here, therefore, is a relatively expensive English Brussels carpet based on a surviving point paper, or diagram, from the archives of an English mill.

105 MOORISH SMOKING ROOM, THE JOHN D. ROCKEFELLER HOUSE

New York, New York
Circa 1885
17½ × 15½ feet (5.33 × 4.76 meters)
46.43, Gift of John D. Rockefeller, Jr.,
and John D. Rockefeller III

The *Moorish Smoking Room* represents a new trend in American design in terms of both style and execution. Inspired by Moorish motifs, it exemplifies the Oriental and Near Eastern designs that were popular during the last quarter of the nineteenth century.

Changing social structures as well as new living patterns at this time brought about new rooms, such as smoking rooms, conservatories, billiard rooms, and painting galleries. A man's home became not only his castle but a symbol of his social and cultural standing in the community as well. Throughout most of the nineteenth century there were certain styles, like Gothic for libraries, that were considered appropriate for certain rooms. The choices of style increased toward the end of the century, when every room in the house could reflect a different era or culture. To help the confused home owner deal with this plethora of styles the profession of the interior decorator was born in the mid-1870s. As a result, design became less focused on individual furnishings than on the overall appearance and effect of the room.

The John D. Rockefeller House was a brownstone built between 1864 and 1865 at 4 West Fifty-fourth Street in New York City. Rockefeller purchased the house in 1884 from Arabella Worsham, who had bought it in 1877. During the last years of her residence she had hired George Schastey, an interior designer, to redecorate and enlarge the house. The *Moorish Smoking Room* is a testament to the complexities and beauty of the Aesthetic Movement.

106 WORGELT STUDY

ALAVOINE OF PARIS
AND NEW YORK
New York, New York

1928, with additions of 1930
10 × 16³/₄ × 14¹/₂ feet
(3.02 × 5.12 × 4.48 meters)
70.23-4, 70.96mn, Gift of Mr. and Mrs.
Raymond Worgelt

The Museum's only twentieth-century period room, a study from a Park Avenue apartment designed by the Parisian decorating firm of Alavoine, is known to visitors as the "Art Deco Study." Though the fashionable modernity of this style of interior is generally associated with the flamboyance and glamour of the Jazz Age, the Roaring Twenties, or luminous, star-studded Hollywood movie sets, the room's design managed to combine traditional comforts with the 1920s style of French interiors that Americans referred to simply as Art Deco or Art Moderne. Alavoine did few modern rooms, mainly specializing in high-style French historical designs.

The effect of the *Worgelt Study* is dependent upon the geometric design, contrasting colors, and subtle textures of the olive and palisander wood wall paneling that formed the basis of the original 1928 room design. In 1930 the paneling was made slightly more complex and several new features were added to the room: a bold metal modernist window replaced a smaller, traditional double-hung one that had been covered with a fringed curtain, and a large abstract lacquer panel designed by Henri Redard and executed by Jean Dunand was inserted above the couch, replacing a series of simple geometric wood squares. (Redard also designed a group of etched glass panels with views of Paris for a small walk-in bar that, because of Prohibition, was hidden discreetly behind a door that blended into the wall decoration.) The room was completed by the addition of glass by René Lalique and sculptures by Raymond Rivoire and Jan and Joel Martel.

107 Curaca's Hat

Peru
17th century (?)
Silver with damasked velvet and cotton
 flannel
4^{15}/$_{16}$ × 13^{1}/$_{4}$ inches (12.6 × 33.7 cm)
41.1275.274c, Frank L. Babbott Fund

During the three hundred years it was subject to Spain, the region of South America comprising the modern states of Peru, Bolivia, and Ecuador produced immense quantities of silver. One-fifth was sent to the king; the rest was traded as money or fashioned into domestic, devotional, and ritual articles by local craftsmen—both European and Native American.

The elaborate work these indigenous craftsmen were capable of is demonstrated in the Museum's collection by this silver hat, part of a ceremonial costume made for a *curaca* (native noble). The brim of the hat is covered with two semicircular plates, each featuring a complex floral and foliate pattern bracketed by cornucopias, while the decoration of the crown is arranged in a cosmological scheme. Just above the brim is a procession of animals and birds—elephants, dogs, lions, a fox, and a variety of fowl and game birds—that on the front of the hat pass under an unusual triangular church or shrine with crosses in arched niches. Above the church appear a solar disk and a crescent moon whose ends have been extended to

form a matching circle enclosing a floral spray. Flanking the sun and moon are a facing pair of quadrupeds (possibly llamas) and opposite them a pair of guitar-playing mermaids. Interspersed among these figures are a variety of blossoms climaxing in a blossom at the top of the hat with stamens of coiled wire beads.

The native craftsmen in Spain's American colonies created complex syntheses of indigenous and foreign imagery. European visual ideas were transmitted by means of prints and book illustrations. The images on this native costume, for instance, may well have been copied from the title-page decorations of religious books or from the borders of biblical illustrations or devotional prints.

108 COVERED GOBLET

English
Circa 1685
Glass
18 inches (45.7 cm) high, 5 inches (12.7
  cm) diameter at rim, 5½ inches (14.0
  cm) diameter at foot
Ex-Leckie Collection
  13.706a and 13.706b, Museum
  Purchase

After the Restoration of Charles II to the throne of England in 1660, the English glass industry flourished, recovering from a period of disruption caused by the Civil War. With the renowned glass of Venice serving as inspiration, English glassmakers strove to develop a clear glass resembling rock crystal, and by the mid-1670s George Ravenscroft achieved success with the addition of lead.

The masterfully manipulated decoration on this splendid standing cup with cover displays the late seventeenth-century English vocabulary of glass ornament. On both the body and the lid of the piece, decorative prunts are applied over a double thread; the lid is crowned with a finial of a serpentine work with pincered fringe; and near the stem and near the finial, a diaper pattern—called "nipped diamond waies" in the seventeenth century—has been worked into the molten glass. This is the most impressive piece in the Leckie Collection, a group of more than nine hundred pieces of English glass acquired by The Brooklyn Museum in 1913.

109 CHEST OF DRAWERS

American, Massachusetts
1680–1700
Oak and pine, 36 × 40 × 21 1/2 inches
(91.5 × 101.6 × 54.6 cm)
49.190.2, Bequest of Mrs. William
Sterling Peters by exchange

Furniture made in New England in the seventeenth century reflects the English heritage of the early settlers of that area. Since the colonists attempted to re-create the familiar surroundings they left behind, outdated styles continued to be produced in America after they became obsolete in English style centers.

This chest of drawers, which descended in the Hancock family of Bradford, Massachusetts, is in the tradition of English seventeenth-century furniture. Oak was the primary wood used in its construction. The facade of the piece is divided into a vigorous series of geometric compartments that give the piece visual strength and rhythm. The top and bottom drawers each have two boldly blocked panels articulated with applied molding, and the smaller middle drawers repeat the pattern of the larger drawers in the outline of their applied moldings. The total effect of the surface pattern

was originally greatly enhanced by vivid color; strong traces of red paint remain in the panels of the center drawers, which are decorated with facing pairs of birds. The panels of the larger drawers are ornamented with black fleur-de-lis, and the applied moldings were originally painted black as well. Those areas of the facade that were originally unpainted were covered with an overall pattern of undulating black lines. Such a survival of original paint on a seventeenth-century object is unusual and helps us understand the strong sense of vivid color that dominated the decoration of the period.

110 TANKARD

JACOB BOELEN
(American, born The Netherlands,
active 1657–1729)

New York
Circa 1685
Silver
7 1/8 × 5 3/8 inches (18.1 × 13.7 cm)
26.60, Gift of Mrs. Richard van Wyck
  and Mrs. Henry de Bevoise Schenck in
  memory of Richard van Wyck

When the Amsterdam-born sil-versmith Jacob Boelen made this tankard in New York around 1685, the influence of Dutch culture in the colony was still strong. Although the tankard form is an English one, in-troduced by the new rulers of New York, Boelen adapted it by adding Dutch decoration to suit his local cli-ents. The undulating meander wire at the base of the tankard and the cut-card ornament of applied leaves just above it are typical of both Dutch and New York silver made in the late seventeenth century. Also typical of late seventeenth-century New York tankards are the cocoon, or cork-screw thumbpiece, and the lush and beautifully engraved baroque car-touche surrounding the coat-of-arms of the Thorne family.

The tankard was probably made for Richard Thorne, but when his daughter Hannah married Cor-nelius van Wyck it passed into the van Wyck family, in which it de-scended for over two hundred years until it was given to the Museum. Since silver tankards were not only useful and beautiful objects but also expensive status symbols that were literally made of money, they often passed from generation to generation at the time of marriages. The Thorne/van Wyck tankard is an es-pecially appealing one whose impos-ing presence bespeaks both fine craftsmanship and beautiful design.

111 SIDE CHAIRS

American, Connecticut
Circa 1740–50
Cherry and maple
41 × 19½ × 17½ inches
  (104.1 × 49.5 × 44.5 cm) each
14.708 and 14.709, Henry L.
  Batterman Fund

The sculptural beauty and attenuated elegance of these chairs exemplify the restraint typical of the finest furniture produced in America during the Queen Anne–style period. Made in Wethersfield, Connecticut, near Hartford, the chairs are fashioned in cherry, the local wood most common in Connecticut furniture. The needlework upholstery on the slip seats is a reproduction of the surviving original upholstery, which was no doubt worked by an early owner of the chairs.

The chairs originally belonged to either Dr. Ezekiel Porter (1707–1775), a noted Wethersfield surgeon, or to his son-in-law, Thomas Belden (1732–1782). Once part of a larger set, they remained in the Porter-Belden-Bidwell House in Wethersfield until 1914, when, along with other furniture from the house, they were acquired by The Brooklyn Museum. Three years later, in 1917, the Museum acquired two downstairs rooms from the house as well. Thus the chairs can now be seen installed at The Brooklyn Museum in the parlor of the house in which they have resided since the eighteenth century.

HENRY WILL
(American, active 1761–93)

New York or Albany, New York
Circa 1761–93
Pewter
7⅞ × 4¹¹/₁₆ × 2¼ inches
 (20.0 × 11.9 × 5.7 cm)
Ex-John W. Poole Collection
45.10.142, Museum Purchase

The well-to-do businessman of late eighteenth-century America would have stored his pens, ink, and sander (to dry the ink) in what was then referred to by the English name of a standish. Though marked pewter standishes were common enough two hundred years ago, this example is, surprisingly, the only American one known to exist.

During the eighteenth century, pewter objects were used in nearly every American household that could afford them. Most people in homes and taverns ate and drank from pewter; porcelain was rare and expensive, and the poor used wooden plates. Pewter plates, porringers, tankards, teapots, candlesticks, and sconces were produced for domestic use, while flagons, chalices, beakers, and baptismal basins were made for religious services. Pewterers like Henry Will were skilled craftsmen who poured molten tin mixed with small bits of copper, antimony, and bismuth into brass molds to create their wares. The object was then allowed to cool and harden before being finished to a smooth surface pleasing to the eye and touch.

Following the English tradition, American pewterers stamped their wares with unique marks bearing the name of the maker as well as other hallmarks that signified little more than a desire to be associated with English guilds of silver- and pewter-makers. The markings on this inkstand are so numerous (two full sets of marks) and prominently displayed (on both sides of the hinged top) that it may have belonged to Henry Will himself.

113 SWEETMEAT DISH

GOUSE BONNIN AND GEORGE
ANTHONY MORRIS
(American, active 1770–1772)

Philadelphia
1771–72
Soft-paste porcelain painted in
  underglaze blue
5 1/4 × 7 1/4 inches (13.3 × 18.4 cm)
45.174, Museum Purchase

In 1770 Gouse Bonnin and George Anthony Morris founded a company to produce porcelain tablewares in Philadelphia. Although the company failed after just two years, it was the earliest American attempt at porcelain production to meet with even modest success. Not until 1826 was porcelain once again successfully produced in America—in Philadelphia by William Ellis Tucker.

Of the handful of Bonnin and Morris wares still in existence, this sweetmeat dish is one of the finest examples. Because of its great rarity and early date, it represents the foundation of The Brooklyn Museum's extensive collection of American ceramics.

In order to compete with relatively inexpensive imported English ceramics, Bonnin and Morris closely imitated the production of major English factories. Thus this sweetmeat dish bears a strong similarity to related objects made by the Bow factory in England. Its form, comprising three scallop-shell-shaped dishes and a shell-encrusted central pedestal supporting a circular dish, embodies the rococo spirit in its use of sources from nature to form an object of complex outline.

114 SUGAR BOWL AND COVER

American
Circa 1800
Glass
7⁷/₈ × 6⁵/₈ inches (20.0 × 16.3 cm)
40.7a and 40.7b, Dick S. Ramsay Fund

Fine glass tableware such as this bright blue sugar bowl was much prized in eighteenth-century America. Although the three major glasshouses of the time—those of Caspar Wistar, Henry William Stiegel, and John Frederick Amelung—all had only limited financial success, they established a tradition of glassmaking in America that continued into the nineteenth century.

Even though the earliest makers of glass tableware in America were all men of German descent, many of their clients were English. As a re-

sult, this sugar bowl is modeled after the vividly colored English tablewares produced in Bristol and often exported to America. The molten glass was first blown into a mold and then removed from it and expanded by further blowing; the piece was then finished off by hand. This gave the bowl a shimmering surface in a "Venetian diamond," or ogival, pattern. A spiral-ribbed finial, often considered a Stiegel characteristic, tops the lid of the bowl, creating a vigorous spatial interplay in the fashion of the rococo period.

115 OIL LAMP

JOSIAH WEDGWOOD
(British, 1730–1795)

Manufactured by Wedgwood, Etruria,
England

Circa 1790

Basalt ware

13 1/2 × 7 3/8 × 7 1/8 inches
(34.3 × 18.8 × 18.1 cm)

55.25.3, The Emily Winthrop Miles
Collection

Few names in the history of ceramics are better known or more revered than that of Josiah Wedgwood and the factory that he founded in 1759. Wedgwood's abilities as a potter, businessman, and tastemaker combined to create an enterprise that was unusually successful from its infancy. Best known for cream-colored, glazed earthenwares that came to be called "Queen's ware" after his royal client and patron, Queen Charlotte, he also developed stoneware of un-

usually refined quality in black, red, and the more famous blue. The black stoneware, which he referred to as "black Basaltes," was the first color he developed, around 1768.

Although Wedgwood's basalt ware (as it is now referred to) was not the first black stoneware in England, it was unusual in several respects. Because it was made from hard, fine-grained stoneware, it offered a wide range of decorative possibilities. It could be shaped or decorated by lathe-turning or cutting, and its surfaces could be variously mat or polished. Basalt ware represented Wedgwood's first attempt to concentrate almost exclusively on ornamental rather than functional items such as tablewares. The surfaces were intended to simulate those of Etruscan vases, and the form and decoration of the objects were usually inspired by

classical subjects, as well (or the ancient world viewed through eighteenth-century eyes).

Classical art and neoclassical architecture and interior decoration were very much in fashion among the British aristocracy at this time, and decorative accessories that could be used on mantels or in niches were an integral part of the neoclassical interior. Oil lamps like the one pictured here represented an attempt to evoke the spirit of ancient Rome. The figures lifting the oil basin on this lamp were based on those by Michelangelo on the tomb of Pope Julius II in Florence. Such lamps are remarkable for the strength and delicacy of their sculptural modeling, the sensitive attention to their proportion and detail, and the fine workmanship of the finished object, which was, after all, a factory product.

CHARLES-HONORÉ LANNUIER
(American, born France, active 1779–
1819)

New York
Circa 1804–19
White marble top supported by
  rosewood veneer frame with applied
  ormolu and gesso
36 × 55⁷/₈ × 21¹/₄ inches
  (91.4 × 141.9 × 54.6 cm)
41.1, Gift of the Pierrepont family

After the first decade of the nineteenth century, the neoclassical style in America became more robust and began to reflect French taste more strongly than ever. During the War of 1812, France was an ally and England the enemy. It is therefore not surprising that the finest furniture of the period, such as this pier table, reflects the style popularized by the Emperor Napoleon and the designers he favored. Men like Charles Percier, Pierre Fontaine, and Pierre la Méssangère published neoclassical designs that were disseminated throughout Europe. In turn, English designers such as Thomas Hope and George Smith published books that were influential in transferring the style to America.

This pier table is attributed to Charles-Honoré Lannuier, a French cabinetmaker who emigrated to New York in 1803 and became one of the premier proponents of the late neoclassical style in America. Designed to be placed against a wall, or pier, between two windows, the table is a superb example of the adaptation of classical details—columns, dolphins, and winged caryatids—to a nineteenth-century form. Its rich combination of gilded wood and gilded metal mounts, polished rosewood, marble, and mirrored glass creates a stunning impression of strength and luxury.

The table has a history of ownership in Brooklyn, where it descended in the Pierrepont family.

117 PITCHER AND GOBLET

ZALMON BOSTWICK
(American, active 1846–52)

New York
Circa 1845
Silver; pitcher: 11 inches (28.0 cm)
 high; goblet: 7³/₄ inches (19.5 cm)
 high
81.179.1 and 81.179.2, Gift of the
 estate of May S. Kelley, by exchange

The Gothic style was a popular one in American architecture and furniture design during the 1840s, and the publication of A. J. Downing's *The Architecture of Country Houses* in 1851 further spread the influence of the style. Surprisingly, however, the Gothic Revival was never widespread among American silversmiths. This pitcher and goblet, along with their mates at the High Museum in Atlanta, are therefore extremely rare examples of Gothic Revival silver in addition to being extraordinarily fine representations of the silversmith's art.

The pieces were made by the New York silversmith Zalmon Bostwick, who worked at 128 Williams Street in 1848 and 1849. An inscription on the base of the pitcher indicates that they were presented by John W. Livingston, a descendant of an old New York family, to his son-in-law Joseph Sampson in 1845. Both pitcher and goblet bear the Sampson crest and the initial S.

The pitcher is closely modeled on an English prototype produced in stoneware by Charles Meigh beginning in 1842. These English stoneware pitchers were no doubt popular in America, for they were copied not only by Bostwick but also by ceramicists like Daniel Greatbach, who modeled a similar pitcher for the American Pottery Company of Jersey City, New Jersey, in the early 1840s. In this way, English style interpretations were spread to America and adapted here into new expressions.

118 BED

JOHN HENRY BELTER
(American, b. Germany,
1804–1863)

New York
Circa 1856
Rosewood; headboard: 65½ × 58½
  inches (166.4 × 148.6 cm); footboard:
  36 × 58½ inches (91.4 × 148.6 cm);
  depth: 83 inches (210.8 cm)
39.30, Gift of Mrs. Ernest Vietor

In both form and decoration, this bed embodies the robust exuberance of the rococo revival style in America. In construction, it reflects the nineteenth-century fascination with technological innovation. Although the bed has its stylistic roots in the rococo style of the eighteenth century, its manufacture was entirely modern. It was made in the shop of John Henry Belter, a German-born craftsman who began working in New York City in the 1840s. Belter used laminated construction in his furniture, a system of manufacture that allowed a strong and relatively lightweight material to be bent into the elaborate serpentine shapes so much a part of the fashion of the time. Although laminated wood was not his invention, Belter did patent a number of innovations throughout his career. The patent for this bed, dated August 19, 1856, specifies a bed constructed entirely of wood and glue in a limited number of parts. According to the patent, the bed can be disassembled easily in case of fire and eliminates the intricate joints and recesses around the individual parts of ordinary bedsteads, areas "notorious as hiding places for bugs." The Belter bed at The Brooklyn Museum, with its extraordinary pierced carving of vines, acorns, and cherub heads, is the most elaborate one known. Along with a related bureau, it descended in the Vietor family of New York.

119 CENTURY VASE

Union Porcelain Works, Greenpoint,
  Brooklyn
1876
Hard paste porcelain
24¹/₄ × 10 inches (56.5 × 25.4 cm)
43.25, Gift of Carll and Franklin
  Chase, in memory of their mother,
  Pastora Forest Smith Chase, daughter
  of Thomas Carll Smith, the founder of
  the Union Porcelain Works

Conceived by Thomas C. Smith,
owner of the Union Porcelain Works,
and designed by Karl L. H. Mueller,
the company's chief designer, the
Century Vase celebrates the optimism and national pride of America at
the time of the country's centennial.
The vase, which was exhibited in the
Union Porcelain Works booth at the

Centennial Exhibition in Philadelphia in 1876, is replete with
American symbolism. Examples of
native animals appear as trophy
heads around the midband of the
base and, most notably, at the handles, which are in the form of bison
heads. On the neck of the vase, an
American eagle clutches bolts of
lightning in its talons. Below the
midband of the piece are scenes from
American history in white bisque.
These were described by a writer at
the time: "in bas-relief, we find Penn
treating with the Indians, a log cabin
with the early settler, ax in hand,
resting from his toil and the story of
the tea-riot in Boston harbor, and a
soldier standing by his cannon." The

same writer went on to describe the
scenes, painted in color, that sur-
round a profile of Washington on the
upper part of the vase: "Above these
there are some representative paintings of the progress of the [indus-
trial] arts. The telegraph is illustrated by a pole upon which a
workman is placing the last of a
number of wires; the steamer, a sewing machine and a reaper are also
shown."

The Union Porcelain Works of
Greenpoint, Brooklyn, was one of the
most important manufacturers of ceramics in America in the late nineteenth century. This monumental
vase displays the eclectic vigor seen
in the artistic production of the age.

Made by Herter Brothers (1865–1905)
New York City
1875
Ebonized cherry with painted and inlaid
 decoration
42⅝ × 66 × 16¾ inches
 (107.7 × 167.7 × 42.5 cm)
76.63, H. Randolph Lever Fund

In the third quarter of the nineteenth century, a coming together of many diverse forces contributed to a growing American interest in art forms of all kinds. This interest gave rise to the Aesthetic Movement, which encompassed everything from painting to book covers and promoted "art furniture," "art pottery," and "art glass."

One of the preeminent furniture and decorating firms during this period was Herter Brothers of New York City. The firm was founded in 1865 by Gustave Herter (1830–1898) and his half brother Christian (1840–1883), both of whom had emigrated from Stuttgart, Germany. Their name became synonymous with the Anglo-Japanesque style, an aspect of the Aesthetic Movement popular during the 1870s and 1880s. This style was the inspiration of the English designer E. W. Godwin, whose work Christian Herter probably saw on a visit to England in the early 1870s.

This Herter Brothers cabinet, with its delicate, rectilinear form, ebonized wood, contrasting light-colored marquetry, and painted panels, exemplifies the best of the Aesthetic Movement. It was part of a parlor suite owned by George Beale Sloan (1831–1904), a prominent Oswego, New York, businessman and a member of the State Senate.

121 SIDE CHAIR

FRANK LLOYD WRIGHT
(American, 1867–1959)

Oak Park, Illinois
1904
Oak with leather upholstery
40 1/8 × 14 3/4 × 18 1/2 inches
(101.9 × 37.5 × 47.0 cm)
83.157, Museum Purchase

Frank Lloyd Wright is the most important and influential American architect of the twentieth century. In his architectural, especially domestic, designs he conceived of furniture and interior fittings as integral to the conception of a house. Following the ideas of nineteenth-century European designers, he spoke of a house as a total work of art where exterior and interior were both part of a grand scheme, the design of one dependent on the other. Furniture had an important architectural function within the interior: it defined the space within a room as clearly as exterior walls defined the building itself.

The side chair illustrated here was a design Wright employed in a number of commissions around 1904; this particular example belonged to the architect himself and was used in his Oak Park, Illinois, home and studio. The conception of the chair begins with certain conventions of turn-of-the-century Arts and Crafts furniture: the material is oak, stained to reveal the natural characteristics of the wood; the chair's construction is straightforward and clear, with nothing hidden from view; and the overall design is simple and uncomplicated.

Yet in terms of subtlety and artistry, this chair goes far beyond the "simplicity" that Arts and Crafts furniture was supposed to embody. (Wright mocked the simplicity of that type of furniture when he described it as "plain as an old barn door.") This side chair is more than a mere chair to be sat upon; it is a sophisticated architectural construction in which artistic intention is more important than comfort or practicality. Its forceful abstract design reveals the uncompromising nature of Wright's work and looks forward to the geometric abstraction that was to become central to modern architecture and design in the early twentieth century.

122 CORNER CABINET

ÉMILE-JACQUES RUHLMANN
(French, 1879–1933)

From a room designed for the Weitz family, Lyon, France
1923
Kingwood (amaranthe) veneer on mahogany with ivory inlay
49⁷/₈ × 31³/₄ × 23¹/₂ inches
(126.6 × 80.6 × 59.7 cm)
71.150.1, Purchased with funds given by Joseph F. McCrindle, Mrs. Richard M. Palmer, Charles C. Paterson, Raymond Worgelt, and others

The furniture of Émile-Jacques Ruhlmann represents the highest achievement of what is now generally called Art Deco. The term is derived from the name of an important exhibition held in Paris in 1925—Exposition Internationale des Arts Décoratifs et Industriels Modernes— and covers a wide variety of modern French decorative art produced during the 1910s and 1920s.

Ruhlmann was the foremost decorator and cabinetmaker in Paris during the decade following World War I. His luxurious furniture was made strictly for wealthy clients who were interested in associating themselves—much as the designer was— with the venerable traditions of high-style French cabinetmaking. Ruhlmann prided himself on the extraordinarily high cost of his furniture, commenting that "Only the very rich can pay for what is new and they alone can make it fashionable. Along with satisfying a desire for change, fashion's real purpose is to display wealth." In the victorious post–World War I era, Ruhlmann's elite clients enjoyed the opulence of his furniture, its suggestion of the grandeur of pre-Revolutionary France, and its implication— through the use of exotic materials gathered from French colonies throughout the world—of the continuation of the French Empire.

The beautifully proportioned and superbly crafted cabinet pictured here is one of the finest examples of the art of the cabinetmaker. It is an exquisitely detailed object whose decorative effect is dependent on the beautifully figured veneers and variously treated ivory inlays that cover its surfaces. The flowers that spill out of the large vase on its center are illusionistically and intricately rendered; the thin lines of white ivory and the dark wood between inlays create a sense of space and turn the flat decoration into something dynamic and living.

123 "Beta" Chair (prototype)

NATHAN GEORGE HORWITT
(American, b. 1898)

Manufactured by Howell Manufacturing
Co., Geneva, Illinois
1930
Chrome-plated tubular steel, wood and
upholstery (not original)
26 × 22⅞ × 27½ inches
(66.0 × 58.1 × 69.9 cm)
85.155, Gift of Nathan George Horwitt

Tubular steel furniture made from chrome-plated extruded steel was one of the most significant achievements of modernist European design of the 1920s. Symbolic of the avant-garde's desire for a brave new world of architecture and interior and object design, metal furniture, with its gleaming surfaces, skeletal structure, futuristic look, and implication of mass production, boldly proclaimed the arrival of what contemporaries termed a new "Machine Age."

American designers began working with tubular steel only at the end of the 1920s, and their designs tended to be more conservative and less ideological than contemporary European work. Whereas European architects freely used metal furniture in their domestic interiors, few Americans allowed their steel chairs to leave the kitchen, sun room, or terrace.

Nathan Horwitt's dynamic and structurally daring *"Beta" Chair* was clearly intended for domestic use and is one of the finest examples of modernist American metal furniture. Its bold use of the structural cantilever—the means by which the seat and back extend beyond their supporting element—allowed the sitter to hover miraculously in midair without visible means of support. In fact, the chair's very structure, with its two C-curves, is the main aesthetic feature of its design.

The name of the chair suggested that it was somehow the result of scientific inquiry. In fact, industrial designers argued at the time that their recently organized profession was a science that could be rigorous, objective, and completely detached from the traditional world of decorative design. They presented themselves to the public as wanting to infuse the elevating principles of art into design while assuring manufacturers that annual restyling of products would result in increased sales and a healthy American economy.

124 "NORMANDIE" PITCHER

PETER MÜLLER-MUNK
(American, b. Germany, 1904–1967)

1935
Chrome-plated brass
12 × 3 × 9 1/2 inches
(30.5 × 7.6 × 24.2 cm)
Manufactured by Revere Copper and
Brass Co., Rome, New York
84.67, H. Randolph Lever Fund

During the 1930s American industrial designers seized upon the principles of aerodynamic streamlining as the perfect aesthetic expression for the dynamic, optimistic, and forward-looking period in which they were living. The shiny, chrome-plated surfaces of objects like this pitcher embodied faith in the symbol of the machine and the processes of mass production as a panacea for what had been, in economic terms, hard times.

Though streamlining was a mode of design most suitable for vehicles of transportation—airplanes, ships, and automobiles—its symbolism was so potent that it came to be applied to all manner of stationary domestic objects. In the case of this pitcher, the designer was inspired by the imposing smokestacks of the famous ocean liner *Normandie*, which had just sailed on its maiden voyage. Like the liner itself, the pitcher's form was sleek, windswept, and elegant. Though the pitcher did not have to cut its way through water and air at the highest speed possible, it was upon the evocation of that illusion that manufacturers based their sales pitch.

Prints,
Drawings,
and Photography

125 THE GREAT TRIUMPHAL CHARIOT OF THE EMPEROR MAXIMILIAN I

ALBRECHT DÜRER
(German, 1471–1528)

1522
Woodcut from eight blocks on eight sheets, overall size approximately 16 × 95 inches (40.5 × 241.3 cm)
83.43, Gift of The Roebling Society

Albrecht Dürer completed his first drawing for the *Great Triumphal Chariot* (now in the Albertina, Vienna) in 1512–13. It was originally intended to form the climax of a frieze in woodcut commissioned by the emperor and, had it been completed, would have been sixty yards long. Approximately half the design was to be by Hans Burgkmair, while other "little masters" contributing to the project were Albrecht Altdorfer, Leonard Beck, Wolf Huber, Hans Schäufelein, and Hans Springinklee. As the leading artist of the highly intellectual, humanistic court surrounding Maximilian, Dürer was entrusted with the honor of depicting the emperor's chariot. His position in Maximilian's court was similar to that of Michelangelo in Pope Julius II's, and a conscious rivalry may well have existed between the spiritual and temporal rulers.

At the insistence of his friend and mentor Willibald Pirckheimer, Dürer revised his design, making it much more allegorical than the earlier drawing by the addition of a regalia of emblems and twenty-two women personifying the Virtues. The second drawing (now also in the Albertina) was submitted in 1518 with a text by Pirckheimer. With the death of Maximilian in 1519, realization of the project seemed unlikely, so Dürer withdrew his drawing, and published it himself as a woodcut in 1522.

The Brooklyn Museum's *Great Triumphal Chariot* is one of eight known impressions of the first of seven editions, the only edition printed by Dürer himself. It is a superb example of what the eminent art historian Edwin Panofsky identified as Dürer's "decorative style" (1512–22), which is characterized by elegant and ornate surface pattern. The Museum's set was formerly in the collection of Count York von Wartenburg of Klein-Oels in Silesia, whose Dürer collection was considered among the most eminent in prewar Germany. Most of the plates are wider and show less loss of the block than the set described in Meder's catalogue raisonné of Dürer's graphic work.

126 THE ROUND TOWER, plate III from INVENZIONI CAPRIC DI CARCERI

GIOVANNI BATTISTA PIRANESI
(Italian, 1720–1778)

Circa 1749
Etching
21 1/2 × 16 1/4 inches (54.7 × 41.4 cm)
37.356.2, Frank L. Babbott and Carll
  H. DeSilver Funds

Giovanni Battista Piranesi, probably the greatest architectural etcher of all time, was best known throughout the eighteenth and early nineteenth centuries for his scenic Roman views. Large in scale and published in albums, these etchings were prized and collected by visitors to Italy. In 1749, a publisher named Bouchard released a series of fourteen etchings by Piranesi that were far more fantastical and imaginative than his images of classical ruins. Scholarly opinion varies widely on the meaning and source of the *Carceri*, as this series is popularly called. A current theory is that the images are closely related to stage sets. For the last hundred years, however, connoisseurs of prints have considered them Piranesi's greatest achievement and one of the most important series in eighteenth-century printmaking.

Because of the somewhat lugubrious subject matter, the *Carceri* did not appeal to print collectors of the time. Bouchard released three issues of the first states between 1749 and 1760, all of which are considered first edition and are characterized by light biting of the plate and a primarily linear treatment, thus reflecting the influence of the great Venetian painter-printmaker Giovanni Battista Tiepolo (1696–1770). The Museum's set is from the second issue of the first edition. In 1761, Piranesi himself published a second edition in which he reworked the plates considerably for a more detailed and tonal effect and added two additional plates. These later states are much more atmospheric and brooding than the first edition and much less rare. Piranesi released four issues during his lifetime, and there have been four posthumous editions.

127 El De La Rollona (Nanny's Boy), plate 4 from Los Caprichos

FRANCISCO GOYA Y LUCIENTES
(Spanish, 1746–1828)

1799
Etching and aquatint
7³/₄ × 5³/₄ inches (19.3 × 13.7 cm)
37.33.4, A. Augustus Healy, Frank L.
Babbott, and Carll H. DeSilver Funds

Goya's famous series of satirical etchings and aquatints, *Los Caprichos*, consists of eighty plates with text. In his announcement of the publication of the suite in the *Diario de Madrid* on February 6, 1799, he wrote of his intentions: "Since the artist is convinced that the censure of human errors and vices (though they may seem to be the province of Eloquence and Poetry) may also be the object of Painting, he has chosen as subjects adequate for his work, from the multitude of follies and blunders common in every civil society, as well as from the vulgar prejudices and lies authorized by custom, ignorance or interest, those that he has thought most suitable matter for ridicule as well as for exercising the artificer's fancy." He commented on the above plate: "Negligence, tolerance and spoiling make children capricious, naughty, vain, greedy, lazy and insufferable. They grow up and yet remain childish. Thus is nanny's little boy." The preparatory drawing for this plate, in red crayon with slight variations, is in the collection of the Prado.

The Brooklyn Museum's *Los Caprichos* is a proof set of first and second states prior to the first edition. It is considered to be the earliest proof set because it contains the largest number of errors in the titles at the bottom of the plates, far more than in any other known proof set. Because of the delicacy of the aquatint, even later impressions of any given plate within the first edition begin to show signs of wear. The quality of impressions in the Museum's set is unsurpassed, with every nuance of tonality fresh and lively. The contrasts of light and dark areas create shimmering patterns that in later editions lose their drama.

128 ROTHERHITHE

JAMES A. MCNEILL WHISTLER
(American, 1834–1903)

1860
Etching
10⅝ × 7¾ inches (27.6 × 20.1 cm)
57.188.65, Gift of Mrs. Charles Pratt

In 1859 James A. McNeill Whistler, who had recently moved to London from Paris, began a series of etchings of scenes along the Thames River, working on his plates directly from nature. Although both Whistler himself and the French printer Auguste Delâtre pulled a number of impressions of the early images, they were not formally published until 1871 as *A Series of Sixteen Etchings of Scenes on the Thames and Other Subjects*, generally called *The Thames Set*. This series, cleanly wiped and linear in treatment, repre-

sents the high point of Whistler's early etching style.

Rotherhithe, originally entitled *Wapping*, was the fifth in the published series. Its composition served as a basis for the 1861–64 painting *Wapping* (National Gallery of Art, Washington, D.C., The John Hay Whitney Collection), the background of which Whistler described as "like an etching." Both works depict the balcony of the Angel, an inn in Cherry Gardens, Rotherhithe. Whereas the painting is horizontal and tighter in focus, the print is verti-

cal, with open sky in the upper two-thirds of the plate.

The most startling and unusual compositional feature of *Rotherhithe* is the asymmetrical vertical division of the space by the large post to the left of center. This radical bisecting of the pictorial space, along with the deliberate flattening of the figures, reflects Whistler's interest in Japanese *ukiyo-e* woodblock prints. The division frames the masts at the left as almost a separate image within the work, emphasizing the complexity of the spatial organization.

129 MARY CASSATT AT THE LOUVRE: THE PAINTINGS GALLERY

EDGAR DEGAS
(French, 1834–1917)

1879–80
Etching, soft-ground etching, aquatint, and drypoint
12 × 5 inches (30.5 × 12.6 cm)
36.955, Collection of The Brooklyn Museum

Edgar Degas made two etchings depicting the American painter Mary Cassatt and her sister Lydia visiting the Louvre in 1879–80, both based on an existing pastel (Lemoisne 581). The first one, *The Etruscan Gallery*, was originally intended for inclusion in a journal of original prints, *Le Jour et la nuit*, for which several of his friends, including Cassatt and Camille Pissarro, made etchings in the same, almost square format. Despite Degas's enthusiasm for the project, the journal was never published.

Degas made a gridded drawing after the pastel that he then used to draw the figures on the plate through a soft ground. He subsequently used the same drawing, with considerable reorganization of the relationship of the figures, for the soft-ground drawing of *The Paintings Gallery*. The format of the latter print is exaggeratedly vertical, strongly resembling the Japanese woodcuts of "pillar" format that were extremely popular in France at that time. The format accentuates the slim elegance of the standing figure of Mary Cassatt in a languid pose leaning on the tapered vertical line of her tightly furled umbrella.

Degas, like many etchers whose work is primarily tonal, often worked his plates through numerous states. He rarely editioned his prints, considering etching a private activity,

and pulled only a few impressions of each state. Rather than selling his prints, he usually gave them to his friends, keeping a few impressions in his studio. The Brooklyn Museum's impression of *The Paintings Gallery* is one of six known impressions of the twentieth (and final) state. It is one of the impressions found during the inventory of his studio after his death and is marked on the verso with the Atelier stamp in red (Lugt 657).

130 IN THE OMNIBUS (THE TRAMWAY)

MARY CASSATT
(American, 1845–1926)

1891
Drypoint and soft-ground etching
14⅝ × 10⅝ inches (36.5 × 26.5 cm)
41.685, Collection of The Brooklyn
  Museum, presented in memory of Dick
  S. Ramsay

At the invitation of her friend and mentor Edgar Degas, Mary Cassatt exhibited her paintings and pastels with the Impressionists, thus becoming one of the few women and the only American to be prominently connected with the Impressionist movement. With Degas, she visited the great Japanese exhibition of 1890 at the École des Beaux-Arts, where she was profoundly influenced by the color woodcuts of Utamaro and Toyokuni, major figurative artists. In 1891 she began a series of ten color prints in which she combined her longtime study of old masters with her new-found enthusiasm for

the simplified areas of flat color and bold, asymmetrical compositions of Japanese woodblock prints. Since she was not conversant with woodblock technique, she devised a method of intaglio printing that approximated the layers of transparent colors of the Japanese prints and, in the process, created some of the most striking and beautiful color prints of the Western tradition.

Cassatt employed several Japanese compositional techniques for *In the Omnibus*. The landscape through the window is divided into three

parts, rather like an image on a screen. The bridge becomes a two-dimensional design bisecting two areas of negative space. The baby's dress, and particularly the bonnet, is treated like a large exotic flower. The structure of the tramway's interior is represented by a series of horizontal lines, with only two strong verticals that both indicate the posts of the windows and serve as a frame for the mother's head. The subjects' dresses are treated as flat areas of color with modeling indicated by rich drypoint lines.

131 LE JOCKEY

HENRI DE TOULOUSE-LAUTREC
(French, 1864–1901)

1899
Lithograph
20¹/₄ × 14¹/₈ inches (51.5 × 36.0 cm)
37.20, Collection of The Brooklyn
  Museum

More than any other graphic artist of the period, Henri de Toulouse-Lautrec was responsible for the great popular revival of lithography in France in the 1890s. He was the first artist whose posters were collected by enthusiasts who either tore them from walls or bribed the poster hangers to sell them pristine examples. Like Edgar Degas, the older contemporary artist he most admired and emulated, Lautrec was a superb draftsman with a particular interest in capturing scenes of popu-lar entertainment and the demi-monde of Paris. Whereas Degas treated his subjects in a generalized, somewhat romantic style, Lautrec had an unfailing ability to capture the telling gesture of his subjects and worked in a more expressive style.

Le Jockey, sometimes known as *Le Galop d'essai*, is one of Lautrec's last lithographs. In the final productive year of his life, he concentrated on animals, particularly horses, one of his childhood passions. His depiction is never disinterested and scientific; he always seems to capture the essence of the particular animal, as he did with his cabaret singers and prostitutes. *Le Jockey* was intended to be part of a series on the races proposed by Pierrefort, a young Parisian print publisher, but was the only image realized. One hundred impressions of the key stone were printed in black and white and another one hundred executed in color.

Lautrec's vantage point and his cropping of the horse on the left are of special interest in *Le Jockey*. Viewed from the rear, with a fore-shortened body, the horse's head appears particularly elegant and graceful. The Brooklyn Museum has both the black-and-white and the color versions of *Le Jockey* in its permanent collection.

132 WOMAN WITH BLACK HAT

ERNST LUDWIG KIRCHNER
(German, 1880–1938)

1910
Lithograph
23½ × 17 inches (59.7 × 43.2 cm)
57.194.1, Carll H. DeSilver Fund

Ernst Ludwig Kirchner was one of the founding members and the strongest, most difficult personality of a group of German artists known as Die Brücke (The Bridge) that was founded in Dresden in 1905 and was extremely influential until its dissolution in May 1913. Die Brücke occupies an important place in the development of German Expressionism as the first distinctly German movement in twentieth-century art. Other key figures in the group were Max Pechstein, Erich Heckel, and Karl Schmidt-Rottluff.

From 1907 on, all the members of Die Brücke were deeply involved in printmaking. Although woodcut is the medium most closely associated with the Expressionists, most were also seriously involved in lithography and etching. Kirchner's approach to lithography was radical for its time, using polished rather than grained stones, as he did not want the prints to look like drawings but to have a rougher, less highly finished look. Like other members of Die Brücke, he eschewed professional printers, preferring to print his own work, often in only a few impressions. His graphic output was the largest of the group, consisting of almost 1,000 woodcuts, more than 650 etchings and drypoints, and over 450 litho-graphs. Since most of his work was never editioned, however, impressions of almost any image are of extreme rarity.

Woman with Black Hat, which is printed in black on slightly greenish-yellow paper, is one of Kirchner's most impressive early portraits. The massed areas of black in the hat and hair create visual weight at the top of the composition and are juxtaposed with the mainly negative space at the lower half. The expressiveness of the thick, somewhat jagged lines describing the neck and shoulders impart energy to the lower half, creating interesting tensions within the composition.

133 Fox

GEORGES BRAQUE
(French, 1881–1963)

1911
Etching and drypoint
21 7/16 × 14 15/16 inches (54.7 × 37.9 cm)
36.59.20, A. Augustus Healy Fund

In the fall of 1907, the poet Guillaume Apollinaire brought Georges Braque to Picasso's studio to see *Les Demoiselles d'Avignon*, thus establishing a friendship crucial to the development of modernism. From early 1909 until August 1914, when Braque entered the army, the two met almost daily and, in their discussions, established the basis of Cubism. Braque etched ten Cubist subjects between 1908 and 1912, but only two, *Fox* and *Job*, were published contemporaneously by his dealer Daniel-Henry Kahnweiler. The other eight were not published until 1950–54.

Fox is a superb example of Braque's analytical phase of Cubism, which is characterized by sparse, rigid articulation with straight lines more richly worked in drypoint than the less-rich curvilinear marks. Braque amplified the composition in a painting of the same year, *Bottle and Glass* (Foundation Hermann and Margrit Rupf, Kunstmuseum, Bern). Because the composition is not reversed, it is almost certain that the etching preceded the oil.

The point of departure for the composition was an English-style bar named Fox near the Gare Saint-Lazare that was frequented by the circle of artists and writers that had formed around Apollinaire. Braque used several references to the actual bar within the composition: a bottle of Old Tom gin, a 15-centimes saucer, and a playing card, as well as "Fox" written in the upper right. The thrust of the composition is vertical, from a broad base to a narrow top with angular lines describing a variety of planes.

134 THE MINOTAUROMACHIA

PABLO PICASSO
(Spanish, 1881–1973)

1935
Etching, scraper and burin
19½ × 27¼ inches (49.8 × 69.3 cm)
59.30, Frank L. Babbott and Loeser Art
 Funds

Picasso created *The Minotauromachia*, arguably his most important single etching, when both the European political situation and his personal life were in a state of upheaval. The Minotaur first appeared in a painting dated June 1, 1928 (Museum of Modern Art, Paris), but did not take its final form in prints until April 11, 1933 (*Walking Minotaur with a Sword*). Half man, half beast, the Minotaur was a symbol not only

of man's unconscious but also of the artist's vision because he could see in the darkness of his labyrinth but was blinded by the natural light of the human world. Being part bull, he is also a symbol of sexual passion and was an emblem to Picasso of his dark and his creative forces. The artist's rational, humanistic side is represented by the bearded figure at the left of the composition, dressed like the crucified Christ. The figure alludes to the iconography of the Crucifixion, where Joseph of Arimathea stands on a ladder to remove the nails for the Descent from the Cross.

At the time he was working on this plate, which went through seven states, Picasso was contemplating a break with his mistress Marie-Thérèse Walter, the inspiration for

his classic period, who was then pregnant. She is depicted five times: as the two spectators in the tower, as the innocent young girl leading the Minotaur, as the wounded mare, and as the *torera* holding the sword of her own destruction. As the artist's enlightened side ascends the ladder out of the scene, his subconscious side blunders blindly through it.

Although an edition of fifty was proposed, only fifteen were numbered. Fifty-five impressions have been located, most of which are trial proofs, dedication proofs, and unsigned proofs in the Picasso estate. The Museum's impression of *The Minotauromachia* is a particularly beautiful proof impression dedicated in the artist's hand to the American artist Man Ray.

135 "Folgen" (Obey/Follow), plate 4 from CAFÉ DEUTSCHLAND GUT

JORG IMMENDORF
(German, b. 1945)

1983
Linoleum cut with overpainting
62¹/₂ × 79 inches (159.0 × 218.0 cm)
84.241, Other Restricted Income Fund

Of the new generation of German Expressionists, Jorg Immendorf brings the most overtly political content to his work, incorporating universally recognizable symbols of Germany with portraiture of some of the shapers of radical twentieth-century thought. In the series of paintings *Café Deutschland*, Immendorf created a revolutionary café that functions as a microcosm of postwar Germany. The composition of the print series *Café Deutschland Gut* is based on one of the paintings in the cycle *Adlerhälfte (Half-Eagle)* but is reversed and distilled.

Café Deutschland Gut consists of ten progressive linoleum cuts, each printed in different color variants in editions of ten. The print is divided vertically by a pole down the center behind the helmeted old soldier in the foreground, representing the division between East and West Germany, East and West Berlin. The rest of the complex composition revolves around this radical bisecting device in a dizzying circular motion. The German eagle banks around the lower left corner while the Brandenburg Gate moves over the shoulder of the central figure. The busts of Stalin and Marx seem to observe the scene dispassionately from an inset in the upper right, while the halo of light over the bar echoes the centrifugal thrust of the composition. A half-hidden figure near the center stands on a ladder removing a block of ice from the central beam.

Folgen is the fourth block in the series of ten. Its closely keyed tones of red and pink render the already dense image even more fascinatingly complex. *Café Deutschland Gut* is one of the landmarks of the renewed German activity in block printing.

136 THE FIRST RIDING
LESSON (LA PREMIÈRE
LEÇON D'ÉQUITATION),

JEAN HONORÉ FRAGONARD
(French, 1732–1806)

Circa 1778
Graphite and brown wash on laid paper
  (watermark D + C BLAUW and fleur-
  de-lys)
13⅝ × 17¾ inches (34.8 × 45.2 cm)
57.189, Gift of Mr. and Mrs. Alastair B.
  Martin

Fragonard is considered one of the best and most versatile draughtsmen of the eighteenth century. His drawings are particularly appealing to the modern sensibility because they are neither overly intellectual nor academic. Although he was François Boucher's student, his vibrant, natural figures filled with movement and life are distinctly different from the elegant, formal studies of his teacher. He worked from memory or direct observation in a loose, fluid style.

This work was traditionally thought to have been a depiction of the artist's family, including his son Evariste, who was born in 1780, caught at a relaxed and intimate moment. However, the drawing has recently been dated to circa 1778 by Eunice Williams, who substantiates this date by citing an etching made after it in 1778 by Marguerite Gérard, the artist's sister-in-law. With this new dating in mind, one can look with fresh eyes and realize that the faces are generalized and not portraits and that the family—barefoot and simple—is not Fragonard's. This is not a mere genre study but probably a scene from the artist's imagination suggesting some universal and generalized statement about human nature.

137A PORTRAIT OF MME. MONNEROT

THÉODORE CHASSÉRIAU
(French, 1819–1856)

1839
Pencil on white wove paper
10¼ × 8¼ inches (26.0 × 21.0 cm)
Inscribed, signed, and dated center right
*à mon ami/Jules/Th. Chassériau/*1839
58.163, Gift of John S. Newberry

137B PORTRAIT OF JULES MONNEROT

1852
Pencil on J. Whatman Turkey Mill 1844
  wove paper
9½ × 7⁷/₁₆ inches (24.2 × 18.8 cm)
Signed, dated, and inscribed lower left
in pencil *à mon ami Jules/Th^r
Chassériau/*1852
39.622, Purchase Check Fund

Théodore Chassériau, a major artist of the mid-nineteenth century, was a student of Ingres who broke away from his neoclassic master to favor the romantic style of Delacroix. In fact, he combined aspects of both of these masters in an original style, which through his heirs, Gustave Moreau and Puvis de Chavannes, ultimately led the way to modern art.

Among his most-admired works are his large legacy of pencil portraits, of which The Brooklyn Museum is fortunate to have these two superb examples. The portrait of Mme. Monnerot dates to 1839, placing it among his early mature works, while the portrait of her son, Jules, dates to 1852, four years before Chassériau died at the age of thirty-seven.

According to a letter written in 1893 by the Comtesse de Gobineau, née Clemence Monnerot, her family became acquainted with the Chassérius in the 1830s. Her brother Jules was a close friend of Théodore, and she was an intimate of his two sisters. From 1837 to 1840, he spent every evening at her mother's house. This fact helps to corroborate the identity of the sitter as that of her mother, for the work is dated 1839, and the dedication indicates that it was a gift to her son. It was not until thirteen years later that he did a portrait of his friend Jules.

Neither work has the fine, delicate, if not slightly cold touch of Ingres or the more intense, looser style of Delacroix. Instead they lie somewhere in between, with finely modeled heads and looser, more relaxed lines forming the rest of the figure. The warmth of both portraits conveys intimately the personalities of the artist's close friends.

The earlier portrait of Mme. Monnerot has a certain naiveté and stiffness of style, but the charm and directness of this rather severe but kindly woman cannot be overlooked as she stares full face at the artist while seated of an evening at home. The three-quarter view of Jules Monnerot, on the other hand, shows his rather impish and lively expression with the sure hand of a mature and sophisticated artist. With these two fine drawings, we are able to see samples of Chassériau's portraiture on paper both at the beginning and end of his career, as well as to attain a deeper understanding of the artist through a close glimpse of his personal life.

138 PORTRAIT OF MADAME LA COMTESSE ADÈLE DE TOULOUSE-LAUTREC

HENRI DE TOULOUSE-LAUTREC
(French, 1864–1901)

1882
Charcoal on L. Berville Salanne paper
25³/₄ × 17 inches (65.5 × 43.0 cm)
Unsigned
38.39, Anonymous gift to commemorate
the 75th birthday of Edward C. Blum,
February 24, 1938

Henri de Toulouse-Lautrec did this portrait of his mother in 1882 when he was eighteen years old. In March of that year he had entered the studio of Léon Bonnat, a highly successful portrait painter in the academic tradition. It was his first formal training, and Bonnat, as was the custom of the day, made him draw careful and precise charcoal studies from plaster casts or nude models.

Returning home in the summer of 1882, Lautrec began to make large charcoal drawings of his family and the workers on the family estate at Albi. These informal and intimate studies are quite removed from the academic precision taught by Bonnat. The loosely conceived three-quarter-length drawing of his mother knitting is a revealing portrait, capturing her personality while revealing the artist's tender feelings for her. It seems that by this time Lautrec had become familiar with the work of the Impressionists, especially Degas's sensitive and relaxed portrait style. This drawing and others of the period contain the incisive psychological insights and profound sensitivity toward humanity characteristic of Lautrec's mature style, without the bitter caricature and pointed observations we have come to associate with his work.

139 CYPRESSES

VINCENT VAN GOGH
(Dutch, 1853–1890)

1889
Pencil, quill, and reed pen, brown and
  black ink on white Latune et Cie
  Blacons paper
24 1/2 × 18 inches (62.3 × 46.8 cm)
38.125.19, Frank L. Babbott and A.
  Augustus Healy Fund

This drawing of cypress trees by Vincent van Gogh, like one now in the collection of The Art Institute of Chicago, was made after a painting of the same subject now in The Metropolitan Museum of Art, New York. Van Gogh was in the habit of making drawings after his paintings to send to his brother Theo to keep him informed of his progress, and in a letter to Theo of June 25, 1889, he expressed his intense feelings about these trees: "The cypresses are always occupying my thoughts; I should like to make something of them like the canvases of the sunflowers, because it astonishes me that they have not been done as I see them. It is as beautiful in lines and proportions as an Egyptian obelisk, and the green is of so distinguished a quality. It is a splash of *black* in a sunny landscape, but it is one of the most interesting black notes, and the most difficult to hit off exactly that I can imagine."

The cypress tree, a subject with which van Gogh is associated almost as much as sunflowers, is a traditional symbol of death in Mediterranean countries. It does not seem accidental, therefore, that he became preoccupied with the great beauty of the cypress trees in the fields around the asylum of St. Paul-de Mausole in Saint-Rémy where he was hospitalized from May 1889 to May 1890.

In this work the broad swirling pen strokes seek a graphic equivalent for van Gogh's vision of the trees as he described them to his brother. The large size and free style of the drawing distinguish it from the smaller, detailed pen copies of his drawings of the Arles period, which were filled with a more studied variety of marks. The monumentality and clarity of this work place it among the artist's finest works on paper.

140 L'Amour en Plâtre

PAUL CÉZANNE
(French, 1839–1906)

1890–95
Pencil on laid paper
19¼ × 12¾ inches (48.9 × 32.4 cm)
39.623, Frank L. Babbott Fund

Paul Cézanne's creativity did not diminish in the last years of his life. To the contrary, his late work has come to be recognized as the source of his most innovative and significant contributions to the art of the twentieth century. The Symbolists, the Fauves, and the Cubists all found justification for the modern styles they developed in the late art of Cézanne.

This drawing from Cézanne's late period is after a plaster of a Baroque statuette that was traditionally attributed to Pierre Puget but is now thought to be by François Duquesnoy. The plaster is still preserved, along with the little wooden table on which Cézanne arranged his still lifes, in his last studio on the hill of Les Lauves in Aix. He made about eleven pencil drawings, four watercolors, and four oil paintings of it in the 1890s, studying it from many different angles. The Brooklyn Museum's is one of the most beautiful and finished studies of the sculpture, and it appears to be the one used for a painting in the National Museum in Stockholm. The angle and position of the sculpture are the same in both works and even the shadows seem to correspond.

Iconographically this statuette plays a significant role in Cézanne's late work. It is one of the many quotations from the art of past centuries that he incorporated in various ways in his paintings.

141   NUDE STANDING IN PROFILE

PABLO PICASSO
(Spanish, 1881–1973)

1906
Charcoal on Ingres laid paper
21 1/8 × 14 1/4 inches (53.6 × 36.2 cm)
43.178, Gift of Arthur Wiesenberger

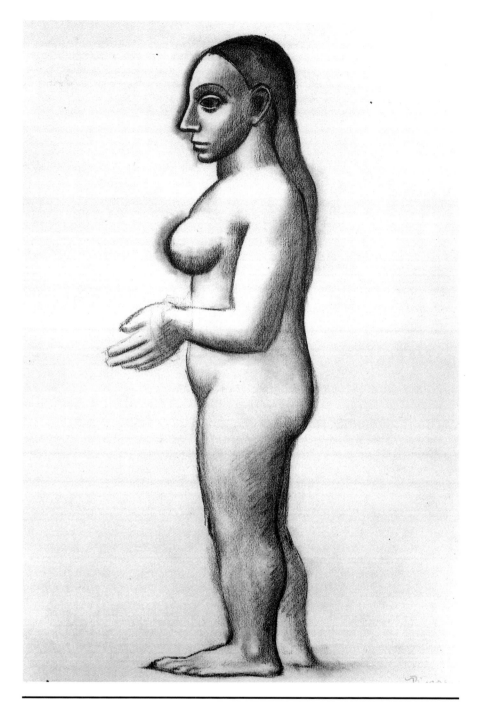

The significance of Picasso's *Nude Standing in Profile* as a historic document of the path to Cubism is indisputable. It is a radical change from the *saltimbanques* of Picasso's rose period that immediately preceded it. In October 1905 Picasso saw Cézanne's *Bathers* at the Salon d'Automne and was affected by the monumentality of the figures. He was also impressed by an exhibition in the spring of 1906 at the Louvre of some recently excavated Iberian sculpture. The sculptural form and stylized features of the figure in this drawing made in the autumn of 1906 show how quickly he could absorb and reconstitute sources.

Nude Standing in Profile is one of a number of studies for the painting *Two Nudes* in The Museum of Modern Art, New York, a significant transitional work that immediately preceded Picasso's 1907 masterpiece *Les Demoiselles d'Avignon.* The drawing is of particular interest in tracing the experiments in geometric simplification that ultimately led to Cubism. The standing nude on the far left of *Les Demoiselles d'Avignon,* although facing the other way, is closely related to it.

Apart from its value as a study, this is a powerful independent drawing of a sculptural blocklike figure standing firmly in the middle of the sheet, looking pensively into space. The female in profile is an image that Picasso returned to in almost every phase of his long and varied career.

142 BILDNIS EINER SCHWANGEREN FRAU (PORTRAIT OF A PREGNANT WOMAN)

PAUL KLEE
(Swiss, 1879–1940)

1907
Pastel, watercolor wash, and brown ink
 on laid paper
9⅝ × 13⁷/₁₆ inches (24.5 × 34.2 cm)
Signed and dated lower right *Paul Klee
 1907*
38.110, Museum Collection Fund

Early in his career Paul Klee made satiric and poetic etchings in an expressive and decorative Art Nouveau style. Around 1905 in Munich he became interested in folk art, especially Bavarian glass painting. This drawing, one of the earliest works by Klee in an American collection, is a preliminary sketch for a painting of the same subject done in Chinese ink on glass, now in the collection of Felix Klee in Bern. A sensitive and charming study of the artist's wife, Lily, it was executed shortly before their son Felix was born.

Art Nouveau influences are still apparent in this work, but it is a tran-

sitional piece looking to a greater naturalism and the Impressionists for new sources. Color was just entering Klee's work, and he wrote in his diary, "Tonality is beginning to mean something to me, in contrast to the past when I seemed to have almost no use for it." The delicate tints of color in this drawing are well suited to the gentleness of the subject. The warmth, wit, and evocative use of line and color displayed here all became trademarks of Klee's mature style.

143 COMPOSITION WITH FOUR FIGURES

MAX WEBER
(American, 1881–1961)

1910
Charcoal on gray laid paper
24½ × 18 inches (62.2 × 46.0 cm)
Signed and dated lower right *Max Weber 1910*
57.17, Dick S. Ramsay Fund

In 1891 Max Weber came with his family from Russia to the United States, settling in Brooklyn. Several years after graduating from Brooklyn's Pratt Institute, he went in 1905 to Paris, where he attended drawing classes at the conservative Académie Julien but soon moved on to the less traditional Académie Colarossi and the Académie de la Grande Chaumière. In these classes he met some of the progressive painters of the day, becoming good friends with the Douanier Rousseau and Matisse.

Back in New York in 1908, Weber associated himself with Alfred Stieglitz's Little Galleries of the Photo-Secession, the 291 Gallery, which was a gathering place for the American avant-garde of the day. There he was included in the 1910 exhibition *Younger American Painters* along with Arthur Dove, John Marin, Marsden Hartley, Alfred Maurer, and Arthur Carles.

Composition with Four Figures (actually three) is a product of this period. Having absorbed the Fauve color and simplified abstracted figures of Matisse, Weber was already moving toward a kind of Cubism. Although the masklike features, mechanical distortions, flattened space, and angular geometric masses of the three female nudes in this drawing, and others of the period, were related to his love of African, Mayan, and Aztec sculpture, they were more likely inspired by an article by Gelett Burgess in the *Architectural Record* of May 1910 that included interviews with Picasso, Braque, and Metzinger and an illustration of Picasso's *Les Demoiselles d'Avignon* of 1906–7. For all its relatedness to the Picasso masterpiece, however, the drawing is by no means a direct copy. The elements of Matisse, the Fauves, and the early Cubists it contains are reconstructed in Weber's own vision to create a unique and compelling work.

144 Le Moulin à Café (The Coffee Grinder)

JUAN GRIS
(Spanish, 1887–1927)

1911
Charcoal on paper
18³/₄ × 12¹/₂ inches (47.6 × 31.7 cm)
86.64, Purchased with funds given by
  Henry and Cheryl Welt

In 1906, at the age of nineteen, Juan Gris moved to Paris from Madrid, where he had studied art and worked as an illustrator. In Paris, he continued to do illustrations, submitting humorous drawings to various journals. It was not until 1910 that he began to paint seriously.

Although Gris knew Picasso and Braque and was certainly aware of their work during this period, he found his own way to Cubism through Cézanne. He did not develop a definitively Cubist style until 1912, when he had his first exhibitions in the Salon des Indépendants and the Section d'Or in Paris and at Der Sturm Gallery in Berlin.

Le Moulin à Café is still strongly rooted in Post-Impressionism, although by 1911 Gris's work had begun to move in the direction of Cubism. The sense of volume, strong angularity, spatial ambiguity, and unusual perspectives seen in this drawing all point toward the more faceted and dislocated forms and broken contours he was to develop in his subsequent Cubist works.

145 Tête de Jeune Homme (Head of a Boy)

PABLO PICASSO
(Spanish, 1881–1973)

1923
Grease crayon on pink Michallet laid
 paper
24¹/₂ × 18⁵/₈ inches (62.1 × 47.4 cm)
Signed lower right, *Picasso*
39.18, Carll H. DeSilver Fund

Although Picasso looked to his Mediterranean heritage for inspiration from time to time throughout his career, the years from 1918 to 1924 in particular have come to be called his classical period. His marriage to Olga Kaklova, a traditional ballerina who tried to lead him from bohemian tendencies to a more refined life-style, his friendship with Jean Cocteau, who was advocating a return to classical tradition, and his experience in 1917 working for Diaghilev in Italy, where he saw Roman marbles and Pompeian paintings, all came together at this time to cause him to break with Cubism.

At the beginning of this period Picasso created paintings and drawings of colossal figures. Around 1923, however, the exaggerated size of these figures disappeared, and he returned to simple, elegant style with a serious feeling for humanity.

The soft, heavy strokes and serene introspective look of *Head of a Boy* are found in other works of the same year, including the charcoal and chalk drawing *Seated Woman with a Hat*, the oil and charcoal painting *The Sigh*, and the figure painting *Pipes of Pan*. The great beauty and serenity of this drawing capture the essence of the ideal classical youth in simple forms and solidly modeled contours. Its extraordinary quality is enhanced by the soft pink paper on which it is created.

146 Study for THEY WILL TAKE MY ISLAND

ARSHILE GORKY
(American, 1904–1948)

1944
Crayon on white wove paper
22 × 30 inches (56.0 × 76.2 cm)
Signed and dated in pencil, lower right,
A. Gorky 1944
57.16, Dick S. Ramsay Fund

Arshile Gorky (born Vosdanik Adoian) was born in 1904 in Armenia. His childhood was a tragic story of flight from his village to escape the Turks, during which his mother died from starvation. After arriving in America in 1920, he took up his studies in art, a career he had long felt destined to pursue.

By 1930 he was an accomplished painter, having studied, absorbed, and copied the masters of modern art from Impressionism through Cézanne to Cubism. During the thirties he absorbed the vocabulary of Surrealism into his work and finally attained his mature style around 1943.

The drawing *They Will Take My Island* was made in the summer of 1944 at a farm owned by his wife's parents in Virginia. As with a number of other highly finished drawings of this period, it became the basis for a closely related painting of the following winter. The drawings of this period reflect the flowers and fields, the bright colors of nature, seen through a Surrealist imagination. The imagery of the outside world, after being absorbed into his unconscious, emerged as his own intensely personal vocabulary and expression.

They Will Take My Island can be read on many levels. Its relationship to Picasso's *Guernica*, a work painted only a few years earlier that Gorky is known to have admired, is particularly significant. The configurations of violence, passion, and destruction are amazingly similar. Both works are intensely personal responses to war, political upheaval, and the loss of homeland.

This drawing, a major work of Gorky's final years, exemplifies how the logic of Cubism, the irrationality of Surrealism, and his own expressive passion were consolidated in his work to form a personal and influential style that anticipated the formation of Abstract Expressionism.

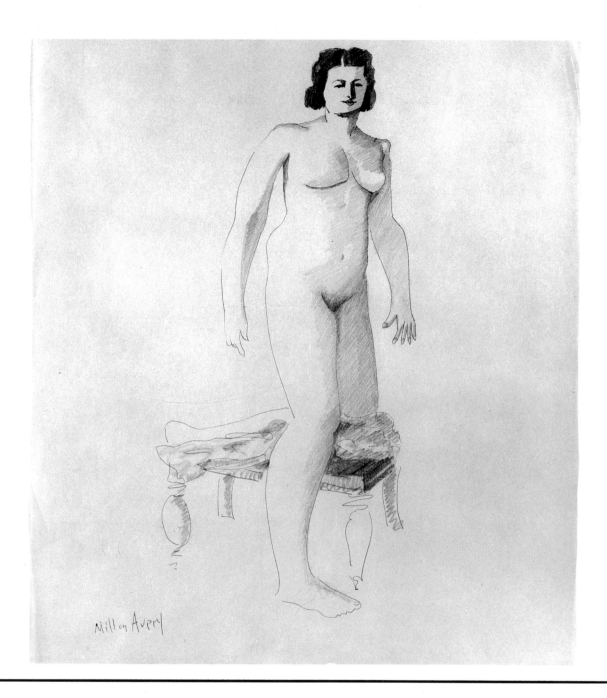

147 NUDE BALANCING

MILTON AVERY
(American, 1892–1965)

1948
Pencil and blue ink on paper
16¾ × 13¾ inches (42.6 × 35.0 cm)
Signed lower left in blue ink; titled and
 signed in pencil verso
86.221, Frank L. Babbott Fund

Milton Avery is one of the pivotal figures of American modernism. Influenced by the artists of the School of Paris, especially Picasso and Matisse, he in turn was a mentor to the next generation of American artists, the Abstract Expressionists. Mark Rothko, Adolph Gottlieb, and Barnett Newman have all acknowledged their debt to him.

Because of his skills as a colorist—he is recognized as one of the most distinguished and original colorists this country has ever produced—Avery's fine draftsmanship has been somewhat overlooked. Yet he drew daily and worked frequently from a model. Indeed, figure drawing was an activity that occupied him continuously throughout his career. It was not so much that he was interested in the figure as he was in simply drawing.

Nude Balancing is outlined in ink and modeled in pencil, a technique characteristic of Avery's drawings of the late 1940s. In it, one can see the influence of the clear and simple outline drawings of Matisse and Picasso. The shading and geometric forms lend it an almost formal solidity typical of Avery's work.

148AB CONEY ISLAND
       BEACH: A DOUBLE
       SIDED DRAWING
       Recto: THE ARTIST
       SKETCHING
       Verso: ACROBATS

REGINALD MARSH
(American, 1898–1954)

Circa 1951
Chinese ink wash on heavy wove paper
22¹/₂ × 30⁷/8 inches (57.2 × 78.6 cm)
Stamped in red, lower right verso, *R. Marsh Collection;* in pencil lower right *Ch* 2294
79.99.1, Gift of the Estate of Felicia Meyer Marsh

Reginald Marsh grew up in an upper-middle-class family and graduated from Yale in 1920. Upon his graduation he came to New York to work as an illustrator. Sometime in the 1920s he was given an assignment by *Vanity Fair* to make sketches of Coney Island. He was so taken with the scene at the beach and with the amusement park that he went back every summer three or four times a week for his entire life to sketch and photograph the musclemen, the acrobats, the bathing beauties—the mass of humanity. He once estimated that one-sixth of his production came from there.

In an article in the *Magazine of Art* of December 1944, "Let's Get Back to Painting," Marsh said, "I go to Coney Island because of the sea, the open air and the crowds—crowds of people in all directions, in all positions, without clothing, moving—like the great compositions of Michelangelo and Rubens."

Marsh's idols were Michelangelo and Rubens. The tangled crowd of bodies provided him with a modern vision of their great machines. The beach supplied him with everything he needed for his art: a continuous crowd of anatomy lessons, a forum for the reconstruction of traditional compositions, and a vehicle for his other great passion, the documentation of the life of New York City, the melting pot of humanity.

Marsh wrote to his wife, "I went to Coney Beach yesterday afternoon. The wind was fresh and strong blowing great white caps in on the seas— the sea a rich blue—the crowd as thick as ever I've seen, much to my delight. The noise of the beach could be heard for miles and there was scarce room to sit down . . ."

The Brooklyn Museum drawing, being double sided, contains many different aspects of these Coney Island drawings. The dense crowd of Rubensian women on the recto is seen being sketched by the artist, who sits in the lower-left corner showing us his role as an observer of life. The drawing on the verso is less complete, although the activities shown are other aspects of life on the Coney Island beach: the acrobats, the guitar player, the ever-present man with a radio.

149 CLIMBING INTO THE PROMISED LAND

LEWIS WICK HINE
(American, 1874–1940)

1908
Gelatin silver print
14 × 10½ inches (35.0 × 26.8 cm)
84.237.1, Gift of Mr. and Mrs. Walter
Rosenblum

Lewis Wick Hine was born in Oshkosh, Wisconsin, and started his working career in an upholstery factory. Soon, however, through his friendship with Professor Frank Manny of the Oshkosh State Normal School, he was appointed superintendent of the Ethical Culture School in New York City. Manny gave Hine a camera and suggested that he teach photography to his students. Although Hine himself only began photographing in 1903, by 1905 he was sufficiently proficient to satisfy an urge to use his camera at Ellis Island, where the phenomenon of immigration fascinated him. *Climbing into the Promised Land* is probably one of his best-known images. This gripping picture of hope, confusion, and excitement is unequaled in its subject matter.

In 1906 Hine joined the National Child Labor Committee. Completely caught up in the lives of the working poor, he began traveling throughout the United States to photograph children working in textile mills, cranberry bogs, fish canneries, coal mines, and so on. Frequently he took his pictures against the wishes of his subjects' employers.

After photographing in Europe during World War I, Hine returned to the United States to resume his travels. By this time labor unions were using his images to get their problems recognized. Always intrigued by the dignity of labor, he undertook one of his greatest projects, *Men At Work*. Once he wrote of the workingman, "Some of them are heroes, all of them, persons it is a privilege to know."

Although Hine obtained work with the W.P.A. in the 1930s, he began to find it harder and harder to achieve recognition. Roy Stryker of the Farm Security Administration, for instance, thought his work outdated. In 1938 he joined the Photo League hoping for new projects, but it was too late. His pioneering achievements all but forgotten, he died penniless and alone, not truly appreciated until at least twenty-five years after his death.

150 MARY PICKFORD, MARCH, 1924

EDWARD STEICHEN
(American, 1879–1973)

1924
Vintage silver print
9¹/₂ × 7¹/₂ inches (24.1 × 19.1 cm)
86.306.2, Anonymous gift in memory of
  Thelma and Ralph Zogg

Born in Luxembourg in 1879, Edward Steichen moved to the United States with his family in 1881. Although he began his career as a painter and continued to paint until after World War I, he took his first photographs in 1896 as design models for lithographs and gradually developed an interest in photography as an end in itself. His early photographic work brought him great acclaim, and Rodin considered him the perfect interpreter of his sculpture.

Steichen's photographs were first exhibited in 1899, and within a few years he had become well known in the Pictorial movement. He exhibited in Europe as well as the United States, was elected to a British photographic society, The Linked Ring, in 1901, and became one of the founders of the Photo-Secession, a group interested in the purely pictorial image, in 1902. He was also instrumental in establishing with Alfred Stieglitz the gallery at 291 Fifth Avenue and designed *Camera Work* magazine as a means of disseminating his ideas.

World War I caused Steichen to change his mind about the pictorial image. As supervisor of aerial photography, he was forced to make sharp, clear pictures. After the war, he gave up painting to devote himself entirely to photography.

Steichen's great talent for sophisticated portraiture led him to a position as chief photographer for Condé Nast publications, for which he took this luminous portrait of the silent-screen star Mary Pickford. He later went on to become Commander of Naval Photography during World War II and eventually Director of Photography for The Museum of Modern Art, New York. There, in 1955, he organized the exhibition *The Family of Man*, perhaps the most popular exhibition of photography ever presented.

151 WOMAN WITH CAMELLIA

CONSUELO KANAGA
(American 1894–1978)

Circa 1930
Gelatin silver print
10¼ × 8⅞ inches (26.0 × 22.2 cm)
82.65.10, Gift of the Consuelo Kanaga
  Estate

Consuelo Kanaga, one of the pioneers of American photography, was born in Astoria, Oregon. She learned how to use a camera and print her own photographs while working as a feature writer for the *San Francisco Chronicle* in the 1920s. Although her work includes a striking range of subject matter, she enjoyed most her portraiture of the struggling poor. As she said, "I thought a medium like photography would change the world."

In the late 1920s Kanaga took a job with the *New York American*, where one of her assignments was to photograph poverty-stricken families living in New York tenements. Here she began to produce some of her most moving work. Her portraiture of black subjects in particular earned her a place in the landmark *Family of Man* exhibition organized by Edward Steichen, who considered her photograph of a young mother and two children, *She Is a Tree of Life to Them*, among his favorites. Another of Kanaga's best-known photographs

was of a camellia in a glass of water. She took it, she explained, "because I thought it needed to be remembered." This portrait of a young black woman with a camellia thus combines two of her best-known images.

The Brooklyn Museum owns the better part of Kanaga's estate, including 1,608 black-and-white negatives, 147 color negatives, and 336 prints. The material was given to the Museum through her estate by her artist husband, Wallace Putnam.

MARGARET BOURKE-WHITE
(American, 1905–1971)

Circa 1930–31
Gelatin silver print
9³/₈ × 13¹/₄ inches (23.7 × 33.7 cm)
79.299.1, Gift of Samuel Goldberg in
  memory of his parents, Sophie and
  Jacob Goldberg, and his brother
  Hyman Goldberg

Margaret Bourke-White started photographing at Rutgers University and the Clarence White School of Photography in New York, where her pictures reflected her first interests — biology and technology. She went on to study at Cornell, where she married Everet Chapman and divorced him two years later. At that time she started hyphenating her name, a compound of her middle and last names.

Although Bourke-White photographed the Cornell campus in the style of the romantic Photopictorialists, by 1927 she had abandoned the Pictorial style and become a freelance industrial photographer. By 1929 her work was appearing regularly in the *Architectural Record*, and her portfolio and reputation won her a job as an editor for *Fortune* magazine. In 1930 the magazine sent her to Russia, where she took this lovely but slightly disturbing photograph of children at table.

By 1936 Bourke-White was working steadily for *Life* magazine, where one of her pictures graced the periodical's first cover. In 1939 she married the novelist Erskine Caldwell, with whom she produced a powerful book on Southern poverty, *You Have Seen Their Faces*. The couple divorced in 1942.

During World War II Bourke-White worked as a war correspondent for *Life*, compiling an unequaled record of photographic firsts. She retired from the magazine in 1969 and died in August 1971 of Parkinson's disease.

153 MULBERRY AND PRINCE STREETS, MANHATTAN

BERENICE ABBOTT
(American, b. 1898)

1935
Gelatin silver print
7 × 9³/8 inches (17.8 × 23.8 cm)
X858.3, Collection of The Brooklyn
  Museum

In 1918, as a young artist, Berenice Abbott left New York and moved to Paris to pursue her studies in sculpture, never dreaming that she would become a photographer. She learned photography as an assistant to the famous Surrealist Man Ray, however, and by 1925 had become a professional portrait photographer to such literary and artistic figures as Marcel Duchamp, André Gide, and James Joyce. No matter what her subject, her photographs never lost the precise, natural, carefully lit quality of her early portraits.

Although thrilled by the writers and artists she met during the 1920s, Abbott was most influenced by the photographer Eugène Atget. After his death in 1927, she purchased thousands of his negatives and prints through the dealer Julian Levy. Until The Museum of Modern Art, New York, bought them in 1968 she acted as curator of this collection by printing, publishing, and exhibiting Atget's work.

Just as Atget documented the streets, storefronts, and country lanes of Paris and its environs, so Abbott photographed New York City, beginning in 1929 in a project for the W.P.A. The stunning detail captured by her 8-by-10 negatives enhances the viewer's belief in their incredible accuracy.

Abbott had a great interest in science, creating photographs that illustrated scientific principles. She said of her work, "I have tried to be objective. What I mean by objectivity is not the objectivity of a machine but of a sensible human being with . . . the mystery of personal selection at the heart of it." For her, "speed and science" were the essence of both photography and the twentieth century.

This picture of Mulberry and Prince streets is one of the few Abbott photographed with people in it. The mysterious shadow figure in the foreground, caused by a time exposure, can be likened to the spirit of Abbott herself, which pervades her work. No matter what the subject, Abbott is always present.

154 Sheik Ali Gournah, Egypt

PAUL STRAND
(American, 1890–1976)

1959
Gelatin silver print
13 3/8 × 10 5/8 inches (34.0 × 27.0 cm)
85.193.2, Gift of Naomi and Walter
Rosenblum

Paul Strand first studied photography with the social photographer Lewis W. Hine at New York's Ethical Culture Society. Hine, in turn, introduced him to Alfred Stieglitz, and it was at Stieglitz's Gallery 291, Strand asserted, that he learned the "modernist aesthetic." Although his first photographs were soft-focus prints, by 1915 he had begun his first experiments with abstraction. His famous image of a white fence, which has been repeated endlessly by other photographers, best expresses his interest in design during that period.

Stieglitz gave Strand a one-man exhibition at Gallery 291 in March and April 1916 and published his photographs in the last two issues of his periodical, *Camera Work*, devoting the final issue entirely to Strand's work. By that time Strand had totally abandoned Pictorialism for "straight" photography, soon to be the dominant form in American photography, and from then until the end of his career he employed simple, straightforward imagery. The unadorned person and object characterized by such portraiture as the moving and powerful *Sheik Ali Gournah* became his hallmark.

Strand moved to France for political reasons in the 1950s. Ever the idealist, he demanded the same standards from those who chose to follow his methods. "Above all, look at the . . . immediate world around you," he said. "If you are alive it will mean something to you, and if you know how to use it, you will want to photograph that meaningness. . . . With clear vision you may make something which is at least a photograph. . . . First learn to photograph. That alone I find for myself is a problem without end."

Strand was among the first photographers to be fascinated by machinery, especially the automobile. He also made films, including the highly acclaimed *Mannahatta* in 1921, and put together extended photographic essays in several countries. He photographed until his death in the United States in 1976.

Painting
and Sculpture

155 The Adoration of the Magi

BERNARDO BUTINONE
(Milanese, circa 1450–circa 1502)

Circa 1480
Tempera on panel
9³/₄ × 8¹/₂ inches (24.9 × 21.5 cm)
78.151.6, Bequest of Helen Babbott
Sanders

This little panel is one of a series of panels of roughly the same size by Butinone that represent scenes from the life of Christ. Originally together, these are now widely scattered in various collections: *The Flight into Egypt* in Chicago, *The Adoration of the Shepherds* in London, *The Massacre of the Innocents* in Detroit, and so on. Scholars differ as to whether the panels were *predelle*—panels beneath the main composition of an altarpiece—or whether they were part of a triptych centering around the widest panel, which represents *The Deposition*.

Butinone is first recorded in 1484, when he was already the head of a successful studio in Milan. The character of his style is clearly that of a North Italian influenced by Paduan and Ferrarese painting and most especially by the great North Italian painter of the previous generation, Andrea Mantegna. The affinities with Mantegna can be seen in the slender figures delineated by tense, wiry lines, in the clarity and precision of detail, and in the motif of the rocky curving hill, with its emphatic linear emphasis and focus on the scattered pebbles. With charming naiveté, the artist has brought this stony decorative motif right into the center of the scene, where there is

no particularly logical connection between it and the architectural form. This architecture is a typical fifteenth-century theme for scenes of the Nativity; the biblical stable is referred to in the thatch-roofed lean-to at the right, but the main structure is a ruined building with classical features, symbolizing the destruction of the pagan world that will be transformed by Christ.

The scene is one of the most significant of the Christian stories centering around the Nativity: the moment at which the most learned and powerful men of the ancient Near Eastern world, symbolized by a black King, a young King, and an old King, come to pay homage to a newborn infant. This paradox is often emphasized, as it is here, by the act of the oldest King taking off his crown (which he would do for no one else) and, in all the dignity of his bearded age, kneeling humbly before a little child. Butinone has presented this theme with the combination of seriousness and charm that is one of the great attractions of *quattrocento* painting. Particularly delightful are the brilliance of color, the costume details, and the presence of the Virgin's little cat, sitting comfortably beneath her stool.

156 Venus and Mars

ATTRIBUTED TO PALMA VECCHIO
(Venetian, circa 1480–1528)

Circa 1510
Oil and tempera on panel
7½ × 6½ inches (19.0 × 16.5 cm)
37.529, Gift of Helen Babbott
McDonald

Though most scholars agree in attributing this luminous little panel to Palma Vecchio, it cannot be established with certainty because there is so little documented information on Palma's career before 1520. What is certain is that the panel is very much under the spell of Giorgione, at a time when the great Venetian painter's influence on Venetian allegorical painting was at its height. The quality of the light, the subtle modeling of the flesh, the gentle reserve of the figures—all place the painting within the poetic orbit of the artist who established the coloristic, atmospheric character of Venetian painting.

The classical deities such as Venus and Mars had by no means been forgotten during the medieval period, but they had been conceived in a way very different from that of antiquity itself. Here, at a moment when the Renaissance was just arriving at that point of aesthetic maturity we call the High Renaissance, the effect of the artist's direct experience of classical sculptures can be clearly felt.

Venus is a fully rounded nude, standing in the pose that would, if seen from the front, be called the *Venus pudica*. Mars is portrayed in the costume of a Roman soldier, which would be known from Roman sculpture. Coexisting with these Graeco-Roman qualities are elements that come out of the artist's more immediate *quattrocento* tradition: the elongated proportions of the figures, the crisp linear play of the drapery, and the delicate detail of the vegetation. An arresting aspect of this painting is its stillness: the figures fill the pictorial field, but they do not carry out any particular action. They are related to each other in their mutual attention, but at the same time they project a mood of inwardness and contemplation.

Like the Butinone panel and other works in the Museum's collection, this one was part of the collection of early Italian paintings formed by Frank L. Babbott, a discerning connoisseur who was President of the Brooklyn Institute in the 1920s.

157 Portrait of Jean Carondelet

JAN CORNELISZ. VERMEYEN
(Netherlandish, 1500–1559)

Circa 1530
Oil on panel
30³/₄ × 24¹/₂ inches (78.0 × 62.2 cm)
47.76, Gift of Horace O. Havemeyer

Though born and trained at Haarlem in the northern Netherlands, Jan Vermeyen worked mostly in the southern Netherlands, particularly Brussels. He was active at the Imperial Habsburg courts of Margaret of Austria and Charles V and was renowned for his portraits, one of the best known of which is this one of Jean Carondelet. Carondelet was a noted cleric and statesman who served, among other posts, as Archbishop of Palermo, Primate of Sicily, and Chancellor of Flanders. He was also provost of the Church of St. Donation in Bruges, where he was buried. It has recently been suggested that the portrait originally hung in the choir of this church.

The type of portrait exemplified here is characteristic for the period: a dark clothed figure silhouetted against a medium-tone ground, with an evenly lit face and naturalistically detailed costume treatment (even fur collars were typical in this northern portrait type). Working within this convention, the artist has given us a painting of great penetration and finesse. The texture of the sitter's hair and his fur collar are masterfully portrayed, as are the gray gloves he grasps so firmly in one hand. The tense activity of the other hand is a counterpoint to the massiveness of the figure and to the strength of the face with its steady, comprehending gaze. This was a period when the art of portrait painting, conceived as an effort to portray character through the accurate rendering of details, had reached a particularly high point in northern Europe, and Vermeyen's portrait is a notable example.

158 THE GREAT RED DRAGON AND THE WOMAN CLOTHED WITH THE SUN

WILLIAM BLAKE
(English, 1757–1827)

Circa 1803–5
Watercolor with pen and black chalk on paper
Image: 17¹/₈ × 13¹/₂ inches (43.5 × 34.5 cm); sheet: 21¹/₂ × 16¹⁵/₁₆ inches (54.5 × 43 cm)
15.368, Gift of William Augustus White

This watercolor belongs to the great series of biblical illustrations that William Blake made for one of his most faithful patrons, a government clerk named Thomas Butts. The first group, done around 1799–1800, consisted of small paintings in tem-pera on canvas; the second and larger group, from about 1800 to about 1809, was made up of watercolors. Of this latter series of more than eighty paintings, twelve are drawn from the Book of Revelation, and four of these concentrate on just two chapters, 12 and 13, in which The Great Red Dragon is a principal fig-ure. The Book of Revelation, with its richly symbolic language and its as-sumptions of a direct link between the supernatural and human history, held an affinity for Blake, and The Great Red Dragon was akin to the kinds of mythological figures that the poet had invented in his own Prophetic Books.

The Dragon, who represents Satan, stands in a threatening pose over The Woman Clothed with the Sun; he is hoping to seize the child that she, symbolizing both Israel and the Church, is about to bear to be the Redeemer of the world. We see him from behind, so that the emphasis is on his great tail, which "drew the third part of the stars of heaven and did cast them to the earth." The fig-ure of the Dragon, with its outspread legs and huge extended wings, forms a powerful cruciform shape that fills the picture plane and dominates, in its tones of ochre and reddish brown, the horizontal curves of the golden woman and the pale yellow moon at her feet. Both figures are conceived in Blake's characteristic style, a very personal interpretation of the neo-classicism of his period, in which can be seen elements not only of classical form but of Michelangelesque anat-omy and the flowing linearity of Gothic sculpture.

159 MLLE. FIOCRE IN THE BALLET "LA SOURCE"

EDGAR DEGAS
(French, 1834–1917)

Circa 1866
Oil on canvas
51 1/2 × 57 1/8 inches (130.8 × 145.2 cm)
21.111, Gift of James H. Post, John T.
  Underwood, and A. Augustus Healy

The subject of this painting is a scene from the ballet *La Source*. This Persian extravaganza shown at the Paris Opera in November 1866 dazzled audiences with its exotic costumes and a sumptuous production that included real water and horses. Degas has portrayed Eugénie Fiocre, a famous dancer of the day, at the height of her career in the role of Nouredda, just after her exciting solo dance in diaphanous pantaloons. Cooling her feet in the stream, she reflects on her fate, for she must abandon her lover to a certain death and journey to her marriage with a foreign prince.

Painted between 1866 and 1868, this painting represents a pivotal moment in Degas's career, poised between his earlier paintings of historical narratives and the contemporary dance subjects that form such a large part of his subsequent work. This is, in fact, the first time that Degas painted a scene from the ballet, although the only clues that he gives us to show that we are witnessing a scene on the stage are the title and the pink satin ballet slippers that Eugénie Fiocre has cast off. While the composition here follows a traditional frontal format, in the next few years, Degas was to move on to a radical, new kind of composition in which unconventional viewpoints incorporate fragmented views of the stage and auditorium, conveying the immediate perceptual experience of a spectator present at the scene.

Although in many of his later portrayals of dancers, Degas displays an obsessive fascination with their highly disciplined poses and movements, here he catches Eugénie Fiocre in an off-beat moment of stillness and introspection. In many of his portraits Degas captures his sitters in such moments of inactivity. As its title makes clear, this painting is as much a portrait of an individual as a painting of a performance. By portraying Eugénie Fiocre in her characteristic milieu—the stage—he pursues his innovative approach to portraiture whereby, in order to capture the modern world realistically, he often shows his sitters—dancers, musicians, writers—in surroundings that reflect their occupations.

The Brooklyn Museum purchased this painting from a sale in New York in 1921 of the seventy-one works by Degas that the great Parisian dealer Jacques Seligman had acquired from the sale of the Degas studio in 1918.

C. Pissarro.

160 THE CLIMBING PATH, L'HERMITAGE, PONTOISE

CAMILLE PISSARRO
(French, 1830–1903)

1875
Oil on canvas
21 1/8 × 25 3/4 inches (54.0 × 65.0 cm)
22.60, Purchased with funds given by
Dikran K. Kelekian

In 1872, not long after his return from London, where he and Monet had lived during the Franco-Prussian War and its aftermath, Pissarro moved to Pontoise, a village on the river Oise to the northwest of Paris where he had worked in the late 1860s. It was during the decade of his residence there that his style was most purely Impressionist in character. In 1874, the year before this painting was made, he was active in helping to organize the first exhibition of the new painting, dubbed Impressionism by a critic of that show. He was the one artist from the original group who stayed with all eight exhibitions, the last of which took place in 1886.

It was during the 1870s also that Pissarro and Cézanne often worked together, sometimes painting the same motifs. While Cézanne learned much from the older artist, the influence was not all one way. *The Climbing Path* is notable for revealing Pissarro's concern, shared with Cézanne, for an overall unity of structure and palette. Both artists were looking at Courbet, whose use of the palette knife is reflected in this painting. The very choice of the motif must have been one that appealed to Cézanne as well: l'Hermitage, the northeastern side of Pontoise, which Pissarro had painted also in the late 1860s, was an area where a steep hillside rose behind the houses, creating a sense of contracted space quite different from the open river views. Here this closing up of space is most vividly expressed in the rising path at the right, seen in ambiguous yet convincing spatial relation to the group of houses in the middle distance.

The Climbing Path, one of the boldest paintings of this period of Pissarro's work, was bought by the Museum in 1922, the year after it was exhibited at the Museum in a controversial exhibition called *Modern French Masters: The Post-Impressionists and their Predecessors.*

161 THE VILLAGE OF GARDANNE

PAUL CÉZANNE
(French, 1839–1906)

1885–86
Oil on canvas,
36¼ × 29⅜ inches (92 × 74.6 cm)
23.105, Ella C. Woodward and A.T.
  White Memorial Funds

In the autumn of 1885 and most of the following year, Cézanne painted in Gardanne, a village near his native Aix-en-Provence, renting a house especially for the purpose. Beside Brooklyn's painting, there are two other views of the subject, one in the Barnes Foundation, Merion, Pennsylvania, and one in The Metropolitan Museum of Art, New York.

In the 1870s, Cézanne had turned away from the morbid, introspective fantasies that are the subjects of many of his early works to concentrate on still lifes, portraits, and landscapes. Schooled by Pissarro, he moved from his violently expressionistic technique of somber colors thickly applied with the palette knife to bright, outdoor colors and a measured, Impressionist stroke. By the mid-1880s, when he painted *The Village of Gardanne*, Cézanne's quest for a disciplined form of painting led him to pursue the underlying structure of nature, a pursuit that resulted in an austerely geometric style which, by the 1890s, would relax into a more opulent and voluptuous mode of painting.

Cézanne must have found Gardanne, with the geometric forms of its little houses stacked steeply up the hill and culminating in the fortresslike church, particularly suited to his purpose. The fact that the canvas is unfinished allows us an insight into his method of constructing his painting. Delicate linear notations, indicated with a sensitive, continually mobile blue line, provide a scaffolding on which he builds the solid forms of the houses. The entire surface of the canvas is kept alive through a constant shift back and forth between hard and soft forms and warm and cool tones; the solid forms of the houses are built up with planes of characteristic Mediterranean, sunbaked color—tawny pinks, ochers, and tans—interspered with feathery areas of blue-green foliage.

Cézanne seems in this work to be exploring, whether consciously or unconsciously, a tension between three-dimensional form and flatness. The solidity of the buildings is denied, to some extent, by the way their densely interlocked forms rise vertically up the canvas and by our awareness of the flat surface of the canvas itself, which is especially apparent here, owing to the unpainted area at the lower right. This sense of an ambiguous relationship between the objects depicted and the space they inhabit was to lead, in the early twentieth century, to the Cubists' revolutionary analysis of space.

The Village of Gardanne is one of a number of adventurous purchases made by the Museum in the early 1920s.

162 Pierre de Wiessant

AUGUSTE RODIN
(French, 1840–1917)

Circa 1886–87, cast 1979
Bronze
84 3/8 × 46 × 39 inches
(214.5 × 116.8 × 96.5 cm)
84.210.9, Gift of Iris and B. Gerald
Cantor

The recent major Cantor gift to the Museum of sculpture by Rodin includes a notable group of twelve studies and figures from one of the artist's best-known monuments, *The Burghers of Calais.* In 1884 the city of Calais, like a number of other French towns during the years after the defeat of France by the Prussians in 1871, decided to erect a monument to their city's most famous hero. This was the fourteenth-century merchant Eustache de St.-Pierre, who had been the first of six prominent citizens to volunteer to surrender to the besieging English king, Edward III, during the Hundred Years War in order to save the city from destruction. Rodin's proposal for a monument that would include not just Eustache de St.-Pierre but all six of the Burghers was accepted, and he was awarded the commission. During the next four years he worked in his characteristic way on many studies of heads, of single figures both nude and draped, and of the figures grouped together.

From the first, the figure of Pierre de Wiessant was conceived in a pose whose torsion and gesture express the inner conflict of a man whose moral will to sacrifice his life for the common good is powerfully resisted by the forces of self-preservation. The exaggerated size of the hands, with their tensely spread fingers, further communicates this sense of psychic conflict.

Like all the Burgher figures, this one is draped in a kind of loose sackcloth. Here it falls back to reveal the powerful chest and shoulders of a strong, mature male, against which the prisoner's rope hangs to remind the viewer of the Burghers' imminent fate. (In fact, having presented themselves to the king in full expectation of death, they were ultimately pardoned on the plea of the pregnant queen.)

Rodin wished to have the group of Burghers placed at ground level, so that citizens could see and relate to them easily; but the late nineteenth-century burghers of Calais, rather put off by the intensity of Rodin's tragic vision, placed them together atop a high pedestal.

163 THE DUCAL PALACE AT VENICE

CLAUDE MONET
(French, 1840–1926)

1908
Oil on canvas
32 × 39⁹/₁₆ inches (81.2 × 100.3 cm)
20.634, Gift of A. Augustus Healy

Monet visited Venice for the first time in 1908 when he was nearly sixty-eight, and returned in the fall of 1909. Captivated by the city's magical light and the way it could transform its churches and palaces, he pursued in a series of twenty-nine paintings his investigations of the effect of light and atmosphere on a particular motif—in this case, architecture—that he had begun with the Rouen Cathedral series in 1892 and 1893 and continued in London with the Thames series in 1903. He started work on a number of canvases in Venice but completed them from memory when he returned home to Giverny. Although he was displeased with the results, thinking that the works had suffered from being painted from memory, his method in this case was, in fact, no different from the way he proceeded with the other serial paintings that preoccupied him during the 1890s. Working in the studio away from the motif allowed him the chance to elaborate his canvases, creating certain correspondences of color and texture between different paintings in the same series.

While in some of the Doge's Palace paintings, Monet takes a distant view looking across the lagoon from San Giorgio Maggiore, in this painting he adopts a closer view facing the palace head on. A soft, chalky pink makes the building radiate with ambient light yet does not dissolve its form. With a sparkling palette of pinks, blues, and violets Monet interweaves thick strokes of paint to create the reflection whose solidity vies with the building itself, making it appear to float on the water.

The Venice works were the last easel paintings Monet was to paint. After this and until his death in 1926 he was to devote himself to the pursuit of light, water, and reflections in his monumental wall paintings of waterlilies.

The Ducal Palace at Venice was presented to the Museum in 1920 by Museum President A. Augustus Healy.

164 NUDE IN A WOOD

HENRI MATISSE
(French, 1860–1954)

1905
Oil on canvas
16 × 12¾ inches (40.6 × 32.5 cm)
52.150, Gift of Mr. George F. Of

This brilliant, small canvas, painted probably in 1905 when Matisse was in Collioure on the Mediterranean, expresses the exuberance of the sunlit south. Yet Matisse has exaggerated the naturally bright colors of the place even further to create a dazzling shower of tangerine, emerald green, mauve, violet, and cyclamen pink strokes that spatter the nude form of the seated woman, making her figure almost indistinguishable from the wood that surrounds her. Although the colors seem to have been applied randomly, Matisse juxtaposes complementary and contrasting hues in order to intensify their brilliance and achieves a dynamic rhythm in the arabesques of the trees that frame the coiled figure. Nevertheless, when Matisse showed other works painted in this style at the Autumn Salon in 1905, the public and the majority of the critics could find in them no pictorial coherence. Shocked by their vivid color and seemingly crude and savage brushwork, one critic named Matisse and his followers—Vlaminck, Derain, and Dufy—"Fauves" or "Wild Beasts." The term has stuck and is still used to describe this style of painting, which Matisse practiced for only a short time, from 1905 to about 1907.

The dramatic impact made by these paintings at the Salon made it seem as if Fauvism was a style that had exploded in a vacuum. In fact, however, it was a natural development from the discoveries the Impressionists had made in rendering light and atmosphere with small, broken touches of paint and the radically new way of using strong, antinaturalistic color for emotive and decorative ends pioneered by van Gogh and Gauguin. In creating this image, Matisse was probably also drawing on his personal interest in Japanese prints and Oriental textiles, and the figure could derive from Persian or Turkish tiles.

Despite its radical technique, the subject of this painting is not new but goes back to a long-established tradition that had prevailed in Western painting since the Renaissance, of depicting the nude in hedonistic harmony with nature. This pastoral strain in Matisse's art culminated in *The Joy of Life*, 1906 (Barnes Foundation, Merion, Pennsylvania), and it has been suggested the *Nude in a Wood* could be one of a number of small studies of nudes that Matisse made in preparation for that painting.

Nude in a Wood has the distinction of being the first Matisse to be acquired by a collector living in America. The American painter and frame maker George F. Of, an early admirer of Matisse's work, purchased the painting from Mrs. Michael Stein in the summer of 1906 and donated it to the Museum in 1952.

165 THE CARPENTER'S SHOP IN NAZARETH

ANONYMOUS
(La Paz)

18th century
Oil on fabric
29³/₄ × 32 inches (75.5 × 81.0 cm)
43.112, Frank L. Babbott Fund

The Brooklyn Museum's collection of Spanish Colonial paintings is one of the most important in North America. It is rich in paintings of the Cuzco School, works central to an understanding of the evolution of Colonial society in Alto Peru. In particular paintings of this school reveal the character of the religious synchretism that resulted as the Catholic priests and governors of the sixteenth and seventeenth centuries communicated Christian concepts and images to the local Andean, post-Incan population.

The Carpenter's Shop in Nazareth is a particularly rich and charming example of the fusion of European themes with the indigenous sensibility. It is one of the foremost examples of the way in which European imagery functioned not as a model to be slavishly imitated but as a medium for the translation of religious ideas into a new context. The theme of the Christ Child working in his father Joseph's carpenter shop, assisted by angels, can be found in Baroque art in Italy, Spain, and northern Europe. Such images were usually transmitted to Andean painters by means of engravings of paintings, which from the later sixteenth century on were produced in large numbers in the printing centers of Flanders.

The Andean artist has composed this theme in an original way full of invention and decorative charm. Included among the tools scattered on the flat ground are the flower patterns so typical of Cuzco painting. A similar motif marks the robe of the Christ Child, who helps Joseph saw a board.

The artist has drawn other themes into the central subject: at the upper right appears God the Father, also in a flower-patterned robe, with a triangular halo symbolizing the Trinity, while at the upper left is a small scene of the Virgin assisted in her needlework by an angel whose kneeling pose is drawn, as is that of the Virgin, from the traditional image of the Annunciation. In the lower left corner, delightfully out of place among the busy angels, is the warrior archangel Michael, in full regalia including plumed hat and high boots. His figure is derived from Baroque sources but is distinctively modified into a type very popular in Peruvian painting.

166 WINTER

WILLIAM RUSH
(1756–1833)

1811
Wood
28 1/8 × 21 × 9 inches (71.4 × 53.3 × 22.9 cm)
42.242, Dick S. Ramsay Fund

Often acknowledged as the first native American sculptor, William Rush gained early training in wood carving from his father, a ship's carpenter, and in 1771 entered formal apprenticeship under Edward Cutbush, an English figurehead carver. Rush's earliest known work dates from around 1789—well after the opening of his own shop and the establishment of an international reputation based on the vital and naturalistic figureheads produced there.

Rush's transition from craftsman to artist seems to have taken place gradually, much of this having to do with his study of modeling with artist Joseph Wright sometime between 1789 and 1793 and his association with Philadelphia's most acclaimed artist, Charles Willson Peale. In addition to being one of the founders of Columbianum artists society in 1794, Rush helped found the Pennsylvania Academy of the Fine Arts in 1805. His involvement in the formation of these important art organizations signals his concern with aesthetic issues grander than those customarily associated with figurehead carving. However, it was not until 1808, with the creation of the freestanding wood figures *Tragedy* and *Comedy* for the New Theatre in Philadelphia, that he made his first true efforts as a sculptor.

Rush went on to create a number of life-size sculptures as well as many portrait busts, all of which demonstrate his desire and remarkable ability to transcend simple craftsmanship. In 1881 he exhibited *Winter* at the First Annual Exhibition of The Society of Artists of the

United States. Described in the exhibition catalogue as "representing a child shrinking from the cold," this successful evocation of the season's chill wind demonstrates the poetic and dramatic nature of his vision.

As the first noted American-born sculptor, Rush achieved a secure position in the history of art early on and was celebrated in an important series of paintings by fellow Philadelphian Thomas Eakins, one of which, *William Rush Carving His Allegorical Figure of the Schuylkill River* (1908), is also in the Museum's collection.

167 THE PIC-NIC

THOMAS COLE
(American, 1801–1848)

1846
Oil on canvas
44 7/8 × 71 7/8 inches (121.6 × 182.6 cm)
Signed lower center: *T Cole/1846*
67.205.2, A. Augustus Healy Fund B

Thomas Cole, America's first great landscape painter, earned his reputation with romanticized views of the American Northeast as well as with grand moralizing allegories and European scenes that challenged his naive audience. English by birth, he emigrated to the United States in 1818 and worked as an engraver and itinerant portrait artist before the success of his first Hudson River landscapes in 1825. His art matured under the influence of European travels (1829 to 1832, and 1841 to 1842), which impressed upon him the allegorical potential of the history-laden landscapes that figured so prominently in the art of Claude Lorraine (1600–1682) and the painters of the English picturesque.

Cole was at the height of his powers in 1845 when he received a commission from James Brown, a wealthy New York banker who expressed a preference for landscapes with interesting figure groups. In an optimistic mood Cole chose the subject of a picnic, using the motif of a popular pastime to describe the ideal coexistence of nature and civilization and thus creating his most important American pastoral. He employed graceful and accommodating natural forms, such as the curved clearing and bending oaks, which he perceived to be a positive influence on man's moral outlook and social capacity. The effect is the suggestion of age in the well-worn features of the landscape, which, in the absence of classical ruins, become the focus for the contemplation of time and human mortality.

The guitarist, a probable self-portrait of Cole, who was also a talented musician, acts as the primary voice of the work, communicating with nature. His music is a traditional *vanitas* symbol, suggesting through its own ephemerality the passage of time. Cole counters this doleful message with the bounty of nature, which provides physical and spiritual nourishment to those who embrace it. Nature's sustaining wealth is accentuated by the dispersal of the trappings of the meal throughout the setting and the flower garlands for which three of the women trade their bonnets, partaking of a tradition long associated with the mythological goddess Proserpina, who returned from the Underworld each year to bring spring to the earth.

168   Mrs. Charles Dodge

CHARLES DODGE
(1806–1886)

Wood
24⅝ × 15¾ × 11 inches
(62.5 × 40.0 × 27.9 cm)
60.36, Dick S. Ramsay Fund

The son of Jeremiah Dodge, the proprietor of a New York shipcarving firm, Charles Dodge became a partner in his father's business in 1833 and by 1842 had established his own shop. While maintaining the carving business in which he would remain active until 1870, Dodge became involved in local politics, and he held a variety of elected and appointed positions including alderman, assessor, deputy tax commissioner, and tax commissioner from the 1840s through the 1860s.

The perennial difficulty of distinguishing art from craft is inherent in Dodge's work as a ship carver and maker of cigar-store Indians. Yet, with this finely wrought bust (believed to be a portrait of his wife), there is no problem in identifying Dodge as an artist as well as an artisan. Its smooth surface and sensitively rendered, though idealized, features betray his knowledge of the neoclassic style then in vogue, and it is possible to interpret his painting of the wood surface white as an effort to imitate the effect of the white marble of the neoclassic models that may have inspired him. Yet the piece remains within the mode of what has been called the American vernacular, a tradition rooted in the pragmatic and utilitarian that gave rise to a unique artistic expression standing at the intersection of folk art, craftsmanship, and fine art.

It is likely that Dodge never considered himself an artist *per se* since the few available facts outlining his activities indicate that his primary interests lay in the commercial and political spheres. However, in this carved portrait, the viewer encounters an extremely rare glimpse of Dodge's potential had he chosen to direct himself fully to the pursuit of artistic goals.

169 THE GREEK SLAVE

HIRAM POWERS
(1805–1873)

1869
Marble
66 × 19³/₄ × 18³/₈ inches
(167.6 × 50.2 × 46.7 cm)
55.14, Gift of Charles F. Bound

Hiram Powers's family moved to Cincinnati, Ohio, from his birthplace, Woodstock, Vermont, when he was about thirteen. With the death of his father shortly after the move, the youth was forced to take on a variety of jobs and finally attained the position of supervisor of the mechanical section of Dorfeuille's Western Museum. During that period he learned to model in clay from Frederick Eckstein, a Prussian sculptor. From 1834 to 1837 he frequented New York, Boston, and Washington and supported himself through commissions for portrait busts, the most notable of which were those of President Andrew Jackson and Daniel Webster.

Powers was one of many nineteenth-century American sculptors who established both home and studio in Florence, Italy. Drawn there by the relative ease with which materials and labor could be procured, these sculptors also sought close proximity to the objects and cultural traditions from which their neoclassic visions derived. Powers sailed for Europe in the fall of 1837 and settled in Florence with the aid of fellow sculptor Horatio Greenough, who had been living in Italy since 1825.

The Greek Slave may be singled out as a paradigm of American neoclassical sculpture. Daring in its de-piction of the female nude, it contains many historical, religious, and political associations that served to mitigate the longstanding public resistance to images of the nude in American art. Although the form is based on classical prototypes, Powers chose to place the content of the work within the modern context of the Greek War of Independence (1821–30) and by it referred to the many Christian Greeks taken prisoner by the Turks and later sold as slaves. The content later expanded, allowing for the work to be interpreted as an allusion to antislavery sentiments then at issue in America.

The last of six full-scale versions of the work to be completed by Powers (the first was finished in 1844 on private commission), The Brooklyn Museum's version differs from its five predecessors in the artist's substitution of bar-manacles for chains as restraints. By 1869, the year of this version, *The Greek Slave* was an important icon of American culture. Known firsthand by thousands (replicas toured major American cities in the 1840s and 1850s, and it received great acclaim at the London Crystal Palace Exhibition in 1851), its image and meaning also entered the American consciousness through countless reproductions in a variety of media as well as through articles in the popular and literary press.

170 Shooting for the Beef

GEORGE CALEB BINGHAM
(American, 1811–1879)

1850
Oil on canvas
35⅝ × 49⅜ inches (85.4 × 125.4 cm)
40.342, Dick S. Ramsay Fund

Born in Virginia and raised in Missouri, George Caleb Bingham had little in his background to suggest the success he would attain as an important painter of portraits and genre subjects. During an apprenticeship in cabinetmaking, however, he met an itinerant portrait painter from whom he received some training and the inspiration to become an artist.

With the exception of a brief period of study in Philadelphia in 1838 and a sojourn in Washington, D.C., from 1841 to 1844, Bingham spent the early part of his career painting portraits of the citizenry of his adopted home state. Around 1845 he turned to genre subjects that provided vivid descriptions of American frontier life. Many of these paintings depicted the workings of the democratic process on the local level and reflected the artist's own role in Missouri politics. (He campaigned vigorously for the Whig Party, served as a member of the Missouri legislature, and held the post of State Treasurer from 1862 to 1865.)

Bingham's genre paintings gained national attention largely through their distribution by the New York–based American Art-Union. *Shooting for the Beef* is the last of twenty works he submitted to the Art-Union before its dissolution in 1851. Here, in what is for him an unusually complex composition, a group of marksmen test their skills in a contest for the bull tethered on the left. While there is no overt reference to political content, the artist's emphasis on the theme of competition within an exclusively male society recalls many of his politically oriented works. The narrative content and the far-ranging view of the frontier landscape combine to make this work an icon of the era of Manifest Destiny in its suggestion of limitless opportunity for those possessed of the pioneering, competitive spirit.

171 LAKE GEORGE

JOHN FREDERICK KENSETT
(American, 1816–1872)

1870
Oil on canvas
14 × 24 1/8 inches (35.5 × 61.2 cm)
33.219, Gift of Mrs. W. W. Phelps in
memory of her mother and father, Ella
M. and John C. Southwick

By 1870, the year he painted this view of Lake George, John Frederick Kensett had already explored and exhausted the Hudson River School aesthetic that had dominated American landscape painting for the greater part of the century. By this time, too, he had fully developed his signature style, now commonly defined by the twentieth-century term "luminism."

Kensett first visited Lake George in 1853. The area had long been a popular sketching site for many artists, and for Kensett it would figure in at least four major oils over the following two decades. His treatment of the subject in the Museum's 1870 painting is unusual for several reasons and may be interpreted as an indication that he was again in the process of reorienting his aesthetic approach. Although he chose to return to a site traditionally linked with the Hudson River School style (which by 1870 was becoming outmoded), he refrained from reiterating the pantheistic sentiments inherent in the work of the previous generation headed by Thomas Cole and Asher B. Durand. In a similar manner, although he adopted the scale and composition of his "luminist" efforts, he exchanged the fixed calm and mirror-smooth surfaces of his earlier luminist works for a sensibility residing in the transitory. The signs of impending atmospheric change—swiftly moving clouds and agitated water—reinforce the idea of transition, as does the artist's uncharacteristic depiction of the lake as it appeared in late autumn.

172 A Storm in the Rocky Mountains — Mt. Rosalie

ALBERT BIERSTADT
(American, 1830–1902)

1866
Oil on canvas
83 × 142 1/4 inches (210.8 × 361.3 cm)
76.79, Dick S. Ramsay Fund, A. Augustus Healy Fund B, Frank L. Babbott Fund, A. Augustus Healy Fund, Ella C. Woodward Memorial Funds, Gift of Daniel M. Kelly, Gift of Charles Simon, Charles Smith Memorial Fund, Caroline Pratt Fund, Frederick Loeser Fund, Augustus Graham School of Design Fund, Bequest of Mrs. William T. Brewster, Gift of Mrs. W. Woodward Phelps, Gift of Seymour Barnard, Charles Stuart Smith Fund, Bequest of Laura L. Barnes, Gift of J. A. H. Bell, John B. Woodward Memorial Fund, Bequest of Mark Finley

Albert Bierstadt was born in Solingen, Germany, and raised in New Bedford, Massachusetts. After returning to Germany in 1853 to study art in Düsseldorf, then the center of an internationally popular school of landscape painting, he came back to the United States in 1857 to begin his career as a landscape painter.

A Storm in the Rocky Mountains — Mt. Rosalie was inspired by Bierstadt's 1863 expedition to the American West in the company of writer Fitz Hugh Ludlow. As he had done in 1859 during his first trip west (an expedition that resulted in his first heroically scaled landscape, *The Rocky Mountains*), he made numerous on-the-spot sketches and studies. Upon returning to his New York studio, he incorporated them into this panoramic vista.

For all its apparent truthfulness in terms of detail, the painting is not topographically accurate. It is, instead, a composition in the literal sense of the word rather than a faithful rendering of a specific site. A highly subjective visual essay on the sublime natural wonders of the New World, it is executed on a scale commensurate with the vastness of the land itself.

Bierstadt's use of large canvases invites comparison of his work to that of Frederic E. Church as well as to the then-popular public attractions of moving panoramas and dioramas. This particular painting also had a personal level of content, for Mt. Rosalie (now Mt. Evans) was named by the artist in honor of his traveling companion's wife, whom Bierstadt married in 1886 following her divorce from the writer.

The painting's history is extraordinary. Purchased in 1867 by an Englishman, Sir Samuel Morton Peto, it remained in obscurity and was reported by a Denver newspaper in 1869 to have perished in a fire. Until its rediscovery in 1974 it was known only by a chromolithograph produced in 1868.

173 JUNE

GEORGE INNESS
(American, 1825–1894)

1882
Oil on canvas
30¹/₄ × 45 inches (77.0 × 114.3 cm)
41.776, Bequest of Mrs. William A.
Putnam

In an important 1878 article, the landscape painter George Inness articulated his views on the purpose of art, saying, in part, "A work of art does not appeal to the moral sense. Its aim is not to instruct, not to edify, but to awaken an emotion." With these words Inness not only expressed his personal aesthetic aims but also confirmed the general displacement of the Hudson River School style in American art by one inspired by the French Barbizon tradition.

Inness, who was born in Newburgh, New York, began his art training when the Hudson River School style was approaching the zenith of its popularity. Yet, his choice of instructor, the French artist Régis François Gignoux, with whom he studied in New York sometime between 1843 and 1845, indicates that his taste extended beyond the mainstream of contemporary American art. While Inness's early paintings reflect his knowledge of the Hudson River aesthetic, he gradually rejected the topographical specificity and moralizing content inherent in that mode. This tendency grew stronger following his second trip to Europe in 1853, for direct contact with the work of the Barbizon painters introduced a looser facture,

brighter palette, and less formulaic composition to his art.

Inness painted *June* (also known as *A Day in June*) at a time when his art was beginning to achieve popular as well as critical admiration. The placid summer scene seems enclosed in an almost palpable atmosphere and exudes a calm serenity that induces the subjective, emotional responses to which he aspired in his art. The painting was shown in several important exhibitions during the artist's lifetime, including the Chicago World's Columbian Exposition of 1893. It stands as a fine representative of Inness's late style and exemplifies what was by 1882 the preferred taste in American landscape painting.

174 LETITIA WILSON JORDAN

THOMAS EAKINS
(American, 1844–1916)

1888
Oil on canvas
60 × 40 inches (152.4 × 101.6 cm)
27.50, Dick S. Ramsay Fund

Today the work of the Philadelphia artist Thomas Eakins holds a place of high esteem in the annals of the history of American art. In his own lifetime, however, his circle of admirers was small, general recognition of his achievements came late in his career, and his greatest impact was felt through his activities as a teacher rather than through the exhibition of his work. Most of his oeuvre falls within the category of portraiture, a genre ordinarily generated as a result of a commission; yet, of the 246 portraits known to have been executed by Eakins, only 25 were commissioned. The rest were largely portraits of his family and close friends that were later given away or kept in his studio.

The subject here, Letitia Wilson Jordan (1852–1931), was the sister of Eakins's friend and pupil David Wilson Jordan, to whom the artist gave the painting on its completion. Apparently, Eakins had seen Miss Jordan at a party one evening and was so taken by her strong good looks that he soon after prevailed upon her to pose for him in the same dress she had worn at the party.

Eakins's portrayal of this handsome woman stands apart from contemporaneous aesthetic norms. In an era primarily disposed to the idealization of women, Eakins expressed his fascination with female beauty in an unconventional manner. Much of this was accomplished through his synthesis of his French academic training and his study of the great Spanish masters Velázquez and Ribera, whose paintings he had seen in Madrid. The meshing of two strong European traditions resulted in a highly naturalistic realism that allowed Eakins to accent rather than veil the personalities of his sitters and to create complex amalgams of physical and psychological realities unique to each subject.

175 **EMBLEMS OF THE CIVIL WAR**

ALEXANDER POPE
(American, 1849–1924)

1888
Oil on canvas
54³/₁₆ × 51¹/₈ inches (137.6 × 129.8 cm)
66.5, Dick S. Ramsay Fund, Governing Committee of The Brooklyn Museum, and anonymous donors

Emblems of the Civil War is a particularly fine example of Alexander Pope's rare but masterful excursions into the genre of trompe-l'oeil still-life painting. A self-taught artist, Pope was involved with his family's Dorchester, Massachusetts, lumber business until it apparently failed in 1879. By the following year the Boston City Directory listed him as an artist. Although he was so well regarded as a painter of animal sub-

jects that he was often referred to as the "American Landseer," the financial stability he achieved in his last decades was obtained primarily through work as a competent but uninspired portrait painter.

Pope's essays in painting vertical trompe-l'oeil still-life compositions may be interpreted as direct responses to the popularity enjoyed by the work of William Michael Harnett (1848–1892), whose several versions of *After the Hunt* had gained fame immediately before Pope executed the first of his works in this genre in 1887. Although most of Pope's still lifes centered on hunting and dead-game subjects, with *Emblems of the Civil War* he created a private, visual memorial commemorating the achievements of a Union

Army major general named William Badger Tibbits (1837–1880).

The calculated symmetry of the objects in this painting—including weapons, army-issue material, and a flag (probably that of Tibbits's own 2nd Regiment New York Cavalry)—functions as a heraldic device, a medallion of sorts that recalls the heroism of the past. The duality imposed by the use of the trompe-l'oeil technique suggests the tangible nature of the objects depicted and at the same time denies to the viewer their existence in the present. No longer meant to function in the roles for which they were originally intended, these "real" objects are now reduced to symbols of Civil War events that by 1888 were fading from the range of firsthand experience.

176 POPPIES ON THE ISLES OF SHOALS

CHILDE HASSAM
(American, 1859–1935)

1890
Oil on canvas
18¹/₈ × 22¹/₈ inches (46.0 × 56.0 cm)
85.286, Gift of Mary Pratt Barringer
and Richardson Pratt, Jr., in memory
of Richardson and Laura Pratt

Of the many American artists who experimented with styles inspired by French Impressionism, Childe Hassam is perhaps the best known. Born in Dorchester, Massachusetts (now a part of Boston), Hassam began his artistic career as a draftsman in an engraving firm and went on to success as a free-lance illustrator. Although his early training in the arts is poorly documented, it is known that he studied for some time with the Munich-trained artist Ignaz Gaugengigl, took classes at the Lowell Institute, and practiced drawing at the Boston Art Club.

During the early 1880s Hassam was known for his work in watercolors and briefly conducted a small class in that medium. One of his students was Celia Thaxter, whose family operated the major hotel on the island of Appledore, one of a group of tiny islands located off the coast of New Hampshire. Hassam first visited the island resort in 1884, and following an extended stay in Paris from 1886 to 1889, where he studied at the Académie Julian, he joined the numerous painters and writers who regularly summered there.

Hassam painted many views of Celia Thaxter's famed garden on Appledore. The garden was widely celebrated in contemporary literature and was the subject of Thaxter's own book, *An Island Garden*, published in 1894, for which Hassam provided the watercolor illustrations.

In *Poppies on the Isles of Shoals* Hassam produced an intense and intimate view of the Appledore garden, concentrating on the wild poppies that carpeted the grassy hills overlooking the bleached white rocks that edged the ocean shore. Painted the year after his return from Paris, the work displays his assimilation of the primary Impressionist concerns of plein-airism, broken and spontaneously applied brushstrokes, and brilliant color. The strict, almost geometric division of the canvas into foreground, sea, and sky, meanwhile, is typical of his garden series. This mixture of compositional discipline and painterly freedom establishes the painting as one of the most pleasing in his oeuvre.

177 PAUL HELLEU SKETCHING WITH HIS WIFE

JOHN SINGER SARGENT
(American, 1856–1925)

1889
Oil on canvas
26¹/₈ × 32¹/₈ inches (66.3 × 81.5 cm)
20.640, Museum Collection Fund

John Singer Sargent, one of America's most famous expatriate artists, was born in Florence, Italy, of American parents and received his artistic training in Paris, where from 1874 to 1878 he studied primarily in the atelier of Émile Carolus-Duran (1838–1917). Although he scored early successes with his submissions to the Paris Salon, his career took a sudden downward turn with the disastrous reception of his portrait of *Madame X* at the Salon of 1884, and in 1885 he moved to London.

In England another London-based American expatriate, Edwin Austin Abbey, introduced Sargent to the art colony of Broadway, a tranquil area that included the small villages of Broadway, Calcot, and Fladbury near the River Avon in Worcestershire. Sargent was a regular summer visitor there from 1885 to 1889, the period of his most concentrated experimentation with the techniques of French Impressionism. Although he had long been aware of Impressionism, having been in Paris when the movement first burst on the scene, his renewed interest in the Impressionist manner at Broadway seems to have stemmed from his natural inclination to experiment with avant-garde methods and his need to establish himself in his new English milieu. While he exhibited his more conservative paintings at the English Royal Academy, he often chose to display his experimental work at the New English Art Club, an organization he helped to found in 1886. The NEAC exhibitions provided the only regular outlet for English artists to promote work that reflected their assimilation of French artistic taste.

At Broadway Sargent usually painted *en plein air*. However, in the case of *Paul Helleu Sketching with His Wife*, he abandoned that practice for one that integrated modern French facture with the careful draftsmanship instilled in him by his academic training. The subjects are the French artist Paul Helleu and his young bride, Alice, who visited Sargent at Fladbury in August 1889 while on their honeymoon. Numerous preparatory drawings of Alice and a photograph of the couple posed as in the painting confirm the belief that the painting was largely a studio production. That the artist considered this painting an experimental work is indicated by his decision to exhibit it at the NEAC in 1892. It is thought that he gave it to the Helleus as a wedding gift. The Museum purchased it directly from Helleu in 1920.

178 THE TURTLE POUND

WINSLOW HOMER
(American, 1836–1910)

1898
Watercolor over pencil
14¹⁵/₁₆ × 21³/₈ inches (38.0 × 54.2 cm)
23.98, Sustaining Membership Fund,
   A. T. White Memorial Fund, and
   A. Augustus Healy Fund

After achieving his first rush of critical and public acclaim with the 1866 exhibition of his painting *Prisoners from the Front*, Winslow Homer experienced several years of disappointment and discouragement. Having been hailed as one of America's most promising and original young artists, he found, by the early 1870s, that his career had not kept pace with his expectations and that his livelihood still rested on his success as an illustrator for *Harper's Weekly*.

This period of inertia in Homer's career coincided with the rise of the watercolor movement in the United States, a movement that seized the attention of artists and public alike in 1873 as a result of a landmark New York exhibition of more than six hundred American and European watercolors sponsored by the American Society of Painters in Water Colors. Although Homer had had a casual interest in watercolor before 1873, that year marked his first sustained efforts in the medium— efforts that lasted more than three decades and yielded close to seven hundred works. His sudden enthusiasm for watercolor may have stemmed not only from the aesthetic appeal of this old but newly validated medium but also from his desire to establish himself in the rapidly expanding market for watercolor paintings.

For the most part Homer executed his watercolors during his many summer trips, concentrating on a particular theme or subject for the duration of each trip. Such is the case with *The Turtle Pound*, one of twenty-five watercolors he is known to have painted during his two-month stay in the Bahamas in the winter of 1898–99. Here, within the simple but dynamic construct of sea and sky, he presents a dignified portrayal of the islanders' way of life, one that he perceived as being closely attuned to nature. While providing a truthful record of a routine task (that of capturing a young sea turtle to be confined in a wooden pound for fattening before going to market), he transcends the level of mere documentation by imbuing his subject with a conceptual monumentality. The universal issue of man's place in nature and the struggle for life as embodied in the captive turtle are given immediacy and physicality through the artist's brilliant handling of the watercolor medium.

179 A Morning Snow— Hudson River

GEORGE BELLOWS
(American, 1882–1925)

1910
Oil on canvas
45 3/8 × 63 1/4 inches (115.2 × 160.7 cm)
51.96, Gift of Mrs. Daniel Catlin

George Bellows arrived in New York City from his native Columbus, Ohio, in 1904 after having dropped out of Ohio State University at the end of his junior year. Intent on becoming an artist and armed with the money earned over the summer playing semiprofessional baseball and selling sketches, Bellows enrolled in William Merritt Chase's New York School of Art. There he attended classes taught by the well-established, albeit controversial, Robert Henri, who along with such associates as John Sloan and George Luks campaigned vigorously against the constraints exerted by the National Academy of Design, then a bastion of artistic conservatism. Although Bellows was never an official member of the group of New York realists headed by Henri (later known as "The Eight" and still later considered part of the Ash Can School), he was deeply influenced by Henri's instruction to create an art based on life. For Bellows as well as his contemporaries that meant the urban realities of New York.

A Morning Snow—Hudson River depicts a scene along the Upper West Side of Manhattan overlooking the Hudson River and the New Jersey Palisades beyond. With the assured, slashing strokes of a heavily loaded brush, Bellows has captured the effects of morning light reflected from the freshly fallen snow.

Although he presents a relatively quiet scene, the artist nonetheless conveys the idea of the city's awakening energies through the inclusion of such small but important narrative elements as a figure shoveling snow, men going to work, and boats plying the river. Even the billowing shapes of smoke and steam seem to signify the hidden power of the city as its inhabitants prepare for another day's activity. Bellows's use of these narrative passages certainly aligns his art with that of the other Henri followers, yet perhaps more than all of them Bellows chose to explore his compositions with an eye for abstract relationships. The elevated vantage point serves to flatten the pictorial space, which is then ordered by a system of horizontal and vertical elements that are in turn relieved by a subtle series of diagonals that occur throughout the painting. Thus, in addition to supplying a satisfying narrative structure, the artist offers a compelling composition that may be appreciated on a purely formal basis.

180 LONGHORN STEER

SOLON BORGLUM
(American, 1869–1922)

1905
Bronze
36 × 76 × 20 inches
(91.5 × 193.0 × 50.8 cm)
Signed lower right
67.274.1, Gift of the City of New York
Department of Real Estate, Benjamin
Kravitz, and the New York City Parks
Department, Joseph Bresnan

Born in Ogden, Utah, Solon Hannibal Borglum grew up in Nebraska, where early in his youth he developed an abiding compassion for animals and a deep respect for the Plains Indians. He started his career in charge of his father's cattle ranch, but his older brother, the sculptor Gutzon Borglum, recognized his talent as an artist and encouraged him while giving him instruction.

After studying at the Cincinnati Art Academy for two years as a pupil of the sculptor Louis Rebisso, he traveled to Paris in 1897 to attend the Académie Julian, where he received criticism from several sculptors, including Augustus Saint-Gaudens. By 1901 he had established a studio in New York City and developed a sound reputation for sculptures of cowboys, Indians, and animals.

This vigorous sculpted portrait of a longhorn steer by Borglum was commissioned in 1905 by Charles A. Schieren, a leather belt manufacturer and one-time mayor of Brooklyn who felt that he owed his considerable fortune to cattle (his leather belting was used in thousands of steam engines throughout the United States). The steer graced the entrance to Schieren's factory at 30-38 Ferry Street at the southwest

corner of Cliff Street in Manhattan, an area near the foot of the Brooklyn Bridge long known as a district for tanners and leather workers.

The head was cast by the Roman Bronze Works of New York. It remained on the Schieren Building from 1905 until the building was condemned and demolished in 1967 to make way for a new entrance to the bridge.

Borglum continued to prosper, receiving many awards for his work and establishing a studio in Silvermine, Connecticut. Although he created several classical statues in the last years of his life, he never gave up his love of the West and Western subjects. His steer's head continues to be one of the most popular sculptures in the Frieda Schiff Warburg Memorial Sculpture Garden, especially among children.

181 NIGHT

ADOLPH A. WEINMAN
(American, 1870–1952)

Circa 1910
Pink granite
120 × 73 × 41 inches
 (304.8 × 185.4 × 104.1 cm)
66.250.1, Gift of Lipsett Demolition Co.
 and Youngstown Cartage

Born in Karlsruhe, Germany, in 1870, Adolph A. Weinman emigrated to New York in 1880 with his widowed mother. By the time he was fifteen, he was apprenticed to a wood and ivory carver. After later studying at Cooper Union and the Art Students League and with Augustus Saint-Gaudens and Phillip Martiny, he opened his own studio in 1904. Today his sculptures grace the Bronx County Building and the Museum of the City of New York, where his statues of Alexander Hamilton and DeWitt Clinton, in two niches, face Central Park.

Weinman was at the height of his career when he completed eight heroic female figures of Day and Night for New York's Pennsylvania Station, a monumental building designed by Charles Follen McKim in the style of the Roman baths at Caracalla. The statues flanked four clocks over the four entrances to the station. Day was depicted holding a sunflower clasped to her breast, while a hooded but half-nude Night was shown with an opium poppy drooping from her hand.

The station, begun in 1906 and completed in 1910, was demolished in 1963 to make way for the new Madison Square Garden and a far more modest and undistinguished skyscraper. Of the pieces of the station, which were buried in the New Jersey Meadowlands, only three statues have been retrieved. Two, Day and Night, can be seen at Ringwood Manor in New Jersey unrestored. Another, this statue of Night, has been pieced together for the Museum's Frieda Schiff Warburg Memorial Sculpture Garden.

182 PAINTING No. 48, BERLIN

MARSDEN HARTLEY
(American, 1877–1943)

1913
Oil on canvas
47⁵/₁₆ × 47⁵/₁₆ inches
(119.8 × 119.8 cm)
58.158, Dick S. Ramsay Fund

As one of the first American artists to receive encouragement and support from the important New York art dealer–photographer Alfred Stieglitz, Marsden Hartley was also among the first to incorporate the effects of European modernism in his work. Even before his first trip to Europe, Hartley had seen examples of the work of Cézanne, Picasso, and Matisse at Stieglitz's gallery at 291 Fifth Avenue and had experimented with their styles. This limited contact with the European avant-garde convinced him of the necessity of European travel, and with financial help arranged by Stieglitz he left for Paris in 1912. There he frequented the famous salon gatherings of the American expatriates Leo and Gertrude Stein, where he could see and discuss the latest developments in Parisian art. Unlike most of his American compatriots, Hartley established his closest friendships with a group of young German artists. Inspired by them and by his reading of Kandinsky's *On the Spiritual in Art*, he went to Germany early in 1913.

Hartley was impressed by the military pageantry that characterized prewar Berlin and was convinced that Berlin provided the environment in which his art could flourish. He returned in May 1913 for a six-month residency and during this sojourn executed *Painting No. 48, Berlin*. Typical of his work of this period, it reveals his assimilation of Picasso's analytic Cubist style, which he had expanded to embrace an iconography incorporating the military atmosphere of Berlin and the mystical associations of numbers, colors, and shapes inspired by his understanding of the works of Kandinsky and the French philosopher Henri Bergson. In a letter to Stieglitz, he noted that the painting represented the mystical embodiment of the number eight (a number generally associated with transcendence from the material to the spiritual) but denied the validity of further explanations of his art.

With the exception of a few pieces left in Paris with the Steins, Hartley's Paris and Berlin paintings were exhibited at Stieglitz's gallery in January 1914. Critical reaction was positive, and the exhibition produced considerable income that permitted Hartley to return to Germany for another extended stay from April 1914 through December 1915.

183   Brooklyn Bridge

GEORGIA O'KEEFFE
(American, 1887–1986)

1948
Oil on masonite panel
47^{15}/$_{16}$ × 51^7/$_8$ inches
(121.6 × 131.5 cm)
77.11, Bequest of Mary Childs Draper

The Brooklyn Bridge, typically a symbol of modernity and industrialism, is here endowed with yet another quality—religious feeling. By depicting a web of cables through a chasm recalling stained-glass windows, Georgia O'Keeffe proclaims this vast structure a modern icon, a contemporary cathedral.

O'Keeffe is known not for her images of manmade objects but for her pictures of the flora and fauna of New Mexico: its desert landscape, bleached animal skulls, and surreal flowers. Yet *Brooklyn Bridge* is not completely detached from her paintings of nature, for it dovetails with her celebration of the American landscape, the bridge being a quintessentially American image.

Moreover, the simplified rendering seen here is found in O'Keeffe's other architectonic images of the same time, specifically her *Patio* series, which she began in the late 1940s. In her *Patio* works, as in this image, space is revealed through a framed opening and is reducible to a geometric form.

184 THE HERO

DAVID SMITH
(American, 1906–1965)

1952
Steel
73¹¹/₁₆ × 25¹/₂ × 11³/₄ inches
  (187.0 × 64.7 × 29.8 cm)
57.185, Dick S. Ramsay Fund

David Smith's oeuvre defies strict art-historical categorization. His early work abstracts nature—animals, plants, insects, and the human figure—while his late work, culminating in the geometric outdoor sculptures of his *Cubi* series, is minimalist.

Smith's *The Hero* conflates the abstract and the figurative, for discernible in this geometric steel sculpture is a life-size female. She is revealed frontally, balanced on a pedestal, with a rectangle for a torso, two triangular forms for breasts, and a tank top for a head.

The Hero is a forerunner of more than ten sculptures produced between 1952 and 1960 that Smith entitled his *Tanktotem* series. "Tank" refers to the industrial tank lids or boiler tops he used to construct his pieces, while "totem" may be indicative of the influence of Sigmund Freud's book *Totem and Taboo*.

The art historian Rosalind Krauss maintained that Smith was "preoccupied" with Freud's discussion of totemism: "The ambiguous attachment of a male name [*The Hero*] to a female sculpture is consistent with the Freudian explanation of totems," she wrote, "in which the male identity—his clan name—is synonymous with the prohibited female object." But the title of this sculpture may also be read as an indication of Smith's interest in classical mythology, for many of his works allude to Greek myth.

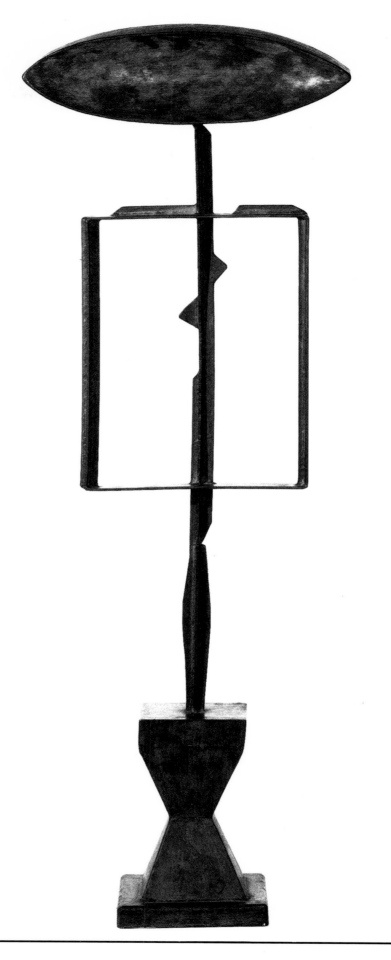

185 WOMAN

WILLEM DE KOONING
(American, b. 1904)

1953–54
Oil on paper
35³/₄ × 24³/₈ inches (91 × 62.2 cm)
57.124, Gift of Mr. and Mrs. Alastair B.
Martin

The female figure was predominant in Willem de Kooning's work from the time of his arrival in America in 1926 until the 1950s. In the 1930s and 1940s, his paintings of women were realistic and detailed. Yet he finally abandoned strict attention to the figure, maintaining, "You could lose your mind" drawing objects so closely resembling nature.

A close rendering of the figure is absent in *Woman*, where the image is neither fully abstracted nor completely representational. Human body parts are discernible but are masked by rich and frenzied painterly lines.

About his *Woman* series, de Kooning remarked: "It's really absurd to make an image, like a human image, with paint, today, when you think about it. . . . But then all of a sudden it was even more absurd not to do it. . . . [Painting *Woman, I,* 1950–52] did one thing for me: it eliminated composition, arrangement, relationships, light—all this talk about line, color and form—because that was the thing I wanted to get hold of. I put it in the center of the canvas because there was no reason to put it a bit on the side. So I thought I might

as well stick to the idea that it's got two eyes, a nose and mouth and neck. . . ."

Facial features are the artist's concession to an identifiable figure. He knew Picasso's *Desmoiselles d'Avignon* of 1907, then on view at The Museum of Modern Art, New York, and its influence is clear in *Woman:* the masklike face, flattened forms, and almond-shaped eyes all recall the Picasso painting. In addition, de

Kooning endowed his subject with ferocity. Fanglike teeth, one of the few recognizable forms in the image, dominate the face. A dozen years after he completed his *Woman* series, the artist found humor in such horrifics: "I look at them [the *Woman* paintings] now and they seem vociferous and ferocious. I think it had to do with the idea of the idol, the oracle, and above all, the hilariousness of it."

186 Untitled (Composition #104)

AD REINHARDT
(American, 1913–1967)

1954–60
Oil on canvas
108¼ × 40⅛ inches (275.0 × 101.9 cm)
67.59, Gift of the artist

Although he was a contemporary of the Abstract Expressionists, Ad Reinhardt produced flat, geometric abstract paintings unrelated to the work of Jackson Pollock or Willem de Kooning. The works of those artists are filled with accidental aspects of the painting process—random brushstrokes and automatic drawing—Surrealism's legacy to the New York School. But Reinhardt maintained that Surrealism was unimportant to his work: "Surrealism never had any fascination for me at all. I would cast out all Expressionist, Dadaist, Futurist, and Surrealist art. They don't fit in with art-as-art at all. In fact, the Surrealists were programmatically anti-art."

Reinhardt championed abstract art. In the late 1930s, he was a member of the American Abstract Artists, the Artists' Union, and the American Artists' Congress. From 1936 to 1941, he was one of the few nonobjective artists employed by the Works Project Administration division of the Federal Arts Project.

In *Composition #104* the artist's control over the work is apparent in solid bricklike blocks of color. The work is strictly composed to deny depth and affirm symmetry.

Reinhardt denied that his paintings contained any content: "The content is not in a subject matter or story, but in the actual painting activity. . . . Abstract painting is not just another school or movement or style but the first truly unmannered and untrammeled and unentangled, styleless, universal painting. No other art or painting is detached or empty or immaterial enough."

Contemporary critics, however, have attempted to find additional meaning in Reinhardt's work. Wrote Thomas McEvilley: "Critics seeking the content of his work should look neither to the Greek Christian cross nor to the problem of the surface, but to the four-limbed mandalas of the Orient—especially the Taoist mandala of 64 squares, which is virtually identical to the internal quadrature of Reinhardt's paintings."

187 OCEAN PARK, NO. 27

RICHARD DIEBENKORN
(American, b. 1922)

1970
Oil on canvas
100 × 81 inches (254.0 × 205.7 cm)
72.7, Gift of The Roebling Society, Mr.
 and Mrs. Charles H. Blatt, and Mr.
 and Mrs. William K. Jacobs, Jr.

In 1967 Richard Diebenkorn began a series of paintings named *Ocean Park* after the section of Santa Monica, California, where his studio was located. In contrast to Diebenkorn's early, figurative works, the *Ocean Park* paintings were abstract, a change that the artist found to permit "an allover light which wasn't possible for me in the representational works, which seem somehow dingy by comparison."

In *Ocean Park, No. 27* Diebenkorn reduces a scene to planes and fragments of color à la Matisse and Mondrian, building up and scraping off layers of paint to signify the Ocean Park landscape. Depth and spatial illusion are suggested by the advance and recession of color. Using a low-key palette devoid of harsh tones, the artist accomplished his stated goal of communicating "a feeling of strength in reserve, tension beneath calm."

188 THE INVERSION

SYLVIA PLIMACK MANGOLD
(American, b. 1938)

1984
Oil on linen
60 × 100 inches (152.4 × 254.0 cm)
86.200, Gift of Henry, Cheryl, Daniel, Michael, and Willie Welt in memory of Abraham Joseph Welt

Sylvia Plimack Mangold's *The Inversion* is a work full of polarities: image competes with void, geometry conflicts with nature, traditional landscape painting faces off with abstraction. The canvas forms a narrative about the painting process.

Plimack Mangold began *The Inversion* as a larger work. "The landscape originally stretched horizontally from left to right, side to side," she wrote. "I cropped it because it didn't work—the negation of some areas becomes a positive element in the support of the total picture." The painting depicts a natural flow of the landscape into a void, a typically American scene in which trees stretch endlessly into the distance.

This places Plimack Mangold in the American landscape painting tradition that culminated in the nineteenth-century Hudson River School.

Until the mid-1970s, Plimack Mangold depicted fragments of flooring or domestic space in an intensely realistic manner. Although she switched to landscapes after moving from New York City to the Catskills, she never completely rejected her early works. Remnants of those interiors are found in the window framelike band that wraps around this landscape, forcing the viewer to peer through a manmade barrier. The color of the band is repeated in the landscape; hence the title of the painting: *Inversion*.

189 HEAD

TOM OTTERNESS
(American, b. 1952)

1984
Bronze
35¹/₂ × 33 × 25 inches
(90.2 × 84 × 63.5 cm)
85.176, Gift of Henry and Cheryl Welt

Though Tom Otterness's *Head* lies within the tradition of bust-length portrait sculpture, it confounds that identification upon first gaze, for the artist has no interest in capturing a sitter's likeness. Rather, *Head* recalls mass-produced, machine-made imagery in which carbon copies predominate and distinction disappears. Rosetta Brooks wrote of this imagery: "As simulation, the clone is 'more real than the real' [Baudrillard], dissolving the past and future into an eternal present."

Much of Otterness's work is humorous. His sculptures—robotlike automatons, body-as-puzzle-piece reliefs, and intertwined pudendal processions—bespeak the artist's glibness as he manipulates and contorts the human figure.

Head, however, has a content apart from humor. About five times the size of an actual human head, it recalls the ancient head of *Constantine,* a colossal sculpture of the fourth century that also denies personal character and concentrates on a sculptural statement of size and anonymity. The resemblance is possibly no coincidence, for Otterness is informed of art history. His travels throughout Europe, the Middle East, and Asia have influenced his work, as have mythology, folklore, and pop culture.

Chronology

1823 A group of concerned citizens of the village of Brooklyn organizes the Brooklyn Apprentices' Library Association for the purpose of "establishing a library, for collecting and for forming a repository of books, maps, drawing apparatus, models of machinery, tools, and implements."

1825 Plans are made for a Library building. On July 4, General Lafayette, on a triumphal tour of America, lays the cornerstone for the new building in Brooklyn Heights.

1831 Art joins the book collection when the Library acquires its first painting—a portrait of Robert Snow, one of the founders and first president of the Library Association.

1841 The Library moves to quarters in the Lyceum building on Washington Street, housing collections previously reported by acting librarian Walt Whitman to have reached 1,200 volumes.

1842 The Library begins a program of exhibitions, including painting, sculpture, models of machinery, and curiosities of nature.

1843 The Apprentices' Library and the Brooklyn Lyceum are legally consolidated and renamed The Brooklyn Institute.

1846 The Institute announces plans for a permanent gallery of fine arts "containing specimens of the finest European artists, with productions of the best painters of our own country."

1851 Augustus Graham, one of the original founders of the Apprentices' Library, dies and leaves a major bequest to the Institute for the acquisition of books, natural history specimens, and paintings by American artists, as well as for support of free lectures and a school of design.

1867 The Washington Street building of the Brooklyn Institute undergoes major renovation to accommodate growing collections and educational activities.

1888 An Institute committee plans for a new building that would be a unique museum combining the arts and sciences. Legislation is passed to set aside land adjacent to Prospect Park for art and educational institutions.

1890 The Institute is reorganized into The Brooklyn Institute of Arts and Sciences, with departments ranging from anthropology to zoology. The new Institute eventually becomes the parent of the Brooklyn Academy of Music, the Brooklyn Botanic Garden, and the Brooklyn Children's Museum as well as The Brooklyn Museum. After fire damages the Institute building, the collections are stored in nearby institutions.

1893 The Institute's Department of Architecture organizes an architectural competition to provide a design for the Museum building. The firm of McKim, Mead & White is selected.

1895 Brooklyn Mayor Charles Schieren lays the cornerstone for the Museum building and construction begins.

1897 The West Wing is completed, collections are installed, and the building is opened to the public.

1899 The organization and growth of the collections are regulated by three departments: Fine Arts, Natural Sciences, and Ethnology.

1905 The Institute Board of Directors sets up an acquisition fund to encourage contributions from the membership.

1906   The Museum begins excavations in Egypt, which continue today in the Precinct of Mut at South Karnak.

1907   The East Wing, Central Pavilion, and Grand Staircase of the Museum are completed. The art collection is composed of 552 paintings, watercolors, and photographs as well as plaster casts and decorative arts. Great quantities of archaeological, ethnographic, and natural history material are accumulated through Museum expeditions.

1909   Thirty statues, designed under the direction of Daniel Chester French, are mounted on the exterior facade of the Museum building. Notable acquisitions include eighty-three John Singer Sargent watercolors, Egyptian antiquities, a model of a humpback whale, and ninety-three Chinese enamel vases.

1915   Colonel Robert Woodward, Institute trustee for twenty-five years, leaves the Museum his private art collection as well as endowment funds.

1916   The Museum begins a major international exhibition program with the *Exhibition of Contemporary Swedish Art*. The heirs of Charles Edwin Wilbour, a pioneer American Egyptologist, donate his collection of art objects and his library to the Museum. These items from Wilbour's collection become the cornerstone of the Museum's world-renowned Egyptian collection and are later augmented by an endowment fund given in Wilbour's honor. William H. Fox, the Institute's Director of Museums from 1914 to 1933, shortens the title of the Central Museum of the Brooklyn Institute of Arts and Sciences to The Brooklyn Museum.

1920   A subway stop is opened in front of the Museum, and attendance increases markedly.

1922   Augustus Healy, President of The Brooklyn Institute for twenty-five years, leaves the Museum his private art collection as well as endowment funds.

1923   The Museum holds a precedent-setting exhibition of objects from its African collection, interpreting them as fine art rather than as ethnographic specimens.

1926   The Museum organizes the *International Exhibition of Modern Art*, one of the largest and most comprehensive showings of modern art yet held in America.

1927   The last two sections of the Museum are completed according to the original McKim, Mead & White plan.

1929   The Museum opens twenty-one American period rooms; in time there are twenty-eight rooms ranging in date from 1675 to 1928.

1934   The Museum establishes a new collecting policy emphasizing the fine arts, cultural history, and the social and industrial aspects of art. The natural history collections are discontinued and dispersed to several institutions, including the Brooklyn Children's Museum, the Brooklyn Botanic Garden, and the American Museum of Natural History. The front stairs are removed and a new entry hall created.

1935   The collections are rearranged in chronological order, beginning with the prehistoric period on the main floor and continuing up to the Gallery for Living Artists on the sixth floor.

1941   The Brooklyn Museum Art School, jointly organized by The Brooklyn Institute and the Brooklyn Art Association in 1891, and previously housed in the Brooklyn Academy of Music, is installed in the Museum.

1948   The Museum purchases the Egyptian holdings of the New-York Historical Society. The Edward C. Blum Design Laboratory is opened to encourage the study of design. Later, in the 1960s, the Design Laboratory is transferred to the Fashion Institute of Technology.

1950   Plans for major renovation of the entire Museum are begun with the architectural firm of Brown, Lawford and Forbes.

1953   The Museum becomes the first American art museum to open a series of nineteenth-century period rooms.

1964   Daniel Chester French's allegorical figures *Brooklyn* and *Manhattan* are removed from the Manhattan Bridge and placed on either side of the Museum's main entrance.

1966   The Frieda Schiff Warburg Memorial Sculpture Garden, containing architectural fragments from demolished New York buildings, is opened in the rear of the Museum. The Brooklyn Museum is designated a landmark by the New York City Landmarks Preservation Commission.

1970   The Brooklyn Academy of Music becomes the first of the departments comprising The Brooklyn Institute of Arts and Sciences to be reorganized as an independent institution.

1976   The New York City Landmarks Preservation Commission approves the addition to the rear of the Museum of a new service extension designed by Prentice & Chan, Ohlhausen. The Brooklyn Museum is added to the National Register of Historic Places.

1985   The size of The Brooklyn Museum collections is estimated at one and a half to two million objects. The organizational structure of the Museum includes seven curatorial departments: African, Oceanic, and New World Art; Costumes and Textiles; Decorative Arts; Egyptian, Classical, and Ancient Middle Eastern Art; Oriental Art; Painting and Sculpture; and Prints and Drawings. There are also two research libraries and an archive. The Art School is closed and the adult classes transferred to Pratt Institute to join a long-established fine arts program.

1986   A Master Plan Competition Jury selects Arata Isozaki & Associates/James Stewart Polshek and Partners to devise a new master plan to improve existing conditions and provide for the Museum's growth into the next century.

Index to Artists and Makers

Photograph Credits

Geoffrey Clements: Plate 189; Gamma One Conversions: 172; W. Hartman: 113; Scott Hyde: 16, 72, 76–99, 123, 147, 162; Justin Kerr: 1, 3, 5, 8–10, 14, 15, 17–19, 25, 32–34, 40, 42, 44–46, 48–52, 54, 59, 60, 64, 66–68, 70, 107, 166, 168, 180, 181; Schecter Lee: 124; John Listopad: 69; Peter Muscato: 186; John Parnell: 6, 12, 22; Philip Pocock: 63, 65, 75, 128, 131, 132, 136, 138a,b, 150–155; Paul Warchol: 100–106.

Catheryn Anders of the Collections Management Department and Kathleen Sloan of the Marketing Department deserve recognition for their splendid support in coordinating the extensive preparation and photography required for this project. Special thanks are also due to the technicians and art handlers for their hard work on this project: Dominique Blasi, Michael Allen, Tony Trapp, Jim Hayes, Andrew Faintych, Rollie Erickson, David Horak, Susan McDonough, Randy Black, Lawrence Anderson, Bob Mizaki, and Polly Willman.